Beyond the Monitor Model

Comments on Current Theory and Practice in Second Language Acquisition

Ronald M. Barasch

C. Vaughan James

Heinle & Heinle Publishers
A Division of Wadsworth, Inc.
Boston, Massachusetts 02116 USA

The publication of *Beyond the Monitor Model* was directed by
the members of the Newbury House Publishing Team at Heinle & Heinle
David C. Lee, Editorial Director
Susan Mraz, Marketing Manager
Kristin Thalheimer, Production Editor

Also participating in the publication of this program were:
Publisher: Stanley J. Galek
Editorial Production Manager: Elizabeth Holthaus
Project Manager: Margaret Cleveland
Assistant Editor: Kenneth Mattsson
Production Assistant: Mary Ellen Eschman
Manufacturing Coordinator: Mary Beth Lynch
Cover Designer: Bortman Design Group
Book Designer: Matthew Dixon Cowles

The editors and publisher gratefully acknowledge the following sources of contributions
included in this volume:
Zielsprache Englisch, 4 (1985). (Dunlop, How do people learn languages?)
TESOL Quarterly, 21 (1987). (Pica et al., The impact of interaction on comprehension)
The Modern Language Journal, 71 (1987). (VanPatten, On babies and bathwater: Input in
foreign language teaching)

ISBN 0-8384-3967-5

Library of Congress Cataloging-in-Publication Data
Beyond the monitor model: comments on current theory and practice in
  second language acquisition/[compiled by] C. Vaughan James, Ronald M. Barasch.
    p. cm.
  Includes bibliographical references.
  ISBN 0-8384-3967-5
  1. Second language acquisition. 2. Language and languages—Study
and teaching. I. James, C. V. (Caradog Vaughan) II. Barasch,
Ronald M.
P118.2.B49 1993
418' .007—dc20   93-27956
                                                          CIP

Manufactured in the United States of America
10 9 8 7 6 5 4 3 2 1

This volume is dedicated to the late
PETER STREVENS,
whose idea it was.

Contents

Contents

Preface

Ronald M. Barasch
C. Vaughan James

The idea for this volume arose out of a natural inclination to bring together a series of articles that, for the first time, addresses Stephen D. Krashen's increasing volume of writing. By its very nature, his impact in second language acquisition and learning cannot be ignored. Fueled by a plethora of articles and books, and energetically and effectively backed by the author's highly professional and entertaining presentations at conferences all over the world, he has provoked strong reactions, both positive and negative, from researchers in second language acquisition and learning.

The lure of the all-embracing theory was arousing the interest of the slumbering masses of language teachers who had hitherto been content to let the linguistic stars converse somewhere out there in the firmament while they earned their daily pittance at the chalkboard. Something was afoot. So let us state at the outset that whatever the long-term effect of what Brumfit calls the Krashen "phenomenon," Stephen D. Krashen has done the language teaching/learning business a significant service by involving more of its participants in the debate than ever before. And this, in itself, is no mean achievement.

The danger—possibly only one of several—was seen as that of seeming to be offering a rallying point to opposing forces in a campaign of "knocking" Krashen. This, let it be said quite clearly, was emphatically not the case. To do so would, in our opinion, have been pointless, and in any case not our intended purpose.

It was a desire to avoid being seen as an anti-Krashen exercise that prompted us to change the title of this volume from the original *Responses to Krashen*—with connotations of riposte—to something less compact but, we hope, having a more neutral and considered ring, appropriate to our aim.

Inevitably, our volume has been somewhat transmuted along the way, and we are grateful to the publisher's readers for comments that have undoubtedly led to improvement. We trust that our contributors will feel we have done them justice, both in our assembling of the whole volume and in our editing of the individual parts. Some time has passed since the idea was first proposed, but this is perhaps all to the good: emotion recollected in tranquillity is a more reliable formula than angry or elated reflex.

In designing this collection of articles we set out to achieve quite clearly formulated aims:

First, to assess the impact of Stephen D. Krashen's theory on different sections of the language teaching/learning constituency. Were we in fact correct in believing that the debate he had sparked really did involve more than an in-group of pundits whose dicta, addressed largely to each other, may have so little immediate or obvious effect on anyone else? And if so—insofar as this can be stated in fairly general terms—precisely what was Krashen's impact?

Second, to examine in some detail the most important hypotheses on which Krashen's theory rests. If, as commonly asserted, what was new lay not in any component part but in the combination or shape of the whole, what could usefully be said about those basic parts that would throw light on the validity of the whole?

Third, to assess the feasibility, wisdom, or usefulness of a universal theory that, while purporting to embrace all circumstances and cases, must surely be appropriate, in the event, to none. If, to many practitioners not normally involved in theoretical disquisitions, the attraction of Krashen's theory was the way it all "came together," was this in fact a genuine aid or a delusion?

Within such a general framework we set out also to meet a number of obvious requirements. First, we wanted to ensure that our contributors represented a proper geographical spread, allowing coverage in particular of points of view from North America, the United Kingdom, and continental Europe. A notable and not always constructive aspect of the Krashen debate has been a tendency to polarize arguments on different sides of the Atlantic, an extreme example, perhaps, being the furor over Krashen's remark at the

Georgetown Round Table (1983) that eclecticism was an "intellectual obscenity" (see Brumfit's contribution to this volume).

As Peter Strevens pointed out (in his address to the IATEFL conference at Brighton in April, 1986), there is a strong tendency and tradition in the USA of beginning always with the formulation of a theory, from which practice is derived, whereas in Europe—and particularly in the UK—a more pragmatic attitude prevails, whereby a body of practice that can be seen to be effective may lead to the evolution of a theory derived from it.

On such a background, the attraction of an all-embracing theory for American teachers and the somewhat startled reaction of their British or European counterparts is certainly worth examination, not least because in each case it may lead to a questioning of accepted ideas, which must surely be a positive step.

At a different level, and possibly of no less ultimate importance, is the contention (put forward strongly in this volume by a number of contributors, notably Freudenstein, Dunlop, and Yalden) that insofar as Krashen's theory is based on empirical evidence, it is drawn almost exclusively from American sources and thus needs to consider work done elsewhere.

To meet this desire for geographical coverage, we have included in the volume contributors not only from North America and the UK, but also from Sweden, Poland, and the Federal Republic of Germany.

Our second requirement was for adequate coverage of different sectors of education, embracing university-based theoretical and applied linguistics, along with teacher training and classroom teaching, including private language schools. This inevitably leads to something of a subdivision into consideration of theory, on the one hand, and practice on the other; but most importantly it covers also the relationship between the two. The main weight is no doubt properly in the area of teacher training, since it is in future teachers that any long-term effect of Krashen's advocacy will become visible.

Third in our requirements was the inclusion of foreign language as well as TEFL/TESL. The need for a rational relationship between the teaching of foreign languages (especially in native English-speaking countries) and the teaching of English (as a second or foreign language) has often been stressed and various bridge-building exercises mounted, unfortunately without conspicuous success. It is remarkable how Krashen's ideas (at least in the UK) have become the focal point of interest in successive conferences of foreign language teachers, coming into productive confrontation with the most powerful home-based influence, that of the Council of Europe Modern Languages Project. It may well be that the influence of Krashen on the European side of the Atlantic will be strongest in the teaching of languages other than English (see Littlewood's article in this volume).

The articles in this volume fall into four main headings:

1. Theoretical Bases
2. Some Hypotheses Examined
3. From Theory to Practice
4. The Panacea Fallacy

However, it should be pointed out that neither individual papers nor groups are as discrete as the headings suggest. In general, each contributor, while concentrating ultimately on one aspect, has felt the need to put it into the broad context of Krashen's theory as a whole, and we have not thought it necessary to avoid this. Indeed, the differences in conception reflected by the various contributors may be said to provide yet another dimension to the argument. In a way we feel Stephen D. Krashen would himself appreciate, there is a certain element of repetition that has a powerful cumulative effect. As an aid to the reader, we have introduced each of the four sections of the book with a brief summary of the main points and some comments of our own.

Whereas we hope this volume will be both informative and thought-provoking on first reading, our basic desire—shared by our publisher—is that it will also have a more lasting value as a textbook for L2 language methods classes. We have therefore included topics for discussion for trainee teachers and other interested persons who, while having ideas of their own, may nevertheless approach the general subject with an open mind. These topics are grouped in an appendix at the end of the book.

We should again stress that we ourselves are not seeking to prove or disprove anything. Although our contributors were invited to work within an agreed general framework, we thought it proper to leave the precise choice of subject to them: apart from obvious respect for expertise, this seemed also the best way to ensure that each contributor wrote because he or she really had something to say! Our aim was to present a possibly contradictory but truly representative selection of the opinions of experts in the field so that readers acquainted with Krashen's original writings plus this volume would be able to make reasoned and informed judgments in the light of their own unique experiences and circumstances.

It is possible, of course, that with a different team of writers we should have produced a different set of judgments, but with the exception of fine nuances we are in fact disposed to doubt this. As we have stated above, there is a certain amount of overlap—and no doubt there are also some gaps. Nevertheless, we are confident that for the discerning reader, this collection will serve its intended purpose.

We would also like to thank the follwing people who gave us helpful comments during the book's development: Ruth Cathcart-Strong, Monterrey Institute of International Studies; James Cummins, Ontario Institute for Studies in Education; Mary McGroarty, Northern Arizona University; Patricia Richard-Amato, California State University, Los Angeles; Sofia Santiesteban, University of Miami; Thomas Scovel, San Francisco State University; Sandra Silberstein, University of Washington; Marguerite Ann Snow, California State University, Los Angeles; Margaret Sokolik, University of California, Berkeley; Margaret Steffensen, Illinois State University; and Earl Stevick, University of Maryland, Baltimore County.

Ronald M. Barasch
C. Vaughan James
1993

Introduction

Sheila M. Shannon,
University of Colorado
at Denver, USA

This book is a collection of articles and essays about the theory of second language acquisition developed over the last two decades by Stephen D. Krashen. Krashen's theory and his application of it to language teaching have been highly controversial. While reactions to his work have appeared over time in journal articles, books, and conference presentations (many authored by the contributors here), this book is the first to bring together responses to Krashen's ideas from diverse areas of the field.

A variety of perspectives on Krashen's theory and its application is included in this volume. However, the overall tone of the book is critical. One might argue that the level of ill will is unfair and uncalled for. However, the amount of antagonism that Krashen's ideas have caused among scholars is one indicator of the energy that he has generated. A major cause of contention is that Krashen claims that the theory accounts for all that is involved in second language acquisition. But all aspects of the theory and its application are vigorously debated. Despite the fact that Krashen's ideas are controversial and because they are, they promote thinking and understanding of second language acquisition and language teaching.

Krashen himself says that he "perhaps audaciously" claims that his is a complete theory of second language acquisition (Krashen, 1985: vii). Therefore, much of the debate is centered on questions about the scientific validity, rigor, and elegance of the theory itself. Despite the steady critique, Krashen continues to have an enormous impact on the practice of language teaching, at least in the U.S. This last point seems to be the cause of as much of the contention as is the scientific evaluation of the theory as such.

Krashen's theory and his suggestions for teaching are the result of his commitment to an understanding of second language acquisition. It is no wonder that the authors of the chapters in this book represent the most prominent scholars in the field of second language research and teaching. Krashen is one of them. Further, the contributors to this book are from the U.S., Canada, and Europe, demonstrating that Krashen's ideas have indeed had a wide influence.

This chapter introduces a sense of the ongoing debate but is not meant to be exhaustive. The contributions to this book each explore in thoughtful detail one or more of the issues mentioned in this chapter. Some areas, particularly where the focus is more on practical implications, will raise new concerns and thoughts. The contributions are written primarily with the language teacher in mind. The reader will be able to appreciate the scope of Krashen's work, consider critiques that help one to keep an informed perspective, and reflect on serious issues and concerns in terms of the fields of scientific inquiry and professional practice. The editors, C. V. James and R. M. Barasch, have provided an introduction to each part of this book, in which they discuss the authors' contributions. They have divided the book into four parts: **Theoretical Bases, Some Hypotheses Considered, From Theory to Practice,** and **The Panacea Fallacy.**

Krashen's Theory of Second Language Acquisition

The title of this book, *Beyond the Monitor Model,* refers to the fact that the Monitor Model does not characterize Krashen's more recent formulations of his overall theory. He began in the seventies with a focus on the Monitor to account for learner performance—the Monitor being the conscious editor of one's own production. Performance varied, according to the Monitor Model, due to the different ways that learners used the Monitor. Eventually, Krashen formulated five hypotheses, one of which is the Monitor. By 1985, Krashen had shifted his focus to the role of input, saying that "it has become clearer to me over the last few years that the Input Hypothesis is the most important part of the theory" (Krashen, 1985: vii). Thus, Krashen's own work goes "beyond the Monitor Model."

Krashen's early work was focused on a number of areas related to second language acquisition, including the lateralization of the brain, the critical period, adult-child differences, acquisition sequences, and the effect of formal learning environments. These explorations, in addition to a consideration of current research, ultimately contributed to his theoretical formulations. For example, Krashen's ideas about how learners monitor or edit their production are ones that he has been developing over a long period of time.

In Krashen's comprehensive theory, he proposes that five hypotheses together account for all second language acquisition. Furthermore, the theory has implications for second language teaching and provides a basis for a model of language teaching called the Natural Approach (Krashen & Terrell, 1983). In the sections that follow, I briefly summarize each hypothesis. A summary of the issues and concerns follows each aspect of the theory. I also include second language teachers' reflections concerning the theory and their teaching practice.

The Five Hypotheses

1. The Acquisition-Learning Hypothesis
2. The Natural Order Hypothesis
3. The Monitor Hypothesis
4. The Input Hypothesis
5. The Affective Filter Hypothesis

The Acquisition-Learning Hypothesis

> There are two independent ways of developing ability in second languages. "Acquisition" is a subconscious process identical in all important ways to the process children utilize in acquiring their first language, while "learning" is a conscious process that results in "knowing about" language. (Krashen, 1985: 1)

Krashen's fundamental principle is that second language acquisition can be just like first language acquisition. How it can be different is accounted for through the other hypotheses. Just as the child is not explicitly taught his or her first language, neither does the second language acquirer need to be "taught." When the second language learner is in a language-rich environment, "the language 'mental organ' will function just as automatically as any other organ" (Krashen, 1985: 4). This mental capacity, the Language Acquisition Device (LAD), was originally proposed only for first language acquisition (Chomsky, 1975). However, Krashen insists that the LAD is available not just for children, but that it continues to function throughout a lifetime and is engaged whenever language is being acquired. Krashen (1985: 4) quotes Chomsky to support his view:

> The learner (acquirer) has no "reason" for acquiring the language; he does not choose to learn (acquire) under normal conditions, any more than he chooses (or can fail) to organize visual space in a certain way—or, for that matter, may more than certain cells in

the embryo choose (or can fail) to become an arm or the visual centers of the brain under appropriate environmental conditions. (Chomsky, 1975: 71)

Krashen assumes that "language" is any language, first or second. This principle, that language acquisition is always innate, underlies the distinction between learning and acquisition.

However, second language learners are very often "taught" language. Krashen argues, though, that many teaching approaches would leave the learner only with knowledge about the language. He maintains that the two systems of learning and acquiring are separate and that conscious learning can be only indirectly related to acquisition. Therefore, for Krashen the implication is that all formal learning environments must be those that are language-rich and that they should not center on teaching about grammar or any other aspect of language. The Natural Approach, which Krashen contributed to, is based on this principle of second language acquisition. Krashen says that the Natural Approach is compatible with those such as Asher's Total Physical Response and Lozanov's Suggestopedia.

Two major criticisms of the distinction between learning and acquisition are that it cannot be tested (Ellis, 1986) and that *learning* and *acquisition* are poorly defined (McLaughlin, 1987). These are considerable weaknesses. The difficulty in testing the distinction can be illustrated with a description of Krashen's own efforts. In order to observe the difference between learning and acquisition, Krashen conducted a study in which learners were to report if judgments of grammaticality were based on a rule that they could state or if their judgments were based on a "feel" they had (Krashen et al., 1978). The rule-based judgments, Krashen posited, would be the product of learning, and the judgments based on "feel" would be the product of acquisition. But some argue that the subjects could try to state a rule that they had never learned or could select the "feel" option as the simpler solution (McLaughlin, 1987).

In responding to the contention that the distinction between learning and acquisition is undefinable, untestable, and unnecessary, Krashen discusses three "interface positions": strong, weak, and weaker (Krashen, 1985). The strong interface position is that learning precedes acquisition. The weak interface position is that conscious learning of the language may be one of a number of ways to acquire a second language. The weaker interface position allows that conscious learning can indirectly influence acquisition. In every case, however, Krashen maintains the distinction between learning and acquisition. For example, he says that the strong interface position suggests that learners learn rules before they acquire them. However, he goes on to assert that unconscious acquisition intervenes as well, and so attributing acquisition to learning is tenuous. The tenacity with which Krashen adheres to the separation of the two systems is what concerns many, who, like Yorio and Marton (separately in this volume), sense that the two are separate but directly related.

Another criticism of this hypothesis addresses the assumption that the processes of first and second language acquisition are the same. Dunlop, Gregg, and Rivers (separately in this volume) point out the weaknesses of this assumption. Each examines the original and current conceptions of the LAD and show how they cannot be directly applied to processes involved in second language acquisition.

The majority of the language teachers with whom I work are experienced and well-informed. They often are familiar with Krashen's ideas before they encounter them in their Masters programs. Their own critiques of the theory are based on their experience and their consideration of the "experts'" critiques. Regarding this first hypothesis, they have remarked that the distinction between learning and acquisition is not something that they have experienced as teachers or as learners. They view learning and acquisition as more interconnected, with each one building on the other. As one teacher stated, "It's cyclical—you get acquisition and you clean it up with learning and then you try it out in acquisition." Another teacher argues that beginning learners are insecure and that learning grammar rules, using a dictionary, and relying on translations provide support and security. Furthermore, teachers assert that their intuition is that learning involves the use of cognitive abilities beyond a process specific to language and that the two systems constantly interact.

The Natural Order Hypothesis

> It states that we acquire the rules of language in a predictable order, some rules tending to come early and others late. The order does not appear to be determined solely by formal simplicity and there is evidence that it is independent of the order in which rules are taught in language classes. (Krashen, 1985: 1)

Krashen arrived at this hypothesis through a review of studies that examined the accuracy of learners' production of morphemes and grammatical structures: "In all these studies some individual variation is found, but it is quite clear that strong tendencies exist—we can certainly speak of some rules as being early-acquired and others as being late-acquired, and of predictable states of acquisition" (Krashen, 1985: 21). Krashen argues that the natural order emerges when language is acquired and that conscious learning interferes with the Natural Order. He sees this as a further requirement that the two systems—learning and acquisition—be kept separate.

Krashen (1987) states that knowing exactly what the Natural Order is is not important for language teaching. He says that "we need to know that an order exists to understand why students make the errors they do and to alter our expectations accordingly, but it is not yet clear that we need to know the determinants of the order" (36). Krashen does not argue for a syllabus based on the Natural Order.

McLaughlin (1987) argues that Krashen's reliance on the morpheme studies to lend support to the Natural Order Hypothesis is flawed. He says that these were not actual studies of the order of acquisition, but of the accuracy of the learners' production of morphemes in obligatory contexts. Further, most of the studies were cross-sectional—learners' production accuracy at a single point in time—so they could not reveal acquisitional sequence. McLaughlin asserts that longitudinal studies indicate that there is variation in acquisition order and that one factor has to do with differences in the learners' first language (how they are different from the language they are learning and how the first languages are different from one another). Moreover, Ellis (in this volume) recognizes the variability that learners display across various linguistic and situational contexts, which calls an invariable order into question.

The issue about an acquisition order that often arises in discussions with teachers is about teaching and the curriculum. When asked how she knew which grammar points to present and in what order, one teacher facetiously replied, "It's in the book." The appeal of a Natural Order is that one could know what to teach and when—like the neatly laid out table of contents of a grammar book. And a Natural Order could be used to assess how well a learner is progressing. Teachers sense that a Natural Order is possible, but express doubts in light of the variations that they see in their students' performance, even among those grouped at the same ability level. Since Krashen does not argue for teaching based on a Natural Order, however, the debate seems to be somewhat of a non-issue for teachers and for Krashen.

The Monitor Hypothesis

This hypothesis states how acquisition and learning are used in production. Our ability to produce utterances in another language comes from our acquired competence, from our subconscious knowledge. Learning, conscious knowledge, serves only as an editor, or Monitor. We appeal to learning to make corrections, to change the output of the acquired system before we speak or write (or sometimes after we speak or write, as in self-correction). I have hypothesized that two conditions need to be met in order to use the Monitor: the performer must be consciously concerned about correctness; and he or she must know the rule. Both these conditions are difficult to meet. (Krashen, 1985: 1–2)

As discussed above, this hypothesis began as a model of learner performance before it was incorporated into Krashen's overall theory. In fact, the Monitor has been relegated to a lesser position in the theory, as evidence has indicated its limited usefulness (Krashen, 1985). In any case, Krashen maintains that the Monitor operates only from learned language and this conscious editing based on learned knowledge is (capital "M") Monitoring. Krashen does allow that unconsciously acquired knowledge can also be used for editing that is based on "feel" or (lower-case "m") monitoring (Larsen-Freeman & Long, 1991; Tarone, 1988). However, the hypothesis is concerned primarily with Monitoring.

A study by Hulstijn and Hulstijn (1984) provides one example of how empirical evidence influenced Krashen to modify his position with respect to the Monitor. Krashen originally postulated that use of the Monitor required three conditions: extra time, knowledge of the rules, and a focus on form. Hulstijn and Hulstijn (1984) found that a focus on form takes extra time, but that providing more time without requiring learners to focus on form did not naturally lead learners to be consciously concerned with the correctness of their production. Krashen (1985) cites this study as evidence that the idea of the Monitor is much less useful than he originally thought.

There are problems associated with the Monitor. First, it is impossible to observe. And if observable, how does one determine if a learner were "Monitoring" (editing by rule) or "monitoring" (editing by "feel")? Finally, McLaughlin (1987) argues that research indicates that adolescents are more successful learners than children. This runs counter to Krashen's claims that children are more successful because they are not burdened by the Monitor. McLaughlin asserts that, having reached a stage of formal operations, an adolescent can use rules and monitor his or her performance and therefore perform better than a child. Thus he argues, contrary to Krashen, that the Monitor would improve performance rather than impede it.

Teachers find the Monitor Hypothesis useful as a metaphor for the learning-acquisition relationship. They rely on their perception that "learned" knowledge of a language goes hand in hand with "acquired" knowledge and that this is a productive interaction. In contrasting students' oral and written performances, however, teachers remarked that the Monitor might be more evident in writing than in speaking. Writers have more time to focus on form and a visible product to aid them in their efforts. In light of the evidence that in oral production time alone does not automatically lead the learner to focus on form, a monitor may not be a useful construct in writing without also asking that writers focus on form (and giving them the extra time). However, Krashen (1987) says that a writing task only "mildly" employs the Monitor and that learners use the Monitor in the way that he originally claimed only with discrete-point grammar tests.

The Input Hypothesis

The Input Hypothesis claims that humans acquire language in only one way—by understanding messages, or by receiving "comprehensible input." We progress along the natural order (hypothesis 2) by understanding input that contains structures at our next "stage"—structures that are a bit beyond our current level of competence. (We move from i, our current level, to $i + 1$, the next level along the natural order, by understanding input containing $i + 1$.) We are able to understand language containing unacquired grammar with the help of context, which includes extra-linguistic information, our knowledge of the world, and previously acquired linguistic competence. (Krashen, 1985: 2)

Krashen states that the Input Hypothesis is his "favourite" and "the most important part" of his theory of second language acquisition (1985: vii). A language-rich environment, he argues, provides comprehensible input in the same way that the environment provides children learning their first language with input. Not all language in a particular context is input; it must be comprehensible. Further, in order for the learner to advance, the comprehensible input must include structures that are just beyond their current stage in the natural order, which is Krashen's notion of $i + 1$.

Another aspect of the Input Hypothesis is that speaking the second language is the result of acquisition rather than the cause. The role of production, or output, is minimalized in the Input Hypothesis. However, Krashen does assign importance to output as it indirectly promotes acquisition by helping learners focus on form. Krashen says, for example, that "it is possible to understand input without appealing to syntactic competence, via the use of perceptual strategies, context, and the meaning of individual words. Output practice might encourage a more syntactic approach to input" (1985: 65).

The Input Hypothesis also supports the notion of a silent period that precedes second language production—a time during which the learner, according to Krashen, takes in language before actual production. The silent period for a second language learner can take anywhere from days to months.

The Input Hypothesis, like the Learning/Acquisition distinction, reveals Krashen's nativist perspective of second language acquisition. Second language acquisition, according to Krashen, is similar to first language acquisition in that input is processed through the LAD, a mental capacity specifically suited to language acquisition. He argues that input in second language acquisition functions in the same way that input does in a child's acquisition of his or her first language. As central as this position is to Krashen's overall theory (recall that it is, according to Krashen, the fundamental principle underlying the theory), Krashen does not explicitly develop it. Larsen-Freeman and Long (1991) argue that Krashen will probably need to include this stance as another hypothesis rather than merely implying it in other hypotheses.

Krashen maintains that conscious learning—that is, a focus on form—can only indirectly influence acquisition. Therefore, the status of input depends on its focus. The input provided by a language lesson that is focused on a discrete grammar point is primarily the text in which it is embedded. The grammar point itself is not input. The text of the lesson contains the potential input. Krashen argues that the ways in which the grammar point itself could indirectly affect acquisition are the following: 1) if the learner uses a form correctly that he or she learned consciously but had not yet acquired, it could help to make the output more comprehensible; 2) hearing or reading a form that the learner may not have yet acquired could make the input comprehensible; and 3) it may lower the affective filter. Thus, for Krashen, instruction should focus only on meaning (comprehensible input) and not on form (learned knowledge about the language). The argument against such thinking is that learners need to focus on form in order to revise incorrect forms that they have acquired. Further, adults have the cognitive skills to benefit from a focus on form. Krashen's theory, with an explicit hypothesis on the function of the LAD in second language acquisition, would not easily allow for other cognitive capacities to play such an important role.

Krashen originally defined comprehensible input as coming from rough-tuned, simplified codes like motherese or caretaker talk and foreigner talk. However, cross-cultural researchers argue that mothers' talk to their children differs across societies and groups and that some mothers do not regard their young children as appropriate conversation partners (see Faltis, 1984, for the discussion). Krashen responds by saying that they also receive input + 1 in any case and that "it is, in fact, valuable data in that it focuses attention on what is essential for language acquisition: not simplified input but comprehensible input containing $i + 1$, structures slightly beyond the acquirer's state of competence" (p. 6). Therefore, Krashen's current position is that simplification does not necessarily make input comprehensible.

McLaughlin (1987: 39) points out that a major concern with the hypothesis is defining or identifying comprehensible input and "which structures constitute the $i + 1$ level." Pica, Rivers, VanPatten, and Marton each separately argue in this volume that $i + 1$ is enhanced if the input is negotiated through interaction. This call for interaction between the learner and the sources of input (teacher, peer, informal interlocutor) is not currently compatible with Krashen's ideas about input. As Marton (this volume) points out, Krashen's learners take in input and formulate hypotheses about the structures of the second language without the benefit of negotiation or as if it did not occur. Rivers (this volume) says that this view of the learner is one of a "silent partner."

Comprehensible input is a slippery notion for some teachers, who sense that it is tautological. They argue (as does Krahnke, this volume) that if input can come from anything, including a grammar lesson, how can teaching discrete grammar points and acquisition-rich environments be distinguished? What teachers find intuitively appealing about the Input Hypothesis is that they already see their formal classrooms as language-rich environments. However, teachers do not agree with a strict distinction between learning and acquisition, as does Krashen. They believe that acquisition occurs in formal instruction as well as in communicative interaction.

The Affective Filter Hypothesis

Comprehensible input is necessary for acquisition, but it is not sufficient. The acquirer needs to be "open" to the input. The "affective filter" is a mental block that prevents acquirers from fully utilizing the comprehensible input they receive for language acquisition. When it is "up," the acquirer may understand what he hears and reads, but the input will not reach the Language Acquisition Device (LAD). This occurs when the acquirer is unmotivated, lacking in self confidence, or anxious . . . when he considers the language class to be a place where his weaknesses will be revealed. The filter is down when the acquirer is not concerned with the possibility of failure in language acquisition. . . . (Krashen, 1985: 3)

Borrowing from contributions from social psychology, Krashen fashioned his Affective Filter Hypothesis. Children have little or no affective filter, Krashen argues, until puberty, when the filter is in place. Krashen primarily targets negative affective factors as those that raise the filter and positive ones as those that lower it. Negative factors include anxiety, embarrassment, and fear of failure, and positive factors are those such as learner confidence and a sense of comfort. This hypothesis and the Monitor Hypothesis are important dimensions to the overall theory because like the Monitor, the Affective Filter is a factor in second language acquisition that is not present with first language acquisition. Krashen asserts that the Affective Filter accounts for individual variation in SLA, which he originally assigned to the Monitor. The Affective Filter, like a monitor mechanism, is also uncharacteristic of first language acquisition. Therefore, Krashen's fundamental principle that second language acquisition can be like first language acquisition is conditioned by these two hypotheses.

However, the primary issue with the Affective Filter is that it is virtually impossible to operationally define. How can one measure its height or its depth or that it is functioning at all? Therefore, Larsen-Freeman and Long (1991) contend that the Affective Filter can be used only as a metaphor. Teachers say that they can "relate to" the Affective Filter as a metaphor in the same way they appreciate the Monitor. Providing a nonthreatening and encouraging environment is what all good teachers see as their job. However, they also describe negative factors that the theory predicts would raise the filter as lowering the filter for some individuals. For example, a learner with a negative perception of the Target Language (TL) group might be motivated to excel in order to deal with the TL group successfully. One teacher commented that teaching discrete grammar points "lowered" some of her students' Affective Filters because it gave them the comfort of the ways that they had studied English for years in their own country (a point with which Krashen agrees).

Summary

To conclude, I will return to Krashen's own summary of the five hypotheses:

> We can summarize the five hypotheses with a single claim: people acquire second languages only if they obtain comprehensible input and if their affective filters are low enough to allow the input "in." When the filter is "down" and appropriate comprehensible input is presented (and comprehended), acquisition is inevitable. (Krashen, 1985: 4)

As I noted at the outset of this chapter, Krashen himself has moved "beyond the Monitor Model." The Monitor and the Natural Order are not mentioned in his own summary of the theory. What lies beyond The Monitor, it appears, is a focus on comprehensible input and the Affective Filter.

The remainder of this book will provide the reader with plenty of food for thought about Krashen's efforts. Nearly every aspect of the theory and its application is critically examined. Much of the book (Parts I and II) are concerned with Krashen's theory as a theory. The contributors pose questions about its validity, support, predictability, and explanatory power. The contributions in Part III examine the application of the theory to practice. As the authors ask, is it realistic, usable, tried, true, or new? And finally, in Part IV, Yalden and Brumfit separately argue against the utility of having a theory of second language acquisition that is directly applied to second language teaching. Unfortunately, Krashen does not respond directly in this volume, but the reader can consider responses that he has made in the past. For example, Krashen (1979) responds directly to McLaughlin's critique of an early formulation of the Monitor Model. Krashen (1985) takes on critics and also states his position on the emergence of the Input Hypothesis as a central tenet to his theory.

One of Krashen's ideas is reminiscent of the work of Russian psychologist L. S. Vygotsky in the area of cognitive development. Vygotsky (1962) posits that what a child can do with assistance or in cooperation with a more competent other today, that child can do independently tomorrow. For Vygotsky, this is the zone of proximal development, which he defines in the following way:

> It is the distance between the actual developmental level as determined by independent problem solving and the level of potential development as determined through problem solving under adult guidance or in collaboration with more capable peers. (Vygotsky, 1978: 86)

Vygotsky argues that the zone is where instruction leads development. Marton (this volume) relates the zone of development to Krashen's input + 1. However, Marton argues that the role of the teacher is that of the more capable other. And Marton contends that eliminating this role for teaching, as Krashen does, is anti-pedagogical.

Providing a language-rich environment that is rough-tuned to the learner's ability is compatible with other prominent theories and popular movements. Holistic approaches to language arts instruction are being transported into second and foreign language classrooms. Those approaches are based on the assertion that reading and writing are elements of language, as are speaking and comprehending (Goodman & Goodman, 1990). Therefore, given authentic and meaningful experiences for using reading and writing, children will use their innate abilities to learn and use language as they did when acquiring their first language. This is similar to the claims that Krashen makes about first and second language acquisition being extensively similar. For example, a teacher asks, "What's the connection between Whole Language and [Krashen's theory of second language] acquisition? I've taught Whole Language this year; I haven't taught any grammar—just thinking that they will get it through input—is that the same?" I would answer affirmatively.

These ideas: comprehensible input + 1, the zone of proximal development, and holistic approaches to literacy instruction are appealing to teachers. They fall under ways of understanding learning and cognitive development as a social phenomenon and also view learners as having a proactive role in the process. These perspectives view learners as being involved in their own construction of that which they are learning. These are ideas that liberate the teacher and give credit to the learner. Viewed critically, ideas such as Krashen's input + 1 stimulate our understanding of second language teaching and learning.

One of the issues that concerns some critics of Krashen is that the theory he promotes, taken uncritically by language teachers, is dangerous. For example, in this volume, Littlewood talks about Krashen's ideas as the possible "basis for a new dogma" (p. 205). Af Trampe discusses the ethics of a zealous promotion of the theory into practice. In my experience of teaching language teachers in Masters programs in TESOL and bilingual education, I have not found that those I teach are swept away by Krashen's theory. Most teachers view all proposals critically. They recognize that what Krashen offers is ambitious but interesting. They enjoy reading Krashen, but they do not find his ideas always equally compelling. More importantly, however, it is through his work that they get a feel for the field of second language acquisition scholarship—the issues, the debates, the requirements, the limitations, and the knowledge it has created. Krashen's ideas continue to spark interest. For the scholar, Krashen has provided an abundant source for research questions and theoretical positions. He has made many of us reconsider our own assumptions. For the teacher, Krashen has led a movement that has great possibilities for making teaching and learning positive experiences.

References

Chomsky, N. (1975). *Reflections on language.* New York: Pantheon.

Ellis, R. (1986). *Understanding second language acquisition.* Oxford: Oxford University Press.

Faltis, C. (1984). A commentary on Krashen's Input Hypothesis. *TESOL Quarterly, 18,* 352–356.

Goodman, Y., & Goodman, K. S. (1990). Vygotsky in a whole-language perspective. In L. C. Moll (Ed.), *Vygotsky and education.* Cambridge: Cambridge University Press.

Hulstijn, J., & Hulstijn W. (1984). Grammatical errors as a function of processing constraints and explicit knowledge. *Language Learning, 34,* 23–43.

Krashen, S. D. (1979). A response to McLaughlin, "The Monitor Model: Some methodological considerations." *Language Learning, 29,* 151–167.

Krashen, S. D. (1985). *The Input Hypothesis: Issues and implications.* London: Longman.

Krashen, S. D. (1987). Applications of pyscholinguistic research to the classroom. In M. H. Long & J. C. Richards (Eds.), *Methodology in TESOL: A book of readings.* New York: Newbury.

Krashen, S. D., Butler, J., Birnbaum, R., & Robertson, J. (1978). Two studies in language acquisition and language learning. *ITL: Review of Applied Linguistics, 39–40,* 73–92.

Krashen, S. D., & Terrell, T. (1983). *The Natural Approach: Language acquisition in the classroom.* Hayward, CA: Alemany.

Larsen-Freeman, D., & Long, M. H. (1991). *An introduction to second language acquisition research.* London: Longman.

McLaughlin, B. (1987). *Theories of second-language learning.* London: Arnold.

Tarone, E. (1988). *Variation in interlanguage.* London: Arnold.

Vygotsky, L. S. (1962). *Thought and language.* Cambridge, MA: MIT Press.

Vygotsky, L. S. (1978). *Mind in society.* (M. Cole, S. Scribner, V. John-Steiner, & E. Souberman, Eds.) Cambridge, MA: Harvard University Press.

Part 1   Theoretical Bases

Introduction
to Part 1:
Theoretical Bases

In this section, Stephen D. Krashen's work is assessed by five contributors—two European, though with widely different specialties and ideological orientation (**Peter af Trampe**, of Stockholm, Sweden and **Waldermar Marton**, of Poznán, Poland) and three Americans (**Kevin Gregg**, currently at Matsuyama University in Japan, **Wilga M. Rivers**, recently retired after a most distinguished period at Harvard, and a team of three researchers—**Pica, Young** and **Doughty**, of the University of Pennsylvania. Of these, af Trampe and Gregg examine Krashen's theory *qua* theory, casting some doubt on its claim to be designated as such, and Marton, while not questioning that there is a serious body of hypotheses worthy of discussion, is disturbed by the author's apparent willingness to disregard both theoretical and practical counter-evidence. Together, the three contributors raise a number of issues that are taken up with various degrees of emphasis and from various points of view by the other contributors to the book. As an introductory section, the articles delineate in broad terms the framework within which subsequent discussion takes place.

In a dispassionate and thoughtful first article, af Trampe acknowledges Krashen's positive achievement in bringing research findings to the attention of a large number of teachers and also sees his value as an incitement to the research community through raising important questions. (Such an inclination to damn with faint praise can be detected in many of the other articles). Examining the Monitor Theory, however, af Trampe finds it both unscientific and simplistic, and introduces several important questions of principle: the theory is formulated in such a way that it is unfalsifiable; no real attempt is made to explain the mechanism of language acquisition or, particularly, of language learning; there are doubts about the way in which much of the research quoted in evidence was conducted and also about the interpretation of the findings of such research; other research giving contrary indications is apparently ignored; where falsifiable predictions are made, no attempt has been mounted to test the hypothesis. In his practical advice to teachers, much of which is sound common sense, Krashen propounds oversimplified dicta that, since unaccompanied by the necessary qualifications, are liable to be taken too literally by harassed language teachers impressed by the repeated references throughout to prestigious research as providing the basis and justification for the author's claims. The same is true of the joint Krashen and Terrell work, *The Natural Approach.*

Our second contributor, Gregg, is more forceful and direct in following a similar line of argument. Stating the two basic requirements of any tenable theory as precision and testability, Gregg finds Krashen imprecise, sometimes contradictory, and always short on examples. Measured alongside Atkinson's requirements for a theory of language acquisition, Krashen's work fails to demarcate the domain in which the theory will operate; it is not based on any fully stated theory of language; it neither adequately describes nor in any way explains the acquisition sequence; and it is similarly incomplete and unconvincing in its treatment of the acquisition mechanism. "No explanation," Gregg says succinctly, "no theory."

Although, as Gregg points out, what Krashen offers is not a pedagogic theory but an acquisition theory, he nevertheless aims at a practical outcome in the classroom, and it is therefore from the pedagogical point of view that our third contributor, Marton, makes his assessment. Marton finds Krashen's service to be threefold: he rightly stresses the importance of input, he questions the value of certain long-standing classroom practices, and his acquisition/learning polarity—while not very convincing—does redirect attention to the problem of the transferability of language skills from the formal learning situation to "real life." Against these obliquely positive aspects, Marton poses what he describes as the "deeply anti-pedagogical" nature of Krashen's thinking. Taking up Krashen's dismissal of the ability of classroom pedagogy to do anything other than simulate real-life input, Marton cites an imposing list of theoreticians/pedagogues—from Sweet and Palmer to Leontiev and Galperin—whose research and experience would suggest otherwise. Krashen makes the basic error of neglecting the all-important question of the *quality* of teaching—a point Marton develops at some length. It is the role of classroom pedagogy to adapt the natural processes to the formal educational context and to make them more efficient. Sound pedagogy will achieve this, and Krashen's rejection of such a viewpoint invalidates much of what he claims.

Rivers and the Pica team are each concerned with the nature and operation of the central element of Krashen's theories, the question of *input*. Rivers examines the mechanics of the predicted galvanization of the learner's productive language powers as a result of subjection to "meaningful" input, while Pica et al. ask what it is that makes input "comprehensible" and therefore "meaningful." Whereas Rivers investigates the problem from a more theoretical point of view, Pica et al. compare two different learning environments to produce empirical evidence of the importance of increasing interaction between teacher and learner. Both illuminate an important area of Krashen's theories while acknowledging that shady corners remain to be explored.

Monitor Theory: Application and Ethics

Peter af Trampe,
University of Stockholm,
Sweden

Stephen D. Krashen has written a large number of papers and books on second language learning, the contents of which can be divided roughly into three groups: research overviews, theoretical expositions of his Monitor Theory, and practical advice to language teachers. The discussion in this paper is concerned with some of my reactions, as a (psycho)linguist, to the second and third groups, but let me just say a few preliminary words about the first.

Research Overviews

Regardless of what you think about Krashen's theories and the methods of language teaching he advocates, he can always be read with profit for his overviews of (almost exclusively North American) research into fields such as language aptitude and attitudes toward language learning, the lateralization of language functions in the brain, and the study of acquisition orders for morphemes. Krashen is only to be commended for his effort in making this research more generally known among the teaching profession.

The Monitor Theory Is Simplistic

Krashen's own theory I find less commendable. Indeed, I find it unscientific and simplistic. It was first critically reviewed by McLaughlin (1978) and Gregg (1984), among others (see also Gregg's contribution to this volume), and there is no need to rehearse their comments here. Let me only briefly give my reasons for calling the Monitor Theory simplistic and unscientific.

The Monitor Theory is built around the distinction between *learning* and *acquisition*. Learning refers to conscious language learning by means of "rules," and acquisition is a subconscious process "very similar to the process children use in acquiring first and second languages" (Krashen, 1981: 1). We can think of this as the setting up of two black boxes—one called "learning" and the other "acquisition." The boxes are somehow thought to reflect psychological processes. Krashen claims that what the language learner has learned consciously (i.e., the content of the learning box) is available to him only as a monitor. This is the "fundamental claim of Monitor Theory" (1981: 2). If one is setting out to build a theory, there is nothing wrong in postulating boxes of this kind: indeed, the distinction between conscious and subconscious learning seems plausible enough, and it is an interesting hypothesis that the result of conscious learning can be accessed and used only in certain ways. Once the distinction has been hypothesized, normal curiosity would lead us to try and lift the lids from the boxes and see what is inside. In particular, we would want to know in some detail how the two different processes work—for instance, what kind of input they need, how they react to different kinds of input, and how they use internalized information in producing their output.

Stated crudely, the input to both the acquisition box and the learning box is a number of utterances and/or written sentences. In the case of acquisition, it consists of utterances, etc. *in* the second language—it is a corpus, or sample, of that language. In the learning case, the utterances are of a very particular kind: they are utterances *about* the second language (i.e., "rules"), and they can be formulated in either the first or the second language. As a linguist, I know that the grammar and lexicon of any natural language are extremely complex. Furthermore, as a psycholinguist I know that both the comprehension and production of utterances are extremely complex and are processes only partly understood. Consequently, both the acquisition and the learning devices have to operate on a complex input to produce complex internal representations of that input to be used in the equally complex process of language production. One would expect that what Krashen had to say about his two boxes would in some way reflect all this complexity.

Regarding the input to the acquisition box, Krashen states that it has to be meaningful for the device to be able to work correctly. The input is often adapted by the use of foreigner talk or teacher talk. The input to the learning device, on the other hand, is simply "rules." As to the inner workings of the devices, the acquisition device is somehow pre-programmed for a natural order (in Krashen's works mostly exemplified by the order of acquisition of certain English morphemes). It is supposed to work in such a fashion that "we acquire (not learn) language by understanding input that is a little beyond our current level of (acquired) competence" (Krashen & Terrell, 1983: 32). This is made possible by the use of contextual cues. Moreover, the process is facilitated by adapted input. About the inner mechanism of the learning device, Krashen has very little to say: it functions only as a monitor, and it works better with "simple" rules (1983: 31) than with rules that are formally or semantically complex. He never discusses how the conscious rules are internalized or what the nature of the mental representations for these rules is. The learning device is a very black box indeed.

The Monitor Theory is indifferent to two important areas of language learning—pronunciation and vocabulary. What aspects of the sound system and the lexicon are, respectively, learned or acquired?

The point at issue is not that Krashen should know how languages are learned/acquired before proposing his theory. Nobody knows that. Besides, quite a lot of research has been done on "natural" language learning, so what Krashen says about acquisition has some support (see, however, Gregg [1984] and this volume for comments on the relevance of the Chomskyan Language Acquisition Device to Krashen's theory). But Krashen has postulated two totally separate mechanisms—acquisition and learning—that serve different purposes in the internalization and production of language, and through them he claims to explain various phenomena. However, especially in his treatment of the learning device, he has failed to take the complexity of language and language processing into account, which means that his model amounts to little more than mere labeling. In this sense it is too simplistic. It reminds me of models that purport to explain the communication process by simply dividing it into a number of components, e.g., sender, receiver, channel, signal, and message. Such models may offer convenient ways of talking about communication, but they do not really explain anything.

The Monitor Theory is unscientific because in the way it is formulated, Krashen makes unfalsifiable claims. If a hypothesis is unfalsifiable, it is consonant with any outcome of any test that you suggest for testing it. It can be neither proved nor disproved by recognizable scientific methods. Of course, whether Krashen's acquisition-learning and monitor hypotheses are true or not is irrelevant: we do not require that a scientist should always be right, but we do require that he or she should formulate hypotheses in such a way that we know under what conditions they would hold and under what conditions they would not. And this, as I think is evident from the following example, Krashen has sometimes failed to do.

The acquisition-learning hypothesis and the monitor hypothesis are the essence of Krashen's theory. As defined by Krashen, the two hypotheses must be considered together, since the results of learning are available only as a monitor. One type of evidence that Krashen adduces as support for his hypotheses is drawn from morpheme studies. The following quotation shows his way of reasoning:

> The value of these studies is considerable. They provide more information than merely showing us the actual order of acquisition. They also show us when performers are using conscious grammar and when they are not. We have hypothesized that when conditions for "Monitor-free" performance are met, when performers are focused on communication and not form, adult errors in English as a second language (for grammatical morphemes in obligatory occasions) are quite similar to errors made by children acquiring English as a second language (some similarities to first language acquisition have been noted as well). When second language speakers "monitor," when they focus on form, this "natural order" is disturbed. The appearance of child-like errors in Monitor-free conditions is hypothesized to be a manifestation of the acquired system operating in isolation, or with little influence of the Monitor. (Krashen, 1981: 6–7)

There are a number of claims involved here. Let us look at some of them.

Children's acquisition of and production in first and second languages are subconscious processes. It is quite obvious that children acquire their first or second language without formal rules or instruction. Furthermore, we can produce and comprehend grammatical utterances without being in the least aware of the rules of language.

Whenever the natural order occurs, this can be taken as evidence of acquisition. There are a number of studies showing that children acquire certain morphemes of English in a specific order. This is called the "natural order." The acquisition-order studies have been criticized on methodological grounds, and there are problems with the interpretation of the results (see, for example, Hatch [1983], Chapter 3). Let us nevertheless regard our assumption as true.

Focus on form causes deviations from the natural order. Again, this seems plausible enough. We know, for instance, from Labov's studies (Labov, 1966) that the speaker's use of language varies as a function of focus of attention. In casual speech, the speaker usually pays attention only to the *content* of the message, whereas in careful speech attention is shifted towards the *form* of the message. This shift of attention can have implications for his or her choice of allophones, allomorphs, syntactic constructions, etc. Indeed, Labov also talks about monitoring: "The most important way in which this attention is exerted is in audio-monitoring one's own speech, though other forms of monitoring also take place" (Labov, 1971: 170). Of course, Labov refers to monitoring in one's first language, i.e., a kind of monitoring that does not require explicit knowledge of the rules of grammar. In Krashen's terms this would be monitoring by means of the acquired (rather than learned) system. Krashen also recognizes this possibility:

> A very important point about the Monitor hypothesis is that it does not say that acquisition is unavailable for self-correction. We often self-correct, or edit, using acquisition, in both first and second languages. (Krashen & Terrell, 1983: 31)

Note that if the natural order is evidence of acquisition, and if acquired knowledge can be used consciously, then the natural order might occur in situations when conscious processing (i.e., "focus on form") is encouraged. However, this causes problems for Krashen's interpretation of the morpheme studies. Some of these studies used conditions that were supposed to be monitor-free, and others used conditions that were thought to induce "focus on form." When speakers' attention is directed at the form of the message— i.e., when they monitor—the natural order is disturbed. But how can we decide if this is acquisition- or learning-driven monitoring? The answer is that without further criteria, we cannot! Figure 1 shows the dilemma.

FIGURE 1

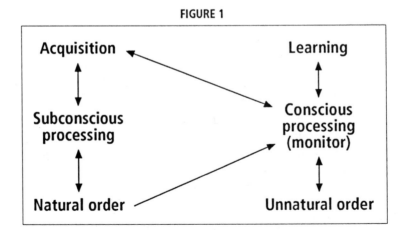

From Figure 1 it can be seen that it is quite possible to relate both natural and unnatural order to both learning and acquisition. Thus the predictions of the Monitor Theory are unfalsifiable, since it predicts every possible state of affairs. It is, of course, a corollary that the morpheme studies offer no evidence for the proposed distinction between learning and acquisition. Notice also that the difference between conscious and subconscious processing is useless for testing the acquisition-learning distinction, as conscious processing can be classified either way. The problem cannot be solved simply by positing two different monitors, unless criteria for deciding which one has been used are specified (cf. Hulstijn, 1982). Even if Krashen did this, the fact remains that a long-standing version of the theory has presented unfalsifiable claims. However, the theory makes one interesting and falsifiable prediction: formally acquired ("learned") rules can never become subconscious and act as the basis of utterance production. It is perhaps symptomatic that Krashen has—at least to my knowledge—made no attempt to test this hypothesis.

Advice to Language Teachers

In Krashen's writings, a great deal of advice on language teaching is offered, and my general impression is that most of it is sound, commonsense advice. Krashen's claim is that this advice follows from his theory of second language acquisition. Chapter 3, for instance, of *The Natural Approach* (Krashen & Terrell, 1983) is called "Implications of Second Language Acquisition Theory for the Classroom." Here, I must make my own standpoint clear. Once again, I find Krashen's theory of second language learning both unscientific and unduly simplistic, though this need not imply that it is worthless. First, it has served as an incitement to the research community because it raises important questions. Second, the theory may be bad, but some of its conclusions, or implications, may nevertheless be correct. This is more likely to be the case when there is independent research to support each conclusion—and there often is—since scientific theories are not usually developed in a vacuum. In fact, Krashen does refer to a lot of recent research on language learning, but questions may arise as to whether the supportive research is correctly interpreted, whether it is good-quality research, and whether there is contradictory data that for some reason has been overlooked.

The most important principle in language teaching, according to Krashen, is that of providing comprehensive input, where *input* refers to the language to which the learner is exposed in the classroom. This should be not only comprehensible but also interesting, because what should be achieved is a focus on message rather than on form. If such input is provided, the learner will automatically learn ("acquire") the forms and rules. I certainly agree that input must be comprehensible, though we do not always know beforehand what kind of input will be comprehensible to any particular category of student, so the teaching must include some means of checking this from time to time.

On the whole, I am inclined also to agree with the focus-on-message requirement. Psycholinguistic experiments have repeatedly shown that we usually process for meaning rather than for form (see, for example, Clark & Clark, 1977), and this is the essential rationale behind much of the communicative competence work on syllabus design and language teaching (see, for example, Wilkins, 1976; Munby, 1978; Brumfit & Johnson, 1979; Candlin, 1981; etc.). However, I cannot leave this point without voicing some doubt. The fact that we have phenomena like pidginization and fossilization can be taken to indicate that focus on message is differentially effective. Perhaps, for instance, it has more effect on vocabulary than on certain aspects of the morphology. If this is true, it would sometimes be beneficial to focus the learner on form (cf. Pienemann, 1985; Long, 1985).

What I have said amounts to agreeing with Krashen that comprehensible and motivating input ("lowering the affective filter") is a necessary condition for foreign language learning. Whether it alone is also a sufficient condition is a moot point. It seems to be implied in Krashen's view that it is, since this kind of input is supposed to lead to acquisition.

As Krashen and Terrell point out, the input hypothesis has the corollary that speaking is not essential in language learning. If we concentrate on listening comprehension, "speaking will emerge on its own" (1983: 58). This is a dictum that must be qualified. Most psycholinguists would agree that in general comprehension/perception precedes production, in the sense that, for a given phonological, morphological, syntactical, or lexical contrast or item, (first-language) learners have perceived the contrast/structure and have grasped part of its meaning or function before spontaneously using it in their own speech. Comprehension, however, is normally a relative and continuous process. For instance, we learn the meaning of a word gradually. This is certainly the case with children (Carey, 1978) and probably also with adult second-language learners (Burling, 1982). Having only a partial grasp of its meaning does not prevent us from using a word. That this can also be the case for grammatical structure is clear from the attested use of prefabricated constructions (see, for example, Hakuta, 1976; Wong-Fillmore, 1979). Furthermore, it may be argued that language learning is a truly interactive process (see Rivers in this volume), in which the learner uses utterances partly for the purpose of testing hypotheses about language. The learner's output may be important as a cue to the caretaker's or teacher's adaptation of his or her output. The nature of the relationship between the child's output and that of the mother is not certain, but Nelson (1981), for instance, found that the frequent use of recasts by mothers seemed to promote the linguistic growth of children. If that were true also in second-language learning, it would mean that the learner's speech production is more important than Krashen and Terrell seem to believe.

To sum up, I have looked at some of the teaching principles that Krashen and Terrell have suggested, and found that while they are basically sound, they should not be treated as the whole truth and nothing but the truth. Rather, they should be looked upon as crude rules of thumb which admit to exceptions and which may have to be qualified and restricted when applied to actual learners in real classrooms. Thus, teachers should approach them with an open mind, while retaining a critical eye. In the face of what is presented as a temptingly simple solution to all their problems, this calls for a considerable degree of discipline.

Ethics

Language teaching, like many other areas where our knowledge is scanty and the relationship between theory and practice cannot be defined once and for all, is a field characterized by strong oscillation between different ideas, where each newly postulated method tends to be regarded as a panacea to remedy all the shortcomings of earlier ones and a shortcut to overcome the arduous intellectual process of learning a new language. There is an almost manic-depressive mixture of pessimism and optimism in this oscillation between polar extremes. Methods to which one has adhered perhaps for years are suddenly renounced, and a new approach is preached with near-missionary zeal. This is all the more baffling, since the fundamental issues are not new. Throughout the history of language teaching there have been, for instance, "naturalists" such as Erasmus of Rotterdam, Michel de Montaigne, Johann Amos Comenius, John Locke, Martin Luther, Francois Gouin, Johann Heinrich Pestalozzi, and David Maximilian Berlitz, who have argued against the scholastic, rationalistic, or grammar-based practices of their day (Hesse, 1975; Hawkins, 1981). In the twentieth century the swings of the pendulum have been more rapid, but the issues remain more or less the same.

In such cases one would expect the truth to lie somewhere between the two extremes. Why then do we still encounter this polarity? I suggest one possible explanation that applies to our own times.

Learning a foreign language is not done in a day. It is a complicated and laborious task. Language teachers, sometimes bitterly, experience this in their daily work, and the mood engendered by this experience disposes them to seize upon and apply new ideas. At least some of these ideas come from people doing research in linguistics, psycholinguistics, educational psychology, etc. Nowadays, science enjoys great prestige: the words *science* and *research* are what Hayakawa calls "purr" words (the opposite is "snarl" words), and this increases the probability that ideas originating in research will reach the teachers in the field. It is unreasonable to expect the teachers to be specialists in linguistics and psychology as well as in language teaching, so many of the ideas will be accepted at face value. Now, in research, generalization is a governing principle—sometimes even a purr word: the researcher tries to stretch his or her theory to the limit, which is totally legitimate in the research community, since this makes the theory more vulnerable to disproof. When we consider the application of the theory to language teaching, however, this state of affairs obviously places a heavy responsibility on the researcher, who knows that his or her theory is likely to be accepted uncritically by the teaching community.

To illustrate what can happen as a consequence of this touching faith in "scientific research," let me give a few examples. In my own professional time, there have been several cases of this kind, and the following three are perhaps the most remarkable:

The wholesale application of generative grammar to foreign language teaching in the sixties. In this case there was nothing wrong with the theory as a theory of grammar, but, as Chomsky himself pointed out, its pedagogical usefulness was very doubtful. Nevertheless, various other linguists ardently advocated its application to FLT. In Sweden, one result of this was a fierce debate on cognitive code learning vs. audio-lingual habit methods. It also resulted in a number of textbooks and grammars that supposedly used the "transformational" approach to teaching. The debate as such was probably a good thing, except that a number of teachers believed that the last word had now been said on the importance of rules of grammar in FLL. This was especially happily accepted by those teachers who had never believed in the newfangled ideas of audio-lingualism anyway; the textbooks, etc. soon fell out of use.

Berstein's distinction between restricted and elaborated codes (see the *Collected Papers* volume, Bernstein, 1971) was widely accepted in Sweden by educationalists and teachers of Swedish as a First Language. In this case, there was a lot wrong with the theory (see Stubbs [1976] for a scathing review), and its consequences were probably more harmful, since it resulted in certain proposals for remedial language teaching (based on misinterpretations of the theory) and induced a false sense of security in some quarters that the last word had been said on the relationship between language and social class and its importance for the success of working-class children at school.

In 1962 Nils Erik Hansegård introduced *the concept of double semi-lingualism* to describe the linguistic situation of a Finnish-speaking minority in the north of Sweden. Some ten years later the concept was adopted by Skutnabb-Kangas (e.g., 1976) and applied to immigrant children in general. The main hypothesis was that the children of immigrants run the risk of becoming deficient (= semi-lingual) in their first as well as their second language. However, little empirical support has to this day been found for such a hypothesis. In spite of this, it was widely accepted among teachers and parents of immigrant children and in many cases also by the school authorities. As a deficiency theory it caused great anxiety, especially among immigrant parents. Among the general public it sometimes led to the stereotype that most immigrant children were linguistically deficient.

With these cases in mind, let us return to the Monitor Theory and the Natural Approach to second language learning. Krashen and Terrell use a number of "purr" expressions—for example, ". . . some of the central findings in language acquisition research. . ."; "Many researchers now believe. . ."; "According to research in second language acquisition. . ."; ". . .the current state of research and theory in adult second and foreign language acquisition. . . ." In this way they appeal to the prestige value of research, and on that count their theories are doubly likely to be favorably received by the teaching community.

Summary

As I hope I have been able to show, the Monitor Theory is basically not viable. As to its application, the teaching principles suggested in Krashen and Terrell should not be looked upon as laws without exceptions, but simply as rules of thumb. The application of bad theories of language and language learning, like the over-application of limited theories, can obviously have serious consequences—the most serious being when their application is downright harmful to the learners, as in the last two cases mentioned above. There is some risk of the over-application of Krashen's distinction between optimal and over-/under-users of the Monitor. We have to accept the fact that language learners differ in terms of personality, learning style, educational background, etc., and that the extent to which a learner relies on conscious rules can be a function of such factors. Krashen's distinction seems to invite unhelpful qualitative judgment of different kinds of learners.

Another serious consequence of bad or limited theories is that they encourage teachers to believe that there is nothing more to be said on a particular issue and thus either reinforce the conservative opinions of some (as in the first case listed above) or discourage further thought about the matter (which happened in all the cases). This is where I see the greatest risk with the Monitor Theory. Apart from being unscientific, it is simplistic, and the suggested implications for language teaching, though formulated as general truths, are open to discussion. I certainly hope that language teachers will not once again fall into the trap and that the theory will eventually be treated with the healthy skepticism it deserves. It would be nice not to have to add a fourth example to the list above.

Krashen's Theory, Acquisition Theory, and Theory*

Kevin Gregg,
St. Andrews University,
Japan

Krashen claims to have developed a comprehensive theory of second language acquisition; I claim he has done no such thing. We can't both be right, and it should be of some interest to settle the matter, especially since Krashen's "theory" currently has no rival in terms either of comprehensiveness or of popularity.[1] Thus if Krashen has not produced a theory of L2A, presumably no one has. What I propose to do here, then, is to show why what Krashen calls a theory is not a theory. I will try to do this by indicating what some of the requirements for a second language acquisition theory are, and pointing out where and how Krashen's theory fails to meet these requirements.[2]

Before we begin, however, two points need to be made. The first is that Krashen's writings are extremely vague, sometimes contradictory, and usually lacking in concrete examples and precise statements. I will thus often be forced to fall back on the method of "rich interpretation" in explicating his work, and this is always risky.

The second point is that it must be remembered that Krashen is offering an acquisition theory, not, for example, a pedagogical theory. Of course, any theory in any field must meet certain criteria, e.g., of precision and testability, and as we will see, Krashen generally fails to meet these. But even putting those problems aside, it would in no way count against my claim if it were shown that an instructional program set up on lines suggested by Krashen (see, e.g., Krashen & Terrell, 1983) actually "worked."

If, for instance, you were to ask me how you could get all the apples from your apple tree to the ground, I could suggest severing their connections with the tree. This would usually do the trick, but I think you would be reluctant to accept my solution as a theory of gravitation. By the same token, telling me that "comprehensible input" in a "low affective filter" environment will lead to acquisition, even if it were true, would not be giving me a theory of second language acquisition that *explains* what the process is and how it works. It is here that Krashen lets us down; he gives us no explanation, hence no theory.

In order to examine Krashen's theory as an acquisition theory, we should measure it against specific criteria for such theories. I will use the conditions elaborated by Atkinson (1982, Chapter 1). And, especially since I claim that there are no L2A theories, it will give us some perspective if we look at some of the more promising work being done in L1A research. For this purpose I will refer whenever possible to work by Kenneth Wexler and his associates (e.g., Wexler & Culicover, 1980), Steven Pinker (e.g., Pinker, 1984), and Robert C. Berwick (Berwick, 1985).

Conditions on Theory Construction

Atkinson (1982) proposes several conditions that he maintains should be met by any language acquisition theory. He is interested in L1A theories, but his conditions are applicable to L2A theory as well and provide a useful framework for investigating the status of Krashen's theory *qua* theory.

An acquisition theory for Atkinson has two components: a sequence of theories $T_1, \ldots T_n$, each accounting for the data in a given domain D for different times $t_1, \ldots t_n$, plus a mechanism M for getting from T_i to T_{i+1}. Atkinson maintains that any such acquisition theory must meet the following conditions, among others:

1) T_i must be explanatory in D at t_i. Specifically, the theory must take into account the problem of explanation in psychological theory (Atkinson's Condition I).
2) T_i must be constructed within the framework of a particular general theory (Condition II).
3) The sequence $(T_1, \ldots T_n)$ must be explicable; specifically, it must admit of an environmental, a reductive, or a teleological explanation (Condition IV; I will distinguish the three types of explanation later).
4) The mechanism M must be specified satisfactorily (Condition V).

We will see that (1) Krashen ignores Condition I completely and thus fails to demarcate a domain within which his theory is to be explanatory, a failure that in itself is fatal to the theory; (2) Krashen's use of linguistic theory barely goes beyond intermittent invocation of a "LAD" whose powers are unspecified and hence totally unconstrained; (3) not only does Krashen fail to explain the acquisition sequence, he generally fails even to describe it; and (4) Krashen's acquisition mechanism is vague and unconvincing, to the extent that it can be said to exist at all.

The Domain of the Theory

In the standard view of explanation—the so-called deductive-nomological paradigm (Hempel & Oppenheim, 1948; see Lass [1980] for a useful discussion in a linguistic context)—we have a datum to be explained (the *explanandum*—call it E) and a set of statements (the *explanans*) consisting of specific observations or conditions (C) and general laws (L) that together logically imply the explanandum, thus: (C & L) → E. To take a simple example: /ŋo/ begins with a velar nasal (C); in English no word may begin with a velar nasal (L); therefore, /ŋo/ is not a possible English word (E). (Note that the explanandum need not be a piece of observable behavior; we will return to this point later.) Atkinson's domain D can be viewed as a set of related explananda.

Of course, the problems still remain of *ceteris paribus* conditions, the accuracy of C, etc., and especially the explanatory depth of L, which can vary according to the needs of the theoretician. Thus, while "The apple fell from the tree because its stem broke" can be accommodated to this paradigm, we are justified in hoping for a more profound explanation, e.g., one that appeals to a precisely defined concept of gravity. An explanans for one explanandum can itself be the explanandum for another explanans.[3] If we want to know why Mary can speak normally, we may properly be satisfied with the explanation that she is a normal adult human being who grew up in normal circumstances; but we may also want an explanation of why growing up in normal circumstances leads to the ability to speak a language. For example, Krashen's Input Hypothesis, which tells us that "humans acquire language in only one way—by understanding messages, or by receiving 'comprehensible input'" (Krashen, 1985: 2), treats what should be an explanandum as if it were only an explanans (see Gregg, 1986).

Another problem, and one that Krashen does not share with most L1A or L2A researchers, is that of defining D, the domain of inquiry. For most researchers, D is fairly limited: the acquisition of a phonological system, say, or the acquisition of the meaning of deictic terms. Even those L1A scholars who have attempted to develop more comprehensive theories of "language acquisition" have made it clear that for them the term *language acquisition* means something more specific than what it seems to mean; that is, they offer theories of the acquisition of a grammar. As Chomsky says, "the central concept throughout is 'grammar,' not 'language.' The latter is derivative, at a higher level of abstraction from actual neural mechanisms; correspondingly, it raises new problems" (1984: 4).

Krashen brings such new problems on himself, since he seems to believe that his theory extends so far as to embrace just about all aspects of language. For instance, in rejecting the idea that production is necessary for acquisition (he calls this idea the Output Hypothesis), he says, "If [the Output Hypothesis] is correct, every item in every component of the grammar, every phonological contrast, morphological, syntactic, sociolinguistic, and discourse rule must be separately tested in production" (1985: 36). I believe Krashen is alone in claiming to be able to account for the acquisition of sociolinguistic and discourse "rules," or in wanting to account for the acquisition of phonological and sociolinguistic rules by one unitary theory of acquisition. It may seem that Krashen is burdening himself unduly by trying to take on all of "language," and indeed he is; but on the other hand, it does give him the opportunity to cite putative evidence indiscriminately, disregarding the actual domain of that evidence. For instance, his discussion of length of residence as a factor in acquisition (1982: 37–42) lumps together studies of syntax and of accent, as if there were a single global factor (rather like "intelligence") called "proficiency," which can be equated with acquisition. This is very convenient for Krashen, albeit a bit troubling for the careful reader.

Let us assume that Krashen is actually restricting himself to the acquisition of a grammar in a more restricted sense. There is still an important problem with our explanandum, one that L1A researchers need not concern themselves with. I refer of course to the fact that in the large majority of cases, a grammar of a second language is not acquired. This will come as news to no one, but the theoretical consequences of this fact have been largely ignored.[4]

L1A theories must address the fact that everyone acquires a first language, what Pinker (1979) calls the Learnability Condition. This is a major constraint on L1A theory; as Pinker says, "a theory that is powerful enough to account for the *fact* of language acquisition may be a more promising first approximation of an ultimately viable theory than one that is able to describe the *course* of language acquisition" (1979: 220; see also Wexler, 1982). But L2A theory cannot avail itself of this constraint. What, then, is the explanandum that is to be accounted for? That some people can acquire a second language? Or that most people don't? In either case, the L2A theorist's job is going to be seriously complicated by the wide variability in terminal states achieved by different learners.

Krashen's solution, of course, is to claim that anyone can acquire a second language and would, if it were not for various affective factors that prevent acquisition to a greater or lesser degree. Although Krashen's account of this putative "Affective Filter" is woefully inadequate (see Gregg, 1984), his approach cannot be denied out of hand. But it is important to notice how this approach shifts the focus of the theory: rather than a theory of acquisition, we have a theory of non-acquisition; or rather, we need one. There is nothing in and of itself wrong with this, of course; but since Krashen insists that the "LAD" does not degenerate in adults, we still need a theory of acquisition as well.

It may seem at first blush that Krashen's position—that the "LAD" continues unimpaired throughout life—has the advantage of theoretical simplicity. Pinker, for instance, makes what he calls his Continuity Assumption on similar grounds. That is, he assumes, following Macnamara (1982: 13), that "the null hypothesis in developmental psychology is that the cognitive mechanisms of children and adults are identical" (Pinker, 1984: 7), so Occam's Razor requires us to start with this hypothesis.[5] Indeed, one would probably prefer the continuity assumption (but see note 5) if adults always acquired second languages and did so with the same speed and facility as children acquiring their first. But since this is far from the case, the simplicity argument won't hold. One could easily argue, for instance, that it isn't the "LAD" that remains the same, but rather the "Affective Filter." After all, while nowhere near every adult has a second language, every single adult *and* child has affect.

We have a choice, then, of trying to explain why most adults don't acquire a second language or trying to explain how those few who do, do; and the choice cannot be made *a priori*. We will see in a moment what Krashen makes of his continuity position when we look at Condition II, but first it would be useful to look at a possible non-continuity position, in order to see more clearly just what is at stake.

We could, for instance, deny that any adult learner actually has native-speaker competence in a second language. We could do, in other words, what few L2A researchers seem to have bothered to do: look into the meaning of the term *competence* in L2A theory.[6] For instance, following Richards (1985), we could distinguish between *competence* and *proficiency*. We could then claim, following a suggestion of Chomsky's (1980: 28), that proficiency (but not competence) can be achieved through other means than the "LAD."[7] We would hope to be able to test this hypothesis, of course, and indeed there seem to be some possible ways of doing so.

For instance, Spolsky et al. (1968) showed that the listening comprehension scores of non-native speakers of English whose scores under normal conditions were equal to those of native speakers were significantly lower under noisy conditions than those of native speakers. Again, it may be that native speakers can make certain kinds of *errors* in their native language that are not possible for even the most proficient non-native (see, e.g., the Japanese slips of the tongue cited in Kamio & Tonoike, 1979: 295–96). Or consider the ability of (native) speakers to "shadow" another speaker's speech (Fodor, 1983: 61, citing Marslen-Wilson, 1973), that is, the ability to repeat the speech with comprehension as they hear it, with a delay of as little as a quarter of a second. It just might be that under extraordinary circumstances as those indicated above, even the most proficient non-native speaker can be distinguished from the native. Practically speaking, of course, this may look like a distinction without a difference; but in terms of acquisition theory, it would undermine the continuity thesis adopted by Krashen.

Of course, these are empirical questions that I cannot hope to answer here; it is enough for my purpose to show that there is nothing untoward in taking a non-continuity position on the "LAD" question. I will sum up by stressing that Atkinson's Condition I, which at first sight may have seemed almost a tautology, is in fact pregnant with consequences for L2A theory, and that Krashen (who is by no means alone in this regard) has not considered the basic problem of what it is that his theory is to explain.

Linguistic Theory

Atkinson's Condition II is intended to preclude ad hoc explanations disguised as theories. More specifically, it demands that we have a linguistic theory of sufficient depth and substance to account for the data we are dealing with. (This is a minimal requirement. We may also need—especially if we are going to be as ambitious as Krashen—theories of pragmatic competence, etc.) As Wexler and Culicover emphasize (1980: 596, n. 10), "If a sufficiently precise theory of what is achieved does not exist, we cannot evaluate (or even do a reasonable job of creating) a theory of the learning of the achievement." In L1A theory this point has at least sometimes been recognized: Wexler and Culicover, for instance, assume that the child acquires a transformational grammar based on Chomsky 1965; Pinker (1984) uses a lexical-functional grammar (Bresnan, 1982). Krashen, on the other hand, has nothing to offer but what he calls the "LAD."

I have been enclosing "LAD" in scare quotes not because I don't accept the concept it represents, but because I do, and because Krashen's use of the term deviates from that of Chomsky and most other generative theorists, who in fact don't use the term much anymore, preferring "universal grammar"

(UG). From now on I will make this distinction, using "LAD" only to refer to Krashen's construct. For Krashen, LAD is simply "the language mental organ," or alternatively, "the internal language processor" (1985: 4, 2). On the one hand, this says next to nothing; on the other hand, it says too much. It says next to nothing since it simply states that there is a language-specific mental faculty, without specifying in any way whatever just what the nature, contents, limits, etc. of that faculty are. As Wexler and Culicover point out, "LAD theories are essentially *any* theory . . . in which the language learner is thought of as forming hypotheses about grammar based on a starting configuration and the input data" (1980: 510, n. 42; emphasis added). Thus if we accept the proposition that there are universal innate properties of language, as Krashen and I and most L2A researchers do, then it is incumbent on the theorist to specify those properties so that specific claims can be made and tested. Research into UG goes on, of course, but there already is a good deal known or thought to be known, and some L2A researchers have begun to make use of this knowledge to attack various well-defined problems in L2A (see, e.g., Ritchie, 1978; Mazurkewich, 1984; White, 1985). Krashen seems content just to brandish Chomsky's name like a talisman.

Krashen's references to "LAD" also say too much when they equate "language mental organ" with "language processor." Language processing— for example, parsing—is not the same thing as language acquisition, and Chomsky's modularity principle is intended in part to capture this fact. Multiple-embedded relative clauses, for instance, violate no principle of UG, but they are nevertheless difficult or impossible to parse and hence to understand. Pinker claims for his theory that "the process of segmenting the continuous sound stream into words and morphemes interacts in only limited ways with the rule acquisition processes . . ." (1984: 28). Of course, interaction is exactly what we would expect from a modular theory of acquisition. But interaction is not the same thing as identity.

This failure to specify the LAD makes it difficult to assess Krashen's continuity claim that "adults can access the same natural 'language acquisition device' that children use" (Krashen, 1982 :10). Since the LAD (*ex my hypothesi*) actually covers a multitude of mental faculties, it is possible that only certain of its functions continue unimpaired to the end. Consider, for instance, Slobin's "operating principles" (Slobin, 1973, 1982), to which Krashen refers from time to time in passing (e.g., 1983: 139, 1985: 3) and which are intended to refer to "predispositions to perceive speech and construct formal systems in particular ways" (Slobin, 1982: 137). Krashen evidently sees these either as part of LAD or as innate constraints on LAD-generated rules. But whereas languages do not violate UG, they often do violate operating principles, for example, Principles D and F ("Avoid interruption or rearrangement of linguistic units," "Avoid exceptions;" Slobin, 1973: 199, 205). Children acquiring English as a first language will sooner or later have to overrule both principles (e.g., questions, irregular verbs), whereas presumably they will never overrule principles of UG. It is possible that the power of the operating principles (or of some of them; they are legion) is significantly reduced in adults.

In a somewhat similar vein, Gleitman and Wanner suggest that for children, the relationship between word and meaning is one to one: ". . . there is a lexical syntax that generates complex items, but youngest learners do not exploit this linguistic resource. For them, the word maps onto a single concept" (1982: 12). Clearly, this isn't true for adults, although there may indeed be a good deal of variation among adults in this area, and it may be one factor in the differential proficiency levels of adults, especially since current generative theory places an increased burden on the lexicon as the domain of learned linguistic information.

Other examples of what appear to be child-specific learning strategies are Pinker's "semantic bootstrapping hypothesis" (Grimshaw, 1981; Pinker, 1982, 1984) and Wexler's Uniqueness Principle (Roeper, 1981). The former says that the child makes certain basic assumptions about the syntax of the input language, based on the semantic role of given words in a sentence (e.g., if X represents the agent of an action, X is the subject of the sentence). The latter says that the child assumes that there can be only one surface structure for any given base structure. Obviously, both strategies will ultimately fail, but Pinker points out that something like semantic bootstrapping will be needed to enable the child to get an initial purchase on the syntactic rules of the language he or she is starting to acquire. It is not at all clear that beginning adults use strategies like bootstrapping or the Uniqueness Principle in learning a second language, although I am not claiming that they do not.

The continuity hypothesis is perfectly plausible, but it is of little value to us unless it is given some empirical content. In Krashen's hands the LAD becomes not the explanatory construct it was intended to be, but simply a new name for the ghost in the machine. Krashen tells us nothing whatever about what the LAD is, and this is in large part because he has nothing to say about the "L." A look at his treatment of acquisition order may help illustrate some of Krashen's confusions about language and linguistic theory.

Explaining the Acquisition Sequence

Given that at two different times a learner will have two more or less different grammars, we want to know not only what these two grammars are (Condition II), but also why the differences appear in that order. Why does the learner proceed from A to A + B rather than from B to A + B? Atkinson accepts three types of possible explanation for a developmental sequence: environmental (e.g., A always appears in the input earlier or more often or perceptually more saliently than B); reductive (e.g., A and B are simply the linguistic reflexes of, say, cognitive structures A' and B', and the latter appear in that order); and teleological explanations, where the order is a logical consequence of the developmental theory (e.g., transformations presuppose phrase-structure rules but not vice versa, so a transformational grammar couldn't be acquired before a phrase-structure grammar).[8]

Where does Krashen's theory fit in here? His Natural Order Hypothesis states that "the acquisition of grammatical structures proceeds in a predictable order" (1982: 12; see also 1983: 136) or, alternatively, that "we acquire the rules of language in a predictable order" (1985: 1). Although Krashen talks of "rules of language" (and seems to mean it, too; see the discussion of the Output Hypothesis above), the actual data available do not extend much further than certain grammatical morphemes in English. Restricting ourselves for the moment to these, how does Krashen explain the fact that, say, -*ing* is acquired before third person -*s*? He rejects environmental explanations (see, e.g., Dulay, Burt, & Krashen, 1982: 201; Krashen, 1981: 53). He does not mention reductive explanations, but his commitment to LAD and to a language-specific "mental organ" seems to imply a rejection of a reductive approach.[9] This leaves teleological explanations (or else an explanation of the fourth kind), but as we have just seen, Krashen has no theory to appeal to.

Not only does he have no theory; it is hard to imagine how he could get one together that would make sense of his vague idea of what a "structure" or "rule" is. The "structures" to be accounted for by the Natural Order Hypothesis include, minimally, rules of syntax and morphology (Krashen [1983], his most detailed discussion, uses the past tense of *sweep* as an example of a rule to be acquired in the Natural Order). These structures seem to exist in total independence of each other, so the Natural Order could evidently include a sequence like X, -*s*, Neg-transportation, the prefix *re-*, Y. This is not encouraging.

Note, by the way, that Krashen's contention that production is not necessary for acquisition (1985: 36) commits him to the possibility that there may be "rules" acquired that *never* appear in the output of a given learner. This makes the empirical status of the Natural Order Hypothesis a good deal less secure.[10] So does the problem of the "acquisition of deviant forms" (1985: 46–49). If we are to accept the Natural Order Hypothesis, English has (or rather, English *is*) a set of "structures" (the number to be determined), that are acquired in a certain order. But where do "deviant forms" fit in in this order? Krashen (1983) suggests that a learner may acquire (a series of) "transitional" rules approaching the real rule with increasing accuracy. But if a learner stops short of "$i + 1$"—acquiring $i + 0.8$, as it were—how can he or she progress to $i + 2$? Or, if the learner can skip from $i + 0.8$ to $i + 2$, then why not skip all the way to $i + 5$? Even if all "deviant forms" are "transitional"—which is unlikely, and in any case Krashen tells us nothing one way or the other about this—the permanent acquisition of just one of them should shut down the acquisition process. And if not all "deviant forms" are "transitional," how do we know what kinds of errors are possible? If we do not have a theoretical means of constraining the acquisition of "deviant forms," then we will have, in principle as well as in fact, no way to determine the Natural Order for a language and hence no way to give the Natural Order Hypothesis any predictive power.[11]

Clearly, there is something wrong here. One thing that is wrong is Krashen's idea of what a language is. He seems to be arguing that a language simply *is* a set of miscellaneous rules. Thus it should make sense to say of a given learner that he or she has acquired, say, 62% of English. I suspect that Krashen is making the same fundamental (and widespread) error that Chomsky warns against: "the assumption that among the things in the world there are languages or dialects, and that individuals come to acquire them" (quoted in Paikeday, 1985: 49). Such a naive view of language as this cannot advance us very far toward an explanation of an acquisition sequence.

The Learning Mechanism

The idea of a language as a collection of individual rules or structures makes it difficult to explain not only the order of acquisition (assuming that there is one), but also the mechanism for acquisition. Still, if Krashen has not succeeded in meeting Condition V, at least he is in good company. As Marshall complained a few years ago about L1A research, "No one has seriously attempted to specify a mechanism that 'drives' language through its 'stages' or along its continuous function" (1979: 443). In L1A research, this challenge has begun to be responded to; in L2A research, Krashen offers us his Input Hypothesis.

The relevant claim of the Input Hypothesis is that "we progress along the natural order . . . by understanding input that contains structures at our next 'stage'—structures that are a bit beyond our current level of competence. . . . We are able to understand language containing unacquired grammar with the help of context, which includes extra-linguistic information, our knowledge of the world, and previously acquired linguistic competence" (1985: 2). The LAD also has a role (1985: 2–3; 1983: 138–139), although this, as one might expect by now, is not specified.

Significantly, Krashen says that we *understand* with the help of context, not that we acquire through context. This is uncontroversial but also unhelpful. There is general agreement that extrasyntactic information, such as information about thematic relations in a sentence, will facilitate acquisition; what is needed is a concrete proposal about how. Pinker's bootstrapping hypothesis is one example; Berwick's parser is another. As Berwick points out (1985: 41–42), "Nearly every grammatical theory posits something like thematic role information." But he then goes on to say that his acquisition procedure "uses this information, but only for simple sentences, and only to fix a few syntactic parameters early in acquisition." Indeed, Berwick considers "minimal use of extrasyntactic information" to be one of the "psychological plausibility criteria" of an acquisition model, and compares his own model favorably with Wexler and Culicover's, which requires input of the complete base structure of a sentence as well as its surface structure. Thus Berwick's model is not data-driven; the acquisition mechanism is internal and is specified by Berwick in detail. Krashen, on the other hand, tells us nothing about what the LAD does; judging from his exposition of the Input Hypothesis, *every* rule or structure in the Natural Order must be (unconsciously) guessed at by using contextual clues. (Remember, it will not do any good to read or hear about the structure at $i + 1$; the Acquisition/Learning Hypothesis precludes learning from becoming acquisition.)

Since Krashen says nothing about the internal acquisition mechanism, I will confine my comments to the external component: the input.[12] Krashen's account of the role of input is rendered problematic by his odd conception of "structure." The Input Hypothesis would seem to require that every structure in a language be present in input in order to be acquired, except that the "creative construction process" (whatever that is) can produce "new forms without the benefit of input by reorganizing the rules that have already been acquired in more general ways" (1983: 138–39).[13] Presumably, Krashen intends this "reorganization" to cover all cases of acquisition where there could be no input—e.g., "deviant forms" like *he go, I no like*, etc.[14] But if all there is to be acquired is "structures," how does one come to know that, say, *I reput the books on the shelf* or *Many earthquakes were happened* are not possible, or that Japanese verbs don't accept a causative suffix if the subject is inanimate?[15] Since we cannot acquire the absence of a rule, we must assume that the LAD creates the relevant constraints, although how that would involve "reorganizing" rules "in more general ways" is not clear.

On the other hand Krashen seems to *require* input to enable a learner to discard a deviant form and acquire the real thing: "intermediate forms" are dropped if they don't reappear in input: "If it does turn up with some minimum frequency, it can be confirmed and acquired. If it does not turn up, it is a 'transitional form' and will eventually be discarded" (1983: 139). This means, as far as I can tell—and I am not confident in my ability to make sense of Krashen here—that although the LAD can *produce* rules, it cannot *acquire* them in the absence of input of those very rules. This brings us back to the problem of acquiring intuitions about constraints on rules, as well as adding the problem of input frequency.

It would seem then that some rules are produced in the absence of input, although these rules form a restricted subset of the rules of (a) language. All other rules must be in the input with some minimum frequency in order to be acquired. This raises two questions: how can we distinguish between the two types of rule, and why, for the second type, is once not enough? Unfortunately, Krashen does not really address either question.

The distinction between input-dependent and input-free rules is, I believe, quite plausible, although I am not happy with Krashen's characterization of the latter. Whatever the case, in Krashen's presentation this distinction, however plausible it may be, is not a principled one; nor could it be, until Krashen tries to satisfy Condition II. In a parameter-setting model of grammar, for instance (see Chomsky, 1984), the setting of a given parameter for the grammar of a given language would entail various other properties of that language and hence the "acquisition" of those properties (see White, 1985, for an example of L2A research using this model). Krashen has no way to account for this kind of possibility, since in his theory there are no parameters, only structures. (Or else parameters *are* structures, in which case the fixing of a parameter and the appearance of various reflexes of the fixing of that parameter would simply be the acquisition of one structure, followed in the Natural Order by the acquisition of several others.)

As for input frequency, it may indeed be that we will need more than one input of a given structure to guarantee acquisition of the structure, but not (or not only) for the reason that Krashen seems to have in mind. Krashen evidently thinks that some sort of mental (but not oral) practice or "review" is necessary (see, e.g., 1982: 24). Actually the problem, at least in L1A, is that one-shot acquisition would entail the risk of the child's hearing a defective example (e.g., a slip of the tongue) the first time and thus acquiring the wrong structure.[16] Now, if one believes as I do, that in L2A one can acquire (some) structures through conscious learning and that negative evidence is sometimes available to (and usable by) an L2 learner, the problem of frequency is mitigated, but probably not obviated. Thus in both L1A theory and L2A theory, the question of input frequency remains very much an open one.

Can This Theory Be Saved?

Krashen's theory, as I said at the beginning, is not a theory. Could it become one? This is hard to say in the absence of a sufficiently detailed revision to evaluate, but at least I think it is fair to say that there is not a prima facie case to be made for flat-out refusing in advance to consider such a candidate. I do not wish to claim that Krashen *cannot* satisfy our criteria for theory construction, merely that he *has* not. It is not self-evident, for example, that Krashen's ideas are *in principle* incommensurate with current linguistic theory or that the domain of inquiry for his ideas cannot be fixed.

Nevertheless, getting these ideas into the shape of a theory will be no easy task, and I'm not sure that even if it were done, the result would be a plausible theory of second language acquisition, let alone a successful one. Still, the effort to make Krashen's ideas conform to the canons of scientific explanation could be a profitable exercise even if unsuccessful, as it could give us a more accurate idea of where the conceptual as well as empirical difficulties in L2A theory really lie. In any case, until such an effort is made, Krashen's second language acquisition theory must remain in that unhappy group that Sir Karl Popper (1972: 39) once characterized as "those impressive and all-explanatory theories which act upon weak minds like revelations."

Notes

*   This paper has benefitted greatly from the many discussions I had with, as well as the many comments I received from, my colleague Bruce W. Hawkins.

1   Ellis (1985, Chapter 10) provides a useful summary of the major "theories," "models," etc. currently popular in L2A research.

2   This paper is intended in part as an extension of, and complement to, Gregg (1984). In that paper (see also Gregg, 1986) I make specific criticisms of each of the five hypotheses that make up Krashen's theory.

3   Needless to say, the problem of explanation in psychology is a good deal more complex than this; for a thorough discussion, see Fodor, 1968. For some interesting comments on the problem of depth of explanation, see Flanagan (1984) and Brainerd (1978, 1979).

4   Notable exceptions are Sharwood Smith (1981) and Zobl (1983).

5   Pinker does, however, accept quantitative changes, e.g., in the power of the mechanisms. It is also worth noting that Borer and Wexler (in process) reject the Continuity Assumption.

6   Not that people don't *use* the term; everybody uses it, usually incorrectly or at least superficially; see Tarone (1984) for an egregious but by no means atypical example. Perhaps the most common misuse of the term *competence* is in conjunction with the word *communicative*. But "communicative competence" evidently is no more than a fancy way of saying "ability to communicate"; it has no *theoretical* content whatever.

7   ". . . language-like systems might be acquired through the exercise of other faculties of mind, though we should expect to find empirical differences in the manner of acquisition and use in this case." Interestingly, Krashen quotes this passage himself (1985: 24, n.6), evidently without noticing its import. It might also be well here to quote Macnamara in this regard, especially as Krashen enlists him in support of the Input Hypothesis: "The [human language learning] device can either extract the nonexplicit rules from the corpus of the language which is to be learned, or *it can construct them on the basis of explicitly stated rules of the sort one finds in grammar books.*" (Macnamara, 1973: 62; emphasis added).

8   Atkinson is silent on the question of maturation, but I assume that he would consider an appeal to maturation—at least, in the context of acquisition order—to be a reductive explanation.

9 On the other hand, Krashen's suggestion that the Affective Filter and the Monitor don't appear until early adolescence, because it is then that Piaget's formal operations stage is reached, can be seen as an attempt at a reductive kind of explanation.

10 Wexler's warning applies to L2A research also: "The task of describing a child's linguistic abilities purely from [output] data available at a given state (or age) is exceedingly difficult. In practical terms it may actually be impossible" (Wexler, 1982: 293). Similarly, Pylyshyn (1973: 45–46) argues that "the form of a grammar (or of any theory of human competence) is settled on for very good reasons—but reasons which do not attempt to take into account any data other than primary linguistic intuitions." Krashen's theory seems to be intended as a competence theory.

11 An L1A researcher such as White, who is not burdened by such odd ideas about "structures," can deal with deviant forms much more easily; she simply argues that "the child's grammar must be seen as 'optimal' at all stages, that his or her grammar is correct for the data, as he or she perceives it" (1982: 2).

12 With the exception of one point (see Note 16), I will omit discussion of caretaker speech (CS) here and simply refer the reader to Gregg (1984, 1986).

13 This quotation pretty much exhausts Krashen's explanation of the internal workings of the LAD.

14 "Deviant," of course, in the dialect of the providers of input; there is nothing deviant about *he go* in certain English dialects.

15 Actually, this last example may be starting to change under the influence of English and specifically of TEFL!

16 This problem may not have attracted Krashen's attention because of his belief that CS is consistently well-formed. And so, indeed, it may be; but as Chomsky points out (Wexler, 1978), this advantage holds true only if CS is the only source of input. Krashen argues for what he calls a "weak interaction position" (1985: 34)—that is, the position that interaction is not a necessary condition for acquisition. This being the case, the child (or the adult L2 learner) is at risk. As Chomsky also points out (Hornstein & Lightfoot, 1981: 11), even a very small percentage of incorrect input could do serious damage.

References

Atkinson, M. (1982). *Explanations in the study of child language development.* Cambridge: Cambridge University Press. (Cambridge studies in linguistics, 35)

Berwick, R. C. (1985). *The acquisition of syntactic knowledge.* Cambridge, MA: MIT Press.

Borer, H. & Wexler, K. (In process.) The maturation of syntax. In T. Roeper & E. Williams (Eds.). *Parameters and linguistic theory.* (Paper prepared for presentation at the Conference on Parameter-Setting, University of Massachusetts, Amherst, May 25–26, 1984)

Brainerd, C. J. (1978). The stage question in cognitive-developmental theory. *The Behavioral and Brain Sciences, 1,* 173–213.

Brainerd, C. J. (1979). Continuing commentary on Brainerd 1978. *The Behavioral and Brain Sciences, 2,* 137–154.

Bresnan, J. (Ed.). (1982). *The mental representation of grammatical relations.* Cambridge, MA: MIT Press.

Chomsky, N. (1965). *Aspects of the theory of syntax.* Cambridge, MA: MIT Press.

Chomsky, N. (1980). *Rules and representations.* New York: Columbia University Press.

Chomsky, N. (1984). *Lectures on government and binding.* 3d. ed. Dordrecht: Foris.

Dulay, H., Burt, M., & Krashen, S. (1982). *Language two.* New York: Oxford University Press.

Ellis, R. (1985). *Understanding second language acquisition.* Oxford: Oxford University Press.

Flanagan, O. J., Jr. (1984). *The science of the mind.* Cambridge, MA: MIT Press.

Fodor, J. A. (1968). *Psychological explanation.* New York: Random.

Fodor, J. A. (1983). *The modularity of mind.* Cambridge, MA: MIT Press.

Gleitman, L. R, & Wanner, E. (1982). Language acquisition: The state of the state of the art. In Wanner & Gleitman (1982).

Gregg, K. R. (1984). Krashen's Monitor and Occam's Razor. *Applied Linguistics, 5,* 79–100.

Gregg, K. R. (1986). Review of Krashen 1985. *TESOL Quarterly, 20,* 116–122.

Grimshaw, J. (1981). Form, function, and the language acquisition device. In C. L. Baker & J. J. McCarthy (Eds.), *The logical problem of language acquisition*. Cambridge, MA: MIT Press.

Hempel, C., & Oppenheim, P. (1948). Studies in the logic of explanation. *Philosophy of Science. 15*, 135–175.

Hornstein, N., & Lightfoot, D. (1981). Introduction. In N. Hornstein & D. Lightfoot (Eds.), *Explanation in linguistics*. London: Longman.

Kamio, A., and Tonoike, S. (1979). Iimatigai no gengogaku. [The linguistics of slips of the tongue.] In K. Imai (Ed.), *Gengo syoogai to gengo riron*. [Language Disorders and Linguistic Theory]. (Siriizu Kotoba no Syoogai [Language Disorders], v. 3). Tokyo: Taishukan.

Krashen, S. (1981). *Second language acquisition and second language learning*. Oxford: Pergamon.

Krashen, S. D. (1982). *Principles and practice in second language acquisition*. Oxford: Pergamon.

Krashen, S. D. (1983). Newmark's "ignorance hypothesis" and current second language acquisition theory. In S. M. Gass & L. Selinker (Eds.). *Language transfer in language learning*. Rowley, MA: Newbury.

Krashen, S. D. (1985). *The input hypothesis: Issues and implications*. London: Longman.

Krashen, S. D. & Terrell, T. (1983). *The natural approach*. Hayward, CA: Alemany.

Lass, R. (1980). *On explaining language change*. Cambridge: Cambridge University Press. (Cambridge studies in linguistics, 27)

Macnamara, J. (1973). The cognitive strategies of language learning. In J. W. Oller, Jr. & J. C. Richards (Eds.), *Focus on the learner: Pragmatic perspectives for the language teacher*. Rowley, MA: Newbury.

Macnamara, J. (1982). *Names for things*. Cambridge, MA: MIT Press.

Marshall, J. C. (1979). Language acquisition in a biological frame of reference. In P. Fletcher & M. Garman (Eds.), *Language acquisition: Studies in first language development*. Cambridge: Cambridge University Press.

Marslen-Wilson, W. (1973). Speech shadowing and speech perception. Ph.D. thesis, MIT.

Mazurkewich, I. 1984. The acquisition of the dative alternation by second language learners and linguistic theory. *Language Learning 34*, 91–109.

Paikeday, T. M. (Ed.). (1985). *The native speaker is dead!* Toronto: Paikeday.

Pinker, S. (1979). Formal models of language learning. *Cognition*, 7, 217–283.

Pinker, S. (1982). A theory of the acquisition of lexical interpretive grammars. In Bresnan (1982).

Pinker, S. (1984). *Language learnability and language development.* Cambridge, MA: Harvard University Press.

Popper, K. R. (1972). *Conjectures and refutations.* 4th ed. London: Routledge and Kegan Paul.

Pylyshyn, Z. W. (1973). The role of competence theories in cognitive psychology. *Journal of Psycholinguistic Research*, 2, 21–50.

Richards, J. C. (1985). Planning for proficiency. Paper presented at the 1985 JALT Conference, Kyoto, Japan, September 14–16.

Ritchie, W. C. (1978). The right roof constraint in an adult-acquired language. In W. C. Ritchie (Ed.), *Second language research: Issues and implications.* New York: Academic.

Roeper, T. (1981). On the deductive model and the acquisition of productive morphology. In Baker and McCarthy (1981).

Sharwood Smith, M. (1981). The competence/performance distinction in the theory of second language acquisition and the "pedagogical grammar hypothesis." Paper presented at the Contrastive Linguistics Conference, Boszkowo, Poland, December.

Slobin, D. I. (1973). Cognitive prerequisites for the development of grammar. In C. A. Ferguson and D. I. Slobin (Eds.), *Studies of child language development.* New York: Holt, Rinehart and Winston.

Slobin, D. I. (1982). Universal and particular in the acquisition of language. In Wanner & Gleitman (1982).

Spolsky, B., Sigurd, B., Sato, M., Walker, E., & Arterburn, C. (1968). Preliminary studies in the development of techniques for testing overall second language proficiency. *Language Learning*, Special issue no. 3, 79–101.

Tarone, E. (1984). On the variability of interlanguage systems. In F. R. Eckman, L. H. Bell, & D. Nelson (Eds.), *Universals of second language acquisition.* Rowley, MA: Newbury.

Wanner, E. & Gleitman, L. R. (Eds.). (1982). *Language acquisition: The state of the art.* Cambridge: Cambridge University Press.

Wexler, K. (1978). Empirical questions about developmental psycholinguistics raised by a theory of language acquisition. In R. N. Campbell & P. T. Smith (Eds.), *Recent advances in the psychology of language*, v. 2. New York: Plenum. (NATO conference series: III, Human factors, v. 4b)

Wexler, K. (1982). A principle theory for language acquisition. In Wanner & Gleitman (1982).

Wexler, K. and Culicover, P. W. (1980). *Formal principles of language acquisition*. Cambridge, MA: MIT Press.

White, L. (1982). *Grammatical theory and language acquisition*. Dordrecht: Foris. (Publications in language sciences, 8)

White, L. (1985). The "pro-drop" parameter in adult second language acquisition. *Language Learning, 35*, 45–62.

Zobl, H. (1983). Markedness and the projection problem. *Language Learning,* 33, 294–313.

The Anti-Pedagogical Aspects of Krashen's Theory of Second Language Acquisition

Waldemar Marton, University of Poznán, Poland

Analyzing Krashen's (1981, 1982, 1985) theory of second language acquisition from the point of view of language pedagogy, one is immediately struck by its anti-pedagogical implications, which are related to the fact that Krashen assigns only a minimal role to language pedagogy in the process of language acquisition. In his opinion, the most important function realized by formal language teaching can be defined as providing comprehensible input to the learner and taking care that this slightly exceeds the learner's current competence. Yet this function is not uniquely connected with the formal educational setting; it can also be realized in naturalistic settings of second language acquisition, where the beginning learner also has a chance of receiving input "roughly tuned" to his actual competence in the form of foreigner-talk (Krashen, 1981: 119–137). Accordingly, Krashen believes that classroom teaching is helpful only when it is the primary source of comprehensible input; where language learning in an informal environment is available, the value of instruction is actually nil (Krashen, 1985: 13–14). Classroom learning cannot improve on the natural processes of language acquisition; at best, it can only try to replicate these processes in the classroom.

Such thinking is deeply anti-pedagogical. The essence of pedagogy resides in the conviction that formal teaching and learning can and should be superior to trial-and-error learning in a natural environment; otherwise, sending our children to schools would not make any sense at all. The same is true of language pedagogy; indeed, it is a necessary assumption of the majority of language courses all over the world, where the learner has incomparably less time and gets incomparably less input than in a natural setting. In many countries, including Poland, school learners get only two to four 45- or 50-minute classes per week, amounting to only a few hundred hours, usually spread over four or five years, for the whole course. Without the assumption that instruction can make a tremendous difference, language learning in such acquisition-poor environments would have to be considered simply a waste of time.

This basic belief that language pedagogy can do better than merely replicate the natural acquisition process in the classroom has been common to the European and American tradition of good and efficient language teaching as practiced and recommended by such outstanding pedagogues as Berlitz, Sweet, Palmer, de Sauzé, Carroll, Strevens, Stevick, and Rivers, who represent not only solid scholarship but also years of successful experience in the teaching of foreign languages. Their witness to the effectiveness of good teaching cannot be jettisoned merely on the basis of self-assured claims from a few not very convincing studies concerning the natural order of acquisition of several grammatical morphemes. Their works are pervaded with the conviction that classroom learning can be not only highly effective but also much more efficient than unaided language acquisition in informal environments, so that the level of proficiency that the classroom learner may reach after, say, 500 hours of good teaching would require five or even more times this number of contact hours with the language on the part of the informal learner. Even Palmer, who was an ardent supporter of basing language pedagogy on some elements of the natural acquisitional processes, had no doubt at all that pedagogical intervention could accelerate these processes and make them more efficient: "We should not conclude that methods involving our powers of study are to be abandoned, and that nature alone is to be responsible for our linguistic education. On the contrary, we suggest that an extensive use be made of powers which are not possessed by the young child or the barbarian" (Palmer, 1964: 16). Elsewhere, the same author pointed out that "by some means or other we have to bridge the gulf between the linguistic capacity of the native child at the age of two and that of the foreign person at whatever age he takes up his studies. We are convinced that this gulf may be bridged by certain procedures which, though 'unnatural,' are nevertheless effective and helpful" (Palmer & Redman, 1969: 104). Similarly de Sauzé, the creator of the famous "Cleveland Plan"—which has probably been one of the most successful language programs ever—although promoting a variety of the direct method that contained a certain number of "natural" elements, believed that a careful gradation of structural difficulty along with the explicit teaching of L2 grammar by way of an inductive method and the systematic correction of learners' errors was an extremely powerful pedagogical device that led to an increased efficiency of the learning process (de Sauzé, 1959). Carroll believes that merely trying to create a rich linguistic environment in the classroom and making the learner experience the totality of the target language without any specifically pedagogical support does not make for maximum efficiency in language teaching. Instead, he recommends a two-stream approach and suggests that "second-language learners appear to be helped by guidance and explanations with respect to particular aspects of instructional content. A program of instruction should contain two parallel streams, one devoted to exposing the learner to materials containing a relatively uncontrolled variety of linguistic elements (for example, vocabulary and grammatical constructions) and the other devoted to a rather carefully developed sequence of instructional content" (Carroll, 1974: 140–141). Strevens never tired of making the point that the quality of teaching, defined by him as the management of learning, is one of the most essential factors determining failure or success in language learning and that, accordingly, language teachers should strive to become highly professional individuals, proud of their expertise in language pedagogy (Strevens, 1980: 20, 23–24, 27).

The same belief in the superiority of well-organized language instruction over the natural processes of language acquisition has been typical of language pedagogy in the former Soviet Union, where it has found its ultimate realization in the application of Galperin's educational theory to foreign language teaching. Galperin's stage theory of the formation of mental operations sees the role of instruction as helping the learner to learn successfully by guiding the mental operations involved in the learning tasks through the use of pedagogical algorithms. As applied to language pedagogy, this means that instead of wasting a lot of time on the unaided formulation and testing of hypotheses about the target language in a trial-and-error manner, the learner follows pedagogical algorithms in productive and receptive tasks at the beginning level (cf. Galperin, 1970; Talyzina, 1970; Leontiev, 1981: 41–48).

The conviction that learning guided by instruction is superior to natural and unaided learning also underlies the thinking of Vygotsky, Bruner, and Ausubel, whose works have exerted a profound influence on present-day educational theory. Vygotsky's concept of the zone of proximal development refers to a learner's ability to successfully acquire a certain part of the instructional material (in the form of knowledge or skill) only when his or her natural learning capacity is supported by the teacher's help and intervention (Vygotsky, 1971: 356–357). Applying this concept to language teaching, we can hypothesize that a given language item, although being in terms of Krashen's theory; at a level higher than $i + 1$, can be acquired by the learner with the help of appropriate instruction—i.e., it need not conform to the natural order of acquisition (assuming, as Krashen does, that such an invariable order really exists). Similarly, Ausubel, while specifically addressing the issue of language learning and teaching, criticizes the assumption that the natural way of learning is the best model for language teaching, pointing out that although the natural method may be the most efficacious for children, it certainly cannot be claimed to be such for adults, who are more cognitively mature and who have already acquired a lot of intellectual skills (Ausubel, 1968: 73–74).

It is clear, then, that Krashen's anti-pedagogical stand flies in the face of opinions and ideas that are based on solid theoretical grounds and on vast teaching experience and have been held by the most outstanding language educators of the last hundred years, as well as being indirectly supported by some of the most prominent thinkers of the twentieth century in the area of general education. It is true that Krashen claims the support of certain empirical evidence, yet it seems to me that this evidence is by no means entirely convincing. In fact, one wonders why so many theorists and practicing language teachers seem to have jumped so readily on the newest anti-pedagogical bandwagon in total disregard of the long tradition of solid scholarship and highly effective teaching. One must rather doubt whether extrapolations from the morpheme studies, which are so important for Krashen's argumentation, are a sufficiently solid foundation on which to base the claim that language instruction *per se* has no effect. Krashen quotes empirical studies that seem to support his position, such as those carried out by Upshur (1968) and Mason (1971), but there are also studies that seem to confirm the view that language instruction increases the effectiveness of learning, as, for instance, the study carried out by Long (1983). In essence, however, none of these studies, irrespective of whether they seem to confirm or disprove Krashen's theory, are truly convincing for the simple reason that none of them in fact take into consideration one decisive factor—*the quality of teaching.*

In language learning, especially, the advantages of formal instruction show up only when this instruction is of a particularly high quality. Bad teaching may indeed have no other effect on learners than to provide them with a certain amount of meaningful input, but in the typical school context this may be too little. Thus learners subjected to a pedagogical treatment that fails to help in their learning may be forced to resort to the natural, unaided acquisitional process and may produce acquisitional orders and developmental sequences similar or even identical to those produced in naturalistic settings. For example, responding to the teacher's question "How did you get to school today?" a learner may produce the following utterance: "Come school bus." Alternatively, especially when the amount of input is insufficient to enable a learner to make hypotheses about the language, he or she may vaguely recall the complexity of a given form that has not yet been acquired and, striving to recreate it, produce one of those "impossible" utterances typical only of classroom learning and probably never appearing in informal settings, such as "I have is went school with bus." Thus teaching that fails to mesh with the learning process may have two different results: it can either promote the natural acquisitional process, which is particularly likely to happen when the learner gets a sufficient amount of comprehensible input, or it can completely fail to lead to any development of L2 competence, leaving the learner with a rather chaotic conglomeration of ill-absorbed bits and pieces of the target language, which may be not sufficient even for performing the simplest receptive or productive tasks.

My own professional experience and my own observations of language teaching in many countries of the world and in various types of institutions have fully convinced me that language instruction does make a difference and that it renders the learning process much more efficient than the process of natural acquisition informal settings, *but only when the teaching is of good quality.* I have seen classes in which most learners—after only 500 to 600 hours of school learning—were able to speak freely and fairly accurately, on a variety of topics, but I have also seen classes where after the same or even a larger number of hours, most learners were not able to make any reasonable use of the target language, even in the receptive mode.

Clearly, assigning such a great role to good teaching begs the question of what good teaching is and how it can be defined. To answer this question is obviously beyond the scope of this paper; for the purpose of our argumentation it is sufficient to claim that the quality of teaching is an extremely important factor, to a large extent determining success or failure of language learning in a formal educational setting. However, I will reflect on certain issues that are connected with the quality of teaching and that point out other anti-pedagogical aspects of Krashen's theorizing. One is that in assessing the quality of teaching we should distinguish between general pedagogical and specifically methodological criteria. The former should be met by any organized teaching process, irrespective of the subject taught; the latter are related only to what is specific to the methodology of teaching foreign languages, that is, to what makes this methodology different from the methodologies of teaching other subjects.

With these two groups of criteria, any language teaching specialist can easily point to those pedagogical procedures that obviously violate the principle of teaching efficiency. Thus if the teacher introduces a technique which, for a longer period of time, keeps only one learner busy while the others go to sleep, this is a serious fault of a general pedagogical nature, since it is obvious that any teaching procedure used in the classroom should, in some manner, activate all the learners. Or if the teacher fails to create a warm and friendly atmosphere in the classroom and thus makes the learner resort to what humanistic psychologists call "defensive learning," it is clear that this is a fault of a general educational nature, since the psychology of learning tells us that the learner's affective domain is as important in any kind of learning as the cognitive one (which also means that the notion of the affective filter, so important to Krashen's theorizing, can be applied to any learning process and not uniquely to second language acquisition).

As far as specifically methodological criteria are concerned, there is a general consensus among contemporary language educators as to which teaching and learning procedures could be described as extremely ineffectual. For example, when we consider François Gouin's pathetically unsuccessful attempts at learning German by memorizing a few grammar books and a dictionary of 30,000 words (Diller, 1971: 51–53), it is obvious that this kind of learning strategy would not be recommended by any language teaching specialist today. Although it is not yet quite clear whether explicitly taught and learned grammar rules can really help in learning a language for spontaneous, communicative uses, certainly nobody believes that any learner could construct (or comprehend) utterances at a more or less normal speed on the basis of totally conscious decisions and operations involving every single language item. The processing capacity of the human mind is simply too limited to cope with such an incredibly complex task. Similarly, a grammar drill of an extremely mechanical kind (that is, one that can be successfully performed without learners being necessarily aware of the meanings of the particular sentences they are manipulating) would also be rejected by most contemporary language educators as obviously not meeting the criterion of methodological efficiency. We cannot totally separate form from meaning in learning procedures, since in doing this we create a barrier against the transfer of linguistic knowledge and skill from exercises to more spontaneous uses of the language.

In spite of the fact that particular language educators today have different recipes for success in teaching, it would not be difficult to find agreement on the exclusion of a number of procedures that obviously do not meet the criterion of maximum teaching efficiency, either from a general educational or from a specifically methodological point of view. By the process of elimination, we may arrive at a set of principles and procedures that might be included in the category of good and effective teaching. Even better, on the basis of accumulated teaching experience and the knowledge provided by related disciplines such as linguistics, psycholinguistics, and the psychology of learning, we may define those language learning strategies that will lead to a successful development of L2 competence.

I think that there are three such strategies. The first can be described as prolonged, silent processing of meaningful input without making any utterances in the target language. By frequent repetition, clear and stable mental representations of particular language items are formed in the learner's cognitive structure. Owing to their clarity and stability, these mental representations are easily recalled and thus can be used for the performance of both receptive and productive tasks. We acquire competence by listening to and reading comprehensible texts in the target language. The second basic strategy can be defined as developing competence through attempted communication in the L2. By participation in communicative situations in which meanings have to be negotiated, the learner also generates input from the interlocutor. This input is particularly useful for learning purposes because it is directly related to the meanings that the learner wants to convey. Thus the learning of the L2 system can be seen as a result or a by-product of attempted communication via this language. The third strategy is a very gradual and controlled development of L2 competence through the performance of reconstructive tasks based on the imitation of language models. Learners following this strategy do not negotiate meaning and do not communicate their own ideas, but gradually absorb the particular language items and learn to combine them into novel utterances by the performance of tasks involving the reproduction, reconstruction, transformation, and adaptation of various source texts.

These three strategies of learning correspond to three basic teaching strategies, defined as globally conceived pedagogical procedures promoting a definite strategy of learning. These strategies, consistently and appropriately applied, are successful by definition, i.e., must lead to the development of a competence in the target language. The term *appropriately* is very important: none of these strategies can work equally successfully under all conditions, and none of them can be considered the best or better than the others in any absolute and abstract sense. Their relative effectiveness and efficiency depends on two essential sets of variables, i.e., the set related to the learner and the set related to the context of language teaching.

Such a relativized approach is truly pedagogical and consistent with contemporary educational theory. It also explains why I consider as antipedagogical Krashen's tendency to reduce all language teaching to only one universal formula, that is, to the providing of comprehensible input. It is true that Krashen also seems to recommend learning by communicating (*Natural Approach*, Krashen & Terrell, 1983), but at the same time he rejects the view that two-way interaction is necessary for language acquisition, claiming that it is no more than helpful and that it only facilitates the acquisitional process (Krashen, 1985: 33–34). He sees the essential pedagogical value of the Natural Approach not in terms of providing learners with the opportunity to communicate and to negotiate meaning, but in skillfully providing comprehensible input in a low-anxiety situation. Comparing Krashen's approach with the concept of a range of basic language teaching strategies, it is evident that the latter also involves the idea that we can successfully learn a language by receiving comprehensible input, but that it sees this possibility as only one of three or perhaps more, and certainly not as the only one. Moreover, the concept of three strategies implies that the receptive strategy cannot be recommended for all types of learners and for all types of teaching contexts, but that it may be fully efficient only in relation to certain more or less predictable configurations of learner and contextual variables.

In presenting the three learning and teaching strategies, I have pointed only to their most essential features, which might give the impression that the receptive and communicative strategies do nothing but replicate the natural acquisitional process in the classroom. In fact, I assume that each of the two strategies should introduce certain pedagogical procedures and make them more efficient. Thus, to make the receptive strategy more efficient and to better provide for transfer from the receptive to the productive skills, the teacher may introduce the explicit teaching of L2 grammar, with appropriately selected grammar exercises that do not require production. If the explicit teaching of grammar is not considered suitable for a given context, the teacher should at least train the learners to pay deliberate attention not only to the contents of the messages they listen to or read but also to the formal features of the target language—such as inflectional affixes, function words, word order, conventions of lexical co-occurrence, etc.—which can be achieved through the application of some specifically designed exercises not involving metalinguistic knowledge. This is essential, since learners can successfully decode messages by applying the semantic strategy, which is based on using the meanings of content words and on anticipation and guessing, and thus can disregard these formal features, whose internalized knowledge is necessary, however, for the performance of productive tasks. (For a description of the semantic and syntactic decoding strategies see Clark & Clark, 1977: 57–85.) We already have evidence that merely receiving meaningful input, even in massive quantities and for a long time, does not automatically lead to the assimilation of all the basic structural features into the learner's productive repertoire. This is indicated by the Canadian immersion programs, also lavishly praised by Krashen as the perfect embodiment of his teaching principle. Other studies have shown that while immersion learners indeed demonstrate superior comprehension skills, their level of productive accuracy is far below that of native speakers, even after some years of participation in the program; some researchers even claim that learners emerging from several years of French or English immersion are not bilingual but speak their native language plus a defective classroom pidgin (Hammerley, 1985: 31–34; Harley, 1985). The introduction of the above-mentioned special pedagogical measures might to a large extent prevent these negative phenomena in language courses that are promoting the receptive way of learning.

Similarly, the communicative strategy of teaching can make learning by communicating more efficient if certain corrective pedagogical measures are introduced. For example, the systematic application of an indirect way of error correction, known in the literature as "expansion," seems to be an excellent pedagogical device that not only provides valuable input but also probably contributes to an increase of accuracy in learners' utterances. Expansion takes place when the teacher picks up a learner's erroneous or incomplete utterance and repeats the intended message in the correct form. That such special pedagogical devices may be useful has again been underlined by studies demonstrating that programs emphasizing "natural" communication may lead to the emergence of a highly inaccurate version of the target language, full of fossilized errors (Omaggio, 1983).

It seems, then, that the wholesale introduction of natural acquisitional strategies into the classroom not only fails to meet the requirements of maximum teaching efficiency but may even produce unwanted and pedagogically harmful consequences. It is not the role of language pedagogy either to just faithfully imitate the natural learning process or to introduce procedures opposing it. The role of pedagogy is to find measures that can both adapt the natural processes to the formal educational context and make them more efficient. We already know a number of such measures that have been associated with various successful language teaching methods and programs and whose value has not been at all disproved by more recent empirical studies or theoretical insights.

One of these traditional pedagogical functions refers to the programming of language courses, that is, to the construction of syllabuses on the principle of the selection and gradation of items to be taught. The importance of this function is obvious when we consider that the time allotted to language courses in formal educational settings is always strictly limited and therefore has to be used very efficiently. To present the learner with at least the basics of the whole L2 system, it is necessary to have a teaching program. This is particularly vital for receptive and reconstructive teaching, though in courses based on the communicative principle, some kind of syllabus probably also makes for greater effectiveness. It is of relatively lesser importance what type of syllabus is adopted for a given course, whether it is, for example, a structural or a notional-functional one. Most syllabus designers today try to incorporate aspects of both linguistic and communicative competence and to correlate them in some way in their pedagogical programs.

Another traditionally important function of language teaching is the systematic provision of feedback related to the learner's performance of various receptive and productive tasks. This may greatly facilitate and accelerate the process of hypothesis testing, even if a lot of hypothesis testing is input-based and takes place subconsciously. The provision of feedback is indispensable if our learners are to achieve accuracy, and it can help in this even within the communicative framework, in which fluency rather than accuracy is emphasized. The exact manner in which feedback should be provided depends on the teaching strategy and should clearly be consistent with it. Within the receptive paradigm, feedback is related to the various types of tests used to assess learners' comprehension and their awareness of the formal features of the L2. In communicative teaching, feedback has primarily the form of expansions. Under the reconstructive strategy, which strongly emphasizes accuracy, feedback is provided in the traditional form of error correction, with induced self-correction being the preferred technique.

Yet another way in which language pedagogy can help learners involves deliberately teaching them to practice linguistic creativity by making novel utterances out of the elements that have already been absorbed. This is the core of the language learning process. Learning a large number of the building elements of the language in the form of lexical items, set phrases, patterns, and routine formulas and gaining the ability to combine them into novel utterances in accordance with the rules of grammar and the conventions of lexical co-occurrence is the most essential and the most difficult task for the learner. Everything else is of relatively lesser importance. There are many very effective pedagogical techniques, particularly compatible with reconstructive teaching and learning, which can be used for the controlled practice of creativity, such as text adaptation and transformation, renarration, summary, retranslation, etc. Certain of these techniques form the core of some very successful language teaching methods, such as the Berlitz Method, Dodson's (1972) Bilingual Method, and Henzel's (1978) Reproductive-Creative Method (which was used experimentally for the teaching of Russian in Polish primary and secondary schools of the Kraków district in southern Poland and proved to be one of the most effective methods of language teaching in the school context).

Explicit teaching of L2 grammar on the basis of metalinguistic terminology, pedagogical grammar rules, and grammar exercises is a matter of considerable controversy, and many educators, including Krashen, support the non-interface position, claiming that metalinguistic knowledge cannot be directly accessed and used in communicative tasks involving spontaneous production of utterances. I hold the opposite view, known as the interface hypothesis, which is also in keeping with the tradition of good and effective language teaching and is supported by many contemporary educators and researchers (e.g., Bialystok & Fröhlich, 1977; Stevick, 1980: 267–282; Sharwood-Smith, 1981; Sorace, 1985). Even Krashen and other scholars of a similar orientation agree that the explicit teaching of grammar can be useful up to a point and that it should be provided, at least for those learners who want it (Krashen, 1985: 75–76). The weak interface position, which I would formulate as the claim that teaching grammar may be helpful in some limited way in the achievement of greater accuracy in speech production by some types of learners, would find the support of most educators and is a sufficient reason for considering instruction in grammar a worthwhile contribution of language pedagogy.

Language pedagogy can also make learning more efficient by the introduction of specially designed teaching materials that can accelerate the process whereby the learner gains semantic experiences in the L2. Such materials may present a great number of language items in the form of lexical units, phrases, collocations, and routine formulas that refer to a certain theme of a certain fragment of reality within the framework of a single text. Thus a text of this kind in a condensed form presents the learner with many semantic experiences, the acquisition of which might require a relatively long time in the course of informal learning. Such specially designed texts are rejected by certain contemporary theorists, who claim that they often do not exhibit proper rhetorical structure and who insist on the exclusive use of authentic materials. This kind of reasoning confuses the end with the means and is, in fact, also deeply anti-pedagogical. The learner may be free to use all sorts of artificial devices in order to learn faster, and although authentic texts certainly have to be introduced at some point, they do not have to be and perhaps even should not be used exclusively in all the stages of the learning/teaching process.

A function of language teaching that has been brought to the fore is related to the notion of strategic competence (Canale & Swain, 1980), which can be defined as the learner's ability to flexibly use various problem-solving strategies (referred to in the literature as "communication strategies") in order to overcome linguistic inadequacy and to successfully get his or her message across. This ability can be very useful for learners in a real-life communication situation, since it will allow them to considerably extend their limited competence and to cope successfully with communication problems. Since we already know something about which of these strategies are most helpful and achieve their purpose particularly well, the explicit training of our learners in the use of communication strategies of the achievement type might be particularly useful. It is compatible, first of all, with the notion of communicative teaching, and within the reconstructive framework occasional sessions devoted to the practicing of communication strategies should be held. Of course, this kind of practice does not directly contribute to the development of competence proper and can be regarded only as a preparation of the learner for an emergency situation and not as an essential learning experience.

Finally, the organization of remedial teaching can also be considered as an important function of language pedagogy. The need for remedial teaching arises very often in the case of a learner or a group of learners marked by some obvious linguistic inadequacy (such as, for example, bad pronunciation) that is incompatible with their overall proficiency level. Remedial teaching is often particularly necessary in language courses for so-called false beginners, who, although formally starting from scratch, have already been subjected to some kind of teaching and have acquired fossilized errors in the process. The eradication of such errors, which is supposed to be effected by remedial teaching, is extremely difficult, and none of the existing recipes for it seems to be fully successful. It continues to be an important acquisitional problem that can be solved only within a formal educational framework.

The above list of pedagogical functions is by no means exhaustive; its aim is only to make the reader aware of the fact that Krashen's assignment of basically only one function to language pedagogy is a gross oversimplification. Certainly, it can be taken for granted that providing meaningful input is also one of the most fundamental functions of language pedagogy, since there can be no acquisition without some prior exposure to the language. Yet I think that raising this function to the position of exclusive importance trivializes the whole idea and role of language education and makes it largely redundant.

In spite of its anti-pedagogical implications, Krashen's theory does contain some elements that make it worthy of consideration even by those who assign to language pedagogy a much greater role than Krashen does. There are, in particular, two such important elements. One is, after all, the emphasis put on the role of meaningful input in the process of language acquisition. Although this role is in fact obvious, it has sometimes been disregarded. Krashen's theorizing has made certain contemporary educators and teachers aware of the principle that input must come first in language learning, and this awareness will contribute positively, both in the sphere of theory and in day-to-day classroom teaching, and will help to eliminate certain misapplications of the new methods and approaches. For example, teachers keen on the application of group work in classroom communicative teaching may avoid the fault of pairing equally incompetent beginning learners and making them negotiate meaning in the L2, since they will realize that this procedure will not provide much useful input to either of them and thus has a very questionable value as a teaching technique.

Another valuable aspect of Krashen's theory is related to his Monitor Model and to the underlying belief that "learned" and "acquired" systems are kept separate in the learner's mind so that there is no transfer of knowledge from the former to the latter. The analysis of this claim and of the evidence (albeit not very convincing) supporting it turns our attention to the extremely important psychological and educational problem of the transfer of knowledge and skill from a learning situation, in which this knowledge or skill has been "acquired," to a less controlled situation involving its application to a new task. The essence of the problem is that very often this desired transfer does not in fact take place. The overcoming of this transfer barrier lies at the very heart of all effective teaching and is extremely relevant to language pedagogy, in particular to the explicit teaching of the L2 grammatical system. Teaching grammar is often so ineffectual precisely because teachers assume that the transfer of knowledge and skills gained in a grammar class to more or less spontaneous production tasks will occur automatically. Yet more often it does not, and it is precisely in this area that the learner should be helped by some special pedagogical devices. Thus the Monitor Model, by questioning the value of explicit teaching, can make us rethink the problem of transfer and look for more satisfying solutions.

Though in this paper I have concentrated on the anti-pedagogical aspects of Krashen's theory, I would like to emphasize that the fact that the theory was even formulated is altogether beneficial to language pedagogy. By challenging the value of language teaching procedures developed over centuries and by questioning the indispensability of the language teaching profession, it has turned our attention to and made us more appreciative of our achievements in language teaching. In spite of the pronouncements of theorists who think that institutional language teaching has had a record of only dismal failure, there exists in language pedagogy a tradition of good and efficient teaching and careful theorizing that weighs the effects of various factors and does not inflate any single one out of proportion. In the era of changing winds and shifting sands, to use Marckwardt's (1975: 41–43) formulation, it is probably wise to take the long and informed view inspired by the accumulated experience of what has been best in the practice and theory of language teaching, and not to be unduly alarmed by yet another hypothesis, however forcefully and convincingly formulated.

A version of this article appeared in "Studia Anglica Poznaniensa," Vol. 23, 1990. We are grateful to Professor Jacek Fisiak for permission to include the article in our volume.

Comprehension and Production: The Interactive Duo*

Wilga M. Rivers
Emerita of Harvard University, USA

Controversy and ferment in the language-teaching world are no novelty. Since the collapse of the monolithic approach to methodology of the audiolingual heyday, we have certainly experienced a "proliferation of competing articulations, the willingness to try anything, the expression of explicit discontent, the recourse to philosophy and to debate over fundamentals," which Raimes takes to be an indication that we are in the midst of a "paradigm shift."[1] Be that as it may, the disparate nostrums of competing "experts" make life very confusing for the classroom teacher.

From audiolingualism's inductive approach of organizing language learning activities strictly in the order of listening first, then speaking, reading, and writing,[2] we moved to deductive, rule-governed cognitive code learning where listening, reading, and speaking came after explanation of grammar rules.[3] Then the stress moved to communicative competence—of the structured kind, emphasizing discourse functions,[4] or the unstructured kind, with an emphasis on pragmatic functions and much talking.[5] Next came the carefully structured Silent Way, with attentive listening to a reduced input, the emphasis being on inductive internalization of language structure, problem solving, and guided production of utterances by the student, with the teacher saying as little as possible.[6] In the unstructured, inductive Total Physical Response[7] there was plenty of what Krashen has called "comprehensible input,"[8] visually accompanied, but with deeds not words in response. In Community Language Learning most of the input was the interlanguage of other students,[9] not the authentic materials from native speakers and writers that were being actively promoted at the same time. With Suggestopaedia, long dialogues were back, read and translated initially, as well as much vocabulary; long sessions of listening then preceded the communicative activities that provided opportunities for students to use what they had absorbed inductively.[10] With the Natural Approach, there is much comprehensible input in the form of simplified, redundant teacher talk, entirely in the new language, as with the direct method, and introducing, as with Suggestopaedia, a wide vocabulary. Speaking is delayed but reading is advanced; and affective, humanistic activities later encourage the productive use of inductively acquired language. The Natural Approach patterns itself, at least in theory, on the way children are believed to acquire their first language.[11]

And so we dance around the act of communication, which is still central, whether we mean communication between speakers or through the written text (as in many Language for Specific Purposes, Language through Literature, and Content-Based Instruction classes). Should we listen a great deal first or read a great deal? Should we speak early in our learning, and when should we write? Nor should we forget that knowledge of the culture of those with whom we wish to interact is also an important aspect of communication,[12] whether absorbed aurally, visually, or from graphic materials.

Why are we so anxious to find one final, all-determining answer? Is it not possible that language is such a multifaceted jewel that there are many ways to approach its acquisition (or the learning of it)?[13] And should not a determining factor in our choice be the objectives of our students?

Krashen[14] asserts that there is one fundamental principle for acquiring a language (in the oral or graphic mode): that students should receive much comprehensible input, in speech or writing, that is just a step ahead of their present linguistic experience ($i + 1$). With such comprehensible input, students will acquire the language, it seems, without the help of grammar or teacher. Production will come naturally and with a naturally developing order of acquisition of grammatical forms that is preprogrammed in each human being, the as yet sketchy research of second language acquisition scholars indicating which are early and which are late acquired items. In fact, according to Krashen's Monitor Model, speaking should not be required or expected until the student feels ready to perform. According to this theory, introducing, teaching, or practicing structural features of the language will not affect students' acquisition of them, since this will inevitably follow an innate natural order. Thus teaching or presenting structural forms in learning activities will only impede natural processes, focusing the student on form rather than meaning, and hindering facility in communication.

What has been learned consciously will not be used to initiate utterances, Krashen tells us, only what has been acquired subconsciously: what has been learned formally is available to us only through the Monitor and can at best help students to make repairs to utterances if they have the time or inclination and know the rules. In other words, the "acquired" system, acquired through listening (or reading), provides all the material necessary for production of utterances in oral or graphic form. Furthermore, Krashen posits, focus on meaning, allowing the acquired system to operate, leads to greater accuracy than relying on the learned system. Provided the affective filter is low (the language learner is not anxious or embarrassed), the acquired system will operate in communication.

There are a number of assertions here that have serious implications for classroom teaching and that warrant reflection and discussion. I shall concentrate here on some aspects of the following, with their associated assumptions:

1. The acquisition-learning distinction and the operation of the Monitor
2. Comprehensible input as the one fundamental principle for language acquisition

Acquisition-Learning Distinction and the Monitor

In his explanation of Monitor theory, Krashen refers to "acquisition" and "learning" as "two separate processes" that "co-exist in the adult."[15] This implies that what one has learned of a language through conscious effort remains in one compartment of the memory and what one has "picked up" informally, or acquired, is retained in another, quite separate compartment, each being available for use only in distinctive circumstances. As a logical consequence, it seems that what is now being "acquired" and used is not interacting with what has previously been "learned" and used (including often the same items). This notion is difficult to sustain in light of what we presently know about the active, dynamic, interacting character of the brain. Recent memory research has emphasized the parallel distributed processing of information in intricate, multiply connected networks. "Parallel" means that information is being processed in many different ways at the same time. Information is "distributed" throughout the system; consequently, it can be accessed at any point in the memory system through these interconnections. Anything one encounters and selectively or peripherally perceives, through whatever sense modality, enters the networks and is immediately bounced around, compared, discriminated, matched, linked up in the networks with information related to it in a multiplicity of obvious and unexpected ways, to serve some purpose eventually along with all the other elements operating in parallel.[16] This model of the processing of information by the human mind makes the kind of artificial barrier that Krashen postulates between what is "acquired" and what is "learned" not only improbable but impossible except in pathological circumstances. It also explains the "din in the head" phenomenon that Krashen reported in 1983. Krashen had been an undergraduate student of German and had spent a year abroad in Austria; on a later visit to a German-speaking area, he found all kinds of expressions in German that he was hearing around him dancing around in his head. He attributed this to the activation of the Language Acquisition Device,[17] whereas cognitive psychological theory would regard this as the interconnecting of what he was hearing about him with elements of the language that he had known and used at an earlier period.

That not everything we know and use was originally learned consciously or formally is true, but most cognitive psychologists would agree that what we learn in any way still interacts with previous knowledge, which frequently facilitates the learning or acquiring of it; new knowledge also modifies existing knowledge.[18] Furthermore, what has been consciously learned may be used without conscious attention once it has become very familiar, after, for instance, much practice in use. This point is discussed in psychological terms by McLaughlin, Rossman, and McLeod in relation to automatic and controlled processes (automatic processes being those that we perform without conscious effort, while controlled processes are those that require our attention as we perform them).[19] What we have learned, Krashen maintains, cannot be used subconsciously at some later date.[20] McLaughlin, Rossman, and McLeod consider, as do other psychologists,[21] that controlled processes can become automatic (or routinized) with much use and that automatic processes can be brought to awareness and developed and refined consciously.

The question of what is "conscious" and what is "subconscious" learning, that is, learning without awareness,[22] is a psychological one that remains as yet unanswered in any definitive way. Whether these two types of learning constitute a dichotomy, as Krashen would maintain, or, rather, are positioned on a continuum is an important issue. If what we have learned consciously can, after a time, be used without conscious attention (a likelihood Krashen does not accept, but which has been a common experience in many domains), and if what we have acquired subconsciously can be brought to conscious awareness, and adapted or acquire new uses, we are considering a continuum, and a clear demarcation between the two forms of learning cannot be maintained. Such a possibility strikes at the very heart of Monitor theory.

Bialystok (1988) sets out two intersecting continua: *non-analyzed/analyzed* (denoting the degree of awareness of the structure of what is known) and *automatic/non-automatic* (representing the ease with which information may be accessed by the learner), thus allowing for considerable individual difference in how language is acquired and controlled. "It appears reasonable," she says, "to separate the learner's representation of knowledge from access to that knowledge, and each of these variables contributes to the learner's control over that knowledge" (p. 38). Highly sophisticated uses of language, she maintains, are characterized by the combination of analyzed and automatic control (p. 36).[23]

What we have learned in a systematic way, Krashen tells us, is available to us only as a Monitor, when we have time and motivation to self-correct. The Monitor, in this theory, despite the name of the model, appears to be of little use in active interaction, its functions being generally confined to checking over formal speech or writing. It is interesting to compare this with the original notion of the Monitor, as introduced by Carroll.

In discussing the monitor, Carroll refers to the delayed auditory feedback experiments of the sixties, where what subjects were saying was fed back to their ears through headphones with a short time lag of up to one second. From these experiments, it was found that, deprived of the opportunity to "hear" what they were saying in the normal way, subjects began to stutter and falter, and were very soon unable to continue their oral communication (and this happened even with one-fifth of a second of delay). This evidence led Carroll to hypothesize that "normal speech involves a perceptual self-monitoring process" that was "interfered with by the delayed feedback."[24] This monitoring in normal oral production become a barely noticed but habitual accompaniment to the expression of personal meaning.[25] Without it, we would not be able to keep track of our production, to adjust our sentences as we elaborate our meaning and to select in mid-utterance more effective ways of expressing our ideas—a normal communicative process that becomes evident when we read transcriptions of informal speech.[26] In Carroll's original theoretical formulation, then, the Monitor had a much more active and continuous role in communication than in its more recent form in Krashen's theory; in the latter it also acts as an editor, but only when the speaker has time or inclination to reflect on what he or she is saying and is focused on form or correctness rather than on the message being conveyed.[27]

The self-monitoring of which Carroll speaks can be of considerable help to us, even indispensable, in the demanding activity of expressing our intentions through a new language. Further light is thrown on this process by Anderson's ACT* model of learning by doing, with its interaction of declarative and performance memory, the latter being a thinking process that enables us to reflect on what we are doing (and what we have done) and adapt our knowledge base and our performance according to new circumstances and needs. This thinking process is a form of monitoring that we may prefer to call reflective matching for appropriateness, and is an essential part of the execution process.[28]

Comprehensible Input as the
One Fundamental Principle for Language Acquisition

Krashen maintains that there is one fundamental principle for developing communicative ability in the oral or graphic mode: that students should receive much comprehensible input, just a step ahead of their present experience ($i + 1$),[29] without attempts at production for some time, and the rest will follow—structures will appear in an innate natural order, and production (ability to express one's own ideas) will develop spontaneously in its own time. In Krashen's own words, so long as the affective filter is "low enough to allow the input 'in,'" language "acquisition is inevitable. It is, in fact, unavoidable and cannot be prevented—the language 'mental organ' will function just as automatically as any other organ."[30]

A number of methodologies in the history of language teaching have emphasized listening in the initial stages (direct method, audiolingual approach, Gouin's action chains), but always with some production following closely on the listening experience. Here we are considering the necessity for prolonged intensive listening without expectation of production for some time—a "silent period," as it has been called. Terrell suggests a delay between listening and student production of several months at the elementary school level, at least a month for high school students, and a week or so for college students, although he admits some of the latter seem to want to speak already after an hour or two.[31] The suggestion of a week for college level is actually quite modest, since many college language classes meet only three hours per week. We will consider the proposed longer periods, as in elementary schools and high schools.

The proposal for an extended initial listening period represents, we are told, a "natural" approach, based on the learning of the first language by children. Assuming that the process of first-language acquisition is paralleled by second-language acquisition, which is controversial,[32] we may query whether the child does learn the native language without attempts at communication for some time. Recent first-language acquisition studies do not seem to reveal the listening, non-communicating, physically active child that Asher's Total Physical Response (which is advocated in the Natural Approach) seeks to copy.[33] First-language studies are identifying earlier and earlier attempts to communicate in the infant's babbling, as well as in its kinesics and physical behavior. Trevarthen observed that two-month-old babies were already using their lips and tongue and waving their hands as people do in conversation. He considers that "the foundation for interpersonal communication between humans is 'there' at birth, and is remarkably useful by eight weeks when cognitive and memory processes are beginning."[34] Some neonatologists now place these attempts at communication even earlier. Before they are nine months old, infants are reproducing intonation patterns that are noticeably related to the language by which they are surrounded (and Chinese babies produce tones by six months).[35] At twelve months babies are uttering single words and at fifteen months are putting two words together. At two years the normal child is already something of a chatterbox, even when alone.[36] We must take into consideration physical and cognitive development when comparing this progress with that of older children.

When we come to young elementary school children, most have difficulty in refraining from talking for a half hour, let alone several months. Theoretical discussion often blinds us to the realities of human behavior. Only in the most teacher-centered, authoritarian classrooms can one impose silence, or minimal production through gestures or single words (as suggested by Krashen and Terrell[37]) on little children or even high school and college students. Some efforts to do so have foundered on the reefs of student resistance and even hostility; it appears that many students come to the task with the feeling that language learning has something to do with speaking, and they want to vocalize. Human beings are born to talk and talk they will—in the native language if means are not provided for them in the second language. There are many well-known techniques for providing young learners with a basic corpus of useful utterances, from learning action songs and poems with repetitive refrains to acting out short situations in which the children regularly find themselves, or playing games that require standard formulas and simple vocabulary. (Traditional children's games and rhymes, as well as adult folk songs, reveal this type of activity to be a well-loved and natural one.) Uncomplicated utterances are easily acquired; children love to use them and are most imaginative in applying them in new contexts. What may seem theoretically desirable (and this may also be contested) runs up against the pedagogical imperative of motivating naturally active students to participate vocally and expressively in the process of learning, whether it be language or mathematics.

Children, and students generally, are not machines to be manipulated in order to find the most efficient way of producing what we may want them to produce. They are interactive human beings. Students, we now believe, achieve facility in using a language when their attention is focused on conveying and receiving authentic messages—messages that contain information of interest to speaker and listener in a situation of importance to both—that is, through interaction. After twelve years' study of children learning language, Wells and his team concluded that "exchange is the basic unit of discourse. . . . Linguistic interaction is a collaborative activity" involving "the establishment of a triangular relationship between the sender, the receiver and the context of situation," whether the communication be in speech or in writing.[38] For the learning of a new language, whether or not there is a structured sequence or structured activities, whether the learning is inductive or deductive or a mixture of the two, there must be communication of meanings—*interaction between people who have something to share.* It is this interaction that we must keep in mind if effective language learning or acquisition is to take place. Interaction involves both comprehension and production, as immigrants, refugees, and other foreign-language users soon discover.

Immigrants' and visitors' attempts to communicate orally stop dead, of course, when they cannot understand what is being said to them. However, the conversation stops equally quickly when the new arrival tries to say something but "can't find the words" and can only gesture with a hesitant smile (although in this case actual communication may continue through the tactile-kinesic modality). Communication breaks down when the minimally equipped speaker utters a stream of words that are unrecognizable phonologically or do not follow the syntactic conventions of the language. If the utterance is pidginized, it may evoke a response in "foreigner talk," which is comprehensible input but limits the nonnative speaker's opportunities to hear authentic language and acquire the full range of structures.[39] Communication also breaks down when the foreigner utters a grammatical, well-pronounced sentence but doesn't understand, or misinterprets, what is said in response.

Comprehension and production, then, are indissoluble partners in the two-way process of communicative interaction, and here I subsume under comprehension and production the associated kinesics and pragmatic rules of conduct within the culture, which are as essential to comprehension as they are to acceptable and comprehensible production. We are all interested in preparing students for complete acts of communication. Where scholars split is on *how* to prepare students to operate freely and in a meaningful way: comprehending, producing, initiating, responding, assessing, countering, evaluating, informing, negotiating, and expressing. We need to understand both comprehension and production: the difference between them and their interactive essence.

Listening with comprehension is learned by attentive listening, which is motivated listening; in other words, we want to comprehend because the content is important to us or because our curiosity is aroused. For this reason, giving orders in the classroom to which students respond physically, as proposed by Asher,[40] has long been considered useful as an initial learning device, especially if the response required is unexpected or slightly ridiculous and therefore amusing; the same applies to action dances and games. Objects and pictures, as used in the Natural Approach, serve a similar purpose of arousing interest and curiosity at an early stage, as do exchanges among students on matters of common concern (what they are wearing, what they are doing, the weather, and so on); techniques such as these were already familiar to Gouin, Berlitz, and the early direct method proponents. Pestalozzi with his objects, Gattegno with his rods, the audiolingualists with their stick figures and miming, audiovisual exponents with their filmstrip images, and eclecticists with their flashcards and cartoons, were all aware of the importance of visual images, objects, and actions in making early input comprehensible and intriguing.

Research by such scholars as Carroll, Tanenhaus, and Bever (1978) brings out differences between the processes of listening and speaking that make it unlikely, however, that intensive listening of itself will lead to fluent and effective speaking. Listening comprehension (as does reading comprehension) draws on knowledge of the world and expectations aroused by the situation and the persons involved in it, all of this being colored by social and cultural expectations. Comprehension of speech is "an active, knowledge-guided process."[41] Listeners have no control over the elaboration of speech to which they are attending. As Carroll, Tanenhaus, and Bever point out, listeners are guided primarily by the melody and rhythm of the utterance to a segmentation into configurations from which functional relations of noun-verb-noun are extracted; these relations are presumed to represent subject-predicate-object relations, unless semantic elements warn the listener to the contrary.[42] Having decided early in the listening about the probable content and import, they extract elements that create a plausible message, this process being guided not only by previous knowledge but also by expectations aroused by the situation. (If they misinterpret the import early on, they may complain of "not understanding," even though the words were not unknown.)

Consequently, listeners need facility in recognizing the aural form of lexical items. From these they draw semantic elements that are interrelated within their mental networks by inferential processes, which are also influenced by knowledge of the possible and the probable.[43] In this process the natural redundancy of language helps, since all the elements of the input are not usually identified by the listener with equal precision. Where there is some ambiguity or lack of clarity, local sign cues (surface structure cues), such as salient morphology for plurals or tensed endings to verbs, help to elucidate the meaning.[44] What is extracted in listening as perceived meaning is not recoded for storage in its original syntactic form. It is stored in memory in a simpler form that preserves the gist. This recoding can later be expanded as required to re-express the major aspects of meaning selected as important by the listener, but will not necessarily be restated with the original grammatical structure or morphology.[45] If we are teaching effective listening skills that will result in identification and retention of the meaning, we teach students to rely first on semantic cues and *not* to focus on the syntax, unless this becomes essential for resolving an ambiguity.

How does the process of speaking differ? Speaking begins with the intention of the speaker. Unlike the listener, the speaker controls by his or her selection of items the level of language and the elaborated or simplified form that will be used. Thus the learner of a language can keep within a simplified syntax and reduced vocabulary to express meaning, but has little control over the riches of authentic speech uttered by native speakers, except when the latter adjust their speech in the face of incomprehension, bewilderment, or requests for simplification or slower speech. According to Schlesinger, the intention of the speaker takes shape in a pattern of semantic relations (the functional relations of agent, action, object, location, and so on). These semantic relations are expressed through the structural relations the syntax of the language provides.[46] (The writer in the language has similar needs.)

If we accept the well-documented findings of researchers like Bever et al. and Schlesinger, we come to the conclusion that speakers need grammar to express nuances of meaning (in other words they need an ability to express meaning through the morphosyntactic mechanisms of the language and, we may add, the phonological conventions), whereas listeners may bypass much of this grammar by resorting to semantic strategies. *This is the fundamental difference between listening and speaking* (and also between reading and writing). To aurally comprehend material over the complexity of which they have little control, listeners need a large recognition vocabulary. They must be able to recognize elements of the language in various forms in different morphophonemic transformations—according to speed of speech, timbre of voice, and selected register, or in varying conditions of noise and incomplete production (while chewing or laughing, for instance). They need to be able to understand what is half expressed or left to inference and interpretation. Learning to aurally comprehend a new language to any degree of sophistication is a lengthy and demanding process. For fluent speaking, students have to develop automatic control of invariant features of syntax so that, while selecting from the options to express nuances of meaning, they are not squandering cognitive energy on verb endings, plural forms, position of adjectives and adverbs, and other formal features that concern the listener only when interpretation becomes complex.[47]

Krashen and Terrell maintain that with plenty of comprehensible input, "the ability to speak (or write) fluently in a second language will come on its own with time."[48] That one way of using language (namely, comprehension) should in some incidental and effortless way lead to the mastery of another (that is, production), which involves quite different processes and requires control of distinctly different aspects of language, seems difficult to maintain, especially when we observe the effort small children have to devote to developing speaking proficiency long after they have attained a high level of comprehension. That such an effortless transition from listening to speaking (or from reading to writing) takes place in second-language learning has yet to be demonstrated, especially with adolescent and adult learners, who have reached the logico-deductive stage of formal thinking of which Piaget speaks.[49] The various experiments with methods that concentrate on comprehension (of aural and written materials), to the exclusion of production until a later stage, have failed to show that speech of any complexity does emerge effortlessly as promised. Most reports of experiments in this area are found, on examination, to end with the hope that this will be so.[50]

This is not to say that we do not "acquire" some language elements from listening without conscious awareness of the learning process. McLaughlin, Rossman, and McLeod, drawing on information-processing research, point out that some of the automatized or routinized processing required for speaking may have been acquired subconsciously in naturalistic situations and some acquired consciously. Some processes that were consciously learned may gradually have become established through more and more subconscious use, so that they are finally used automatically. Controlled processes may be conscious or subconscious, depending on the amount of practice and regular use to which they have been put.[51]

Unfortunately, because of distance from areas where the language being learned is spoken, a dearth of accessible native speakers in the neighborhood, and societal pressures of various types (such as the perceived acceptability for social interaction of existing pockets of speakers of the language), practice in most language-learning situations worldwide is limited to formal classroom settings, with opportunities to use the language shared among the members of large classes and occasions for naturalistic acquisition severely limited. Age of the learner, as noted earlier, is another important factor that determines how the language will be assimilated, as are differences in personal learning styles. In such formal situations, shortcuts to language use, such as choral practice, small group interactions, and cooperative learning activities, as well as exposure to authentic language through tapes, films, videodiscs, and radio and television programs where available, supply the necessary practice in comprehension and production. Yet despite this restricted access to native speech, students continue to emerge from such settings able to use what they have learned in expressing meaning as circumstances demand it.[52] Experience in study abroad and job situations shows that they rapidly improve their ability to communicate when plunged into a language-rich environment with many opportunities for purposeful interaction, if they have a solid base of knowledge of the language on which to draw. Brecht, Davidson, and Ginsberg's study of students' progress in Russian during a period of residence in St. Petersburg demonstrated clearly that those who had the strongest preparation in the structure of the language made the greatest gains in spoken language proficiency during their stay.[53]

Since the grammar we draw on for effective real-time comprehension is different from the grammar we need to express our ideas explicitly,[54] it would seem clear that without very attentive listening or reading, that is, close monitoring with the intent of inductive analysis of the structures used, listening (or reading) will not result in the internalizing of the production grammar we require for speaking (or writing). If we encourage students to listen (or read) in this way, with close attention to the production syntax, we are not helping them to become efficient listeners (or readers) who infer meaning primarily from semantic elements and from a leaner, less complex comprehension grammar. Terrell became aware of this fact, especially for languages with complex morphosyntax, and in 1991 he advocated that, in order to improve inductive learning of morphosyntactic features through listening, students should be given "advance organizers," in Ausubel's terminology (that is, some "information about target-language forms and structures that will aid in processing the input") and "meaning-form focusers" as "input organizers" to draw attention to non-salient and redundant grammatical morphemes that are, nevertheless, essential to acceptable and comprehensible expression. He admits that in some cases "explicit grammar instruction" may be necessary.[55]

Both comprehension and production are demanding processes that require time and increasing knowledge of vocabulary and language structure to mature and much practice to perfect. Unfortunately, despite all we know about the differences between listening for comprehension and speaking to be comprehended, few materials to date teach the type of recognition grammar listening requires, and even fewer initiate students into the different strategies we employ in receiving and communicating messages. Many students are not even made aware of the need for developing different strategies for these two aspects of communication. They do not learn how to piece together meaning from semantic elements and draw on context and previous knowledge for listening, nor how to develop inferencing skills through intelligent, fact-based guessing and supplementing where the signal is not clear. They are not brought to realize that for speaking we make the most of what we have, daring to create new utterances and judging by the reaction whether we need to paraphrase, expand, or use visual elements to fill out our meaning. In listening, the syntax may be beyond our previous experience, but this does not faze us because we can infer meaning or, if necessary, ask for clarification.

With speaking we are in control, and with practice in the right strategies we can make a little go a long way. But we must possess that little. Developing language control has never been easy and effortless. Even after years it is not so in our first language (in speaking and, especially, in writing), and achievement is very variable among individuals.

Does it matter how the language we possess was acquired? In this regard a phenomenon reported by the U.S. Government language-teaching agencies is of interest. This is the case of "the terminal 2" and even the "terminal 1+". In the proficiency,[56] 2 or 2+ represents limited working proficiency, enabling the appointee to satisfy routine social demands and limited office requirements. Scores of 3 or 3+ are expected for most positions requiring U.S. representatives to operate in the language in a professional context: that is, to satisfy representation requirements and handle professional discussions within a specified field. For the 3 level an acceptable, but nonnative, control of the structure of the language and a broad vocabulary are required. The "terminal 2's" are those who entered the agency's language program with enough knowledge to qualify at the 2 level but who, despite the intensive training they receive, never advance beyond 2+ in communicative proficiency and so do not reach the minimum professional proficiency required for most positions. "The grammar weaknesses that are typically found in this profile," according to Higgs and Clifford, "are not *missing* grammatical patterns which the student could learn or acquire later on, but are *fossilized* incorrect patterns."[57] Terminal 2's cannot seem to reach the acceptable standard in communication represented by 3 or 3+. Usually they have a wide vocabulary but control a low level of grammar.

"Experience has shown again and again," state Higgs and Clifford, "that such fossilized patterns are not remediable, even in intensive language training programs or additional in-country living experience. . . . A terminal pattern has also been identified at the 1+ level. The terminal 1+ has usually learned the foreign language on the streets. Street learners do not need accurate grammar to survive. As a result, they develop and internalize their own communication strategies. Even though most of these strategies are not linguistically correct, they succeed for Level 1 tasks (able to satisfy routine travel needs and minimum courtesy requirements). They do not, however, work at higher functional levels, when more sophisticated communicative tasks are attempted. This means that these inaccurate strategies, which normally consist of fossilized lexical and grammatical structures, have to be *unlearned* before functional language ability can be improved. Once again remediation in these cases is seldom, if ever, successful."[58]

When pre-service foreign-language teachers were tested at the University of Minnesota, similar terminal cases were identified. Most of these "had begun their language training in unstructured overseas work or study settings."[59] In Krashen's terms, these students had acquired their knowledge of the language through purposeful activities providing comprehensible input, during which they were focusing on meaning in a non-threatening environment—a situation Krashen says leads to greater accuracy as the "acquired system" is allowed to operate.[60] Others "had only school learning experiences. . . . All (of the latter) came from language programs that either were taught by instructors who themselves had not attained grammatical mastery of the target language. . . or by instructors who had chosen not to correct their students' mistakes for philosophical, methodological, or personal reasons.[61] These groups of learners had developed ingrained, or "fossilized" inaccuracies that they were unable to eradicate at a later stage.

The problem of seemingly irremediable fossilization pinpointed by the U.S. Government agencies has to be taken into serious consideration. It tallies with experiential or anecdotal data on those students who go abroad with a glib, communicative fluency, with many inaccuracies and inadequacies, who are gradually surpassed in productive skill by at first inhibited, grammar-trained students, whose passive knowledge of structure and lexicon becomes active in the environment where the language is heard and must be spoken. In other words, the years of conscious learning pay off for these students when active production is required in the pressured situation of using with native speakers the language they have learned.[62]

Perhaps the most widely studied language-learning classes have been French Immersion classes in Canada where students study content in a second language in a home-school language switch situation, focusing on meaning, not form. Swain and Lapkin examined the disturbing fact that students in these classes retained many morphosyntactic errors in their speech after years of content-based immersion classes, where they received much "comprehensible input" but were not required to produce sufficient "comprehensible output" in the form of sustained utterances. They attribute the continuing inadequacies to the fact that the immersion students received a functionally restricted input (their teachers did not regularly use the full array of structures the learners needed for expression) and insufficient and inconsistent feedback on form. They suggest supplementation of such instruction with "activities that will involve the use of the missing forms and functions" and "opportunities for sustained language use by the students, with some form of consistent feedback." They describe successful late immersion programs that adopted such an activity approach. "In the activity-centered program, students worked on projects of their own choice either individually or in small groups;" these activities "provided ample opportunities to engage in a wide variety of speech acts with their teacher and fellow students." The "three essential components of immersion methodology," they maintain, are "consistent and creative error correction strategies, broadening the functional range of classroom discourse, and insisting on varied and extended opportunities for second language use."[63]

Lightbown and Spada[64] studied intensive English as a Second Language classes for native speakers of French in grades 5 and 6 in Quebec elementary schools who had limited contact with English outside of their classes. All the classes studied were communicative in approach, but learners in the class in which the teacher gave the most form-focused instruction were the most accurate in their expression. This form-focused instruction was not explicit grammar instruction, but rather explicit reaction to errors and formal difficulties as they occurred, along the lines of Rutherford and Sharwood Smith's "consciousness-raising."[65]

Krashen's views on conscious learning were not always as dismissive as they now seem to be. In a well-known study, he and Selinger wrote on the "Essential Contributions of Formal Instruction in Adult Second Language Learning," they compared "language teaching methods known to be successful in helping adults learn language" and found that "the universal and presumably crucial ingredients of formal instruction are (1) the isolation of rules and lexical items of the target language, and (2) the possibility of error detection or correction." They hypothesized that "adults who seem to be able to 'pick up' languages or who are [able] to improve their second language proficiency outside the classroom have some means of approaching items in the target language one at a time (via bilingual dictionaries and grammars or through using native speakers as informants) and are also getting feedback (perhaps helpful native speakers correct their errors. . . . If this is so," they conclude, "such 'informal' learners are really using formal instruction and do not constitute counter-examples to the claim that formal instruction is of more benefit than exposure after puberty."[66]

It is interesting that in Pica's 1983 study it was found that "classroom instruction inhibited use of pidgin-like construction for any instructed subjects, even for those who were exposed to naturalistic input," in other words, those instructed used learned morphology, even if overusing it at times, whereas those "acquiring" in naturalistic settings did not. These instructed subjects did not appear to keep what they had "learned" distinct from what they had "acquired" as they used the language. Pica concludes that "as reflected in their production errors, differing conditions of L2 exposure appear to affect acquirers' hypotheses about the target language and their strategies for using it."[67]

To explain "certain apparent cases of fossilization," Krashen posits an Output Filter: "A device that attempts to explain why second-language users do not always perform their competence. These acquirers," he continues, "appear to be fossilized, but in reality have acquired more rules than they normally perform. . . . The output filter prevents acquired rules from being used in performance."[68] This is an interesting development of the theory. If the acquired system alone initiates utterances and learned material is available only as an editor (Monitor) under certain conditions, we may well ask: What is initiating utterances when the output filter is preventing acquired rules from being used? Krashen tells us that apparently fossilized speakers have acquired "imperfect intermediate forms" in certain circumstances and it is these that are being found in utterances.[69] But these intermediate forms that are being used have also been "acquired." How is it possible to use these "acquired" rules when, we are told, the output filter is preventing acquired rules from being used? How is it that the output filter allows some "acquired" rules, imperfect intermediate ones, apparently, to operate but not those that presumably belong to the natural order of acquisition set? If this is so, what is the explanation? Is it possible that some fossilized forms have been "learned" at some stage (taught by teachers whose knowledge of the language was incomplete, or learned from poorly conceived materials as Selinker has suggested[70]), and that these learned forms are initiating utterances at those times when the output filter is preventing acquired rules from operating? Does this mean, then, that "learned competence," which cannot become "acquired," according to Krashen, can become "fossilized" and can initiate utterances in certain cases, despite the theory that only acquired forms can initiate utterances? If so, how does such variation accord with the statement that the "mental organ" for language . . . produces one basic product . . . in one fundamental way"? The Output Filter, it seems, creates more problems for the theory than it solves.

Beyond the Monitor Model: An Interactive Approach

For well-rounded language learning, comprehension and production may be usefully combined, as they are in normal communication and in informal second-language learning situations. Plenty of comprehensible input is, and always has been, important (although a whole paper could be written on what makes input "comprehensible" for specific learners). Students need to learn not only to create meanings from what they hear, without undue attention to details of morphology and syntax, but also to put together their own meanings and to negotiate meaning with others; for this, they need ready access to the syntactic, lexical, and pragmatic resources of the language, as they create utterances that convey their meanings clearly in communicative interaction. For the meanings they receive and express to be comprehensible, they also need early introduction to the cultural assumptions and expectations of the speakers of the language, and this knowledge also increases the probability that their output will be acceptable and appropriate.

These and other considerations discussed in this article point to an interactive approach as an appropriate way of developing ease in communication in a second language, with students listening to authentic materials (on tape, film, disk, radio, or television), to native speakers where they are accessible, to their teachers, and to each other, responding and contributing to the interaction as they engage in purposeful tasks in which each is fully engaged; in this way they will learn to navigate their way comfortably and acceptably in the use of the new language. Comprehension and production thus retrieve their rightful relationship as an interactive duo. We must provide as many opportunities as possible for meaningful interaction while the language is being learned; in this way we help our students build up their confidence as early as possible in language comprehension and use, sparking motivation to persevere with efforts to make the language really their second language. There may be formal learning as well as informal learning, as teachers interact with students, students with teachers, and students with fellow students, as well as with the community of speakers of the language, either by going out into a nearby community or bringing the community into the classroom, in actuality or vicariously.

For genuinely interactive activities, comprehending and producing, conveying information and sharing ideas and experiences, the affective filter must be low, to use Krashen's terminology, that is, students and teachers must care about each other as well as about the meanings being expressed and feel at ease with each other as they cooperate in the learning experience. Authentic interaction, in or out of the classroom, depends on human relations within groups. It requires that individuals seek to understand and appreciate other individuals—not manipulating or directing them or deciding how they can or will learn, but encouraging and drawing them out (educating them) by allowing for their individual, and sometimes culturally determined, preferences in how they will learn. (This applies as much to classes for immigrants and refugees as to formal classes for young children, adolescents, or adults.) Teacher directed and dominated classrooms, where students are expected to learn in the one way the teacher has ordained, are not interactive classrooms, whether "comprehension first" classrooms or those whose procedures are based on some other set of convictions.

An interactive approach requires of the teacher a high degree of indirect leadership and emotional maturity. Teachers are individuals, as are their students; in interactive teaching, the teacher's level of confidence and satisfaction is as important as that of the students. (Teacher relaxation is a prerequisite for student relaxation.) We each teach and interact most effectively according to our own personality, just as students learn in their individual ways.[71] An interactive approach encourages both teacher individuality and student individuality.

Whatever promotes student participation in an atmosphere where students and teacher are relaxed and involved stimulates the interaction, through comprehension and production, that is basic to second-language learning. The interaction may be quiet; it may be noisy; it may be assured and vigorous; it may be indirect, providing almost imperceptible encouragement for self-expression. It may be related to formal study, encouraging students to use immediately what they have been learning in purposeful activity, thus internalizing the way the language works through *performing rules*, not reciting or endlessly discussing them.[72] The interaction may be free-wheeling, allowing opportunities to use a number of structures and a diverse vocabulary (which has been learned on previous occasions or personally collected[73]) to work through interesting and absorbing tasks and projects, student initiated or at least student maintained. The interaction will always provide opportunities for both students and teachers to listen and speak—to create, vary, and experiment.[74] Whatever the mode with which students and teacher feel most at ease, it will always involve as well interaction with interesting and informative content, so that students' minds are being stretched while they develop control of the new language.

Theories of language acquisition and learning are continually changing as they evolve. In classrooms, language learning is taking place in ways theorists may not yet understand, but which teachers observe every day. They must continue with their task while waiting for more definitive answers, employing the best of what has been proposed theoretically, according to their own judgment of its appropriateness in their own situation, and innovating in a practical way in classroom involvement to help students express themselves in the new and unfamiliar language. If we wish to see our students develop the ability to use the language freely and purposefully, we must provide a classroom environment where there is an atmosphere of trust and confidence that develops the students' own confidence and encourages them to plunge in and make the language their own.

Appendix:* Ten Principles of Interactive Language Learning and Teaching

1. The student is the language learner.

    Corollary 1: Motivation springs from within; it can be sparked but not imposed from without.

2. Language learning and teaching are shaped by student needs and objectives in particular circumstances.

    Corollary 2: Language teaching and course design will be very diverse.

3. Language learning and teaching are based on normal uses of language, with communication of meanings in oral or written form basic to all strategies and techniques.

4. Classroom relations reflect mutual liking and respect, allowing for both teacher personality and student personality in a nonthreatening atmosphere of cooperative learning.

5. Basic to language use are knowledge of language and control of language.

6. Development of language control proceeds through creativity, which is nurtured by interactive, participatory activities.

7. Every possible medium and modality are used to aid learning.

8. Testing is an aid to learning.

9. Language learning is penetrating another culture: students learn to operate harmoniously within it or in contact with it.

10. The real world extends beyond the classroom walls; language learning takes place in and out of the classroom.

---

*   For full discussion of the implications of the Ten Principles, see W. M. Rivers, "Ten Principles of Interactive Language Learning and Teaching," chap. 19 in W. M. Rivers, ed. and contrib., *Teaching Languages in College: Curriculum and Content* (Lincolnwood, IL: National Textbook Company, 1992), pp. 372–92.

Notes

* Some sections of this article appeared in an earlier version as "Comprehension and Production in Interactive Language Teaching," *Modern Language Journal* 70 (1986): 1–7.

1 A. Raimes, "Tradition and Revolution in ESL Teaching," *TESOL Quarterly* 17 (1983): 535–52. Raimes is referring to T.S. Kuhn's formulation in *The Structure of Scientific Revolutions,* 2d ed. (Chicago, University of Chicago Press, 1970), p. 91.

2 N. Brooks, *Language and Language Learning: Theory and Practice* (New York: Harcourt, Brace & World, 1960).

3 K. Chastain, *The Development of Modern Language Skills: Theory to Practice* (Philadelphia: Center for Curriculum Development, 1971).

4 J.A. van Ek, *The Threshold Level for Modern Language Learning in Schools* (London: Longman, 1977).

5 S.J. Savignon, *Communicative Competence: An Experiment in Foreign-Language Teaching* (Philadelphia: Center for Curriculum Development, 1972).

6 C. Gattegno, *Teaching Foreign Languages in Schools: The Silent Way,* 2d ed. (New York: Educational Solutions, 1972).

7 J.J. Asher, "The Learning Strategy of the Total Physical Response: A Review," *Modern Language Journal* 50 (1966), 79–84.

8 S.D. Krashen, "Theory versus Practice in Language Training," in R.W. Blair, ed., *Innovative Approaches to Language Teaching* (Rowley, Mass.: Newbury, 1982b), pp.20–21.

9 C.A. Curran, *Counseling-Learning in Second Languages* (Apple River, Ill.: Apple River Press, 1976).

10 G. Lozanov, *Suggestology and Outlines of Suggestopedy* (New York: Gordon and Breach, 1978).

11 T.D. Terrell, "A Natural Approach to Second Language Acquisition and Learning," *Modern Language Journal* 61 (1977): 325–37.

12 For a thorough study of the theoretical and practical aspects of teaching another culture, see G.L.N. Robinson, *Crosscultural Understanding: Process and Approaches for Foreign Language, English as a Second Language and Bilingual Educators* (Englewood Cliffs, NJ: Prentice-Hall, 1985).

13 Note that, in this article, I do not adhere to the distinction between *acquisition* and *learning*, as Krashen defines them in his Monitor model. I maintain this distinction only when discussing Krashen's hypotheses. I personally follow the practice of Dulay, Burt, and Krashen in *Language Two* (New York: Oxford University Press, 1982), in which they state: "We use the words 'learning' and 'acquisition' interchangeably, although they are sometimes used in the L2 literature to distinguish between *conscious* and *subconscious* language development. To express this important distinction, we use 'conscious' and 'subconscious' respectively" (p.11).

14 The summary of the Monitor Model in this and the following paragraph is derived from Krashen (1981); S.D. Krashen, *Principles and Practice in Second-Language Acquisition* (Oxford: Pergamon Press, 1982a); Krashen, in Blair, ed. (1982b); S.D. Krashen and T.D. Terrell, *The Natural Approach: Language Acquisition in the Classroom* (Hayward, CA: Alemany Press, and Oxford: Pergamon Press, 1983); and S.D. Krashen, *The Input Hypothesis: Issues and Implications* (London and New York: Longman, 1985).

15 Krashen (1982a), p. 15.

16 For a detailed discussion of the active, dynamic nature of mental processes, see W.M. Rivers, "Mental Representations and Language in Action," in J.E. Alatis, ed., *Linguistics, Language Teaching and Language Acquisition: The Interdependence of Theory, Practice and Research.* GURT 1990: 46–63 (Washington, D.C.: Georgetown University Press, 1990). Reprinted in *Canadian Modern Language Review* 47(1991): 1–16.

17 Krashen (1983), "The Din in the Head, Input, and the Language Acquisition Dance." *Foreign Language Annals,* v. 16, n. 1, pp. 41–44.

18 D.P. Ausubel, *Educational Psychology: A Cognitive View* (New York: Holt, Rinehart and Winston, 1968), pp. 99–103.

19 B. McLaughlin, T. Rossman, and B. McLeod, "Second Language Learning: An Information-Processing Perspective," *Language Learning* 33 (1983): 135–58, applies the theory of automatic and controlled processes to second language learning.

20 Krashen (1985), pp. 42–43.

21 As one example, see J.R. Anderson, *The Architecture of Cognition* (Cambridge, MA: Harvard University, 1983).

22 Krashen and Terrell (1983), p. 26.

23 E. Bialystok, "Psychological Dimensions of Second Language Proficiency," in W. Rutherford and M. Sharwood Smith, eds., *Grammar and Second Language Teaching: A Book of Readings* (New York: Newbury, 1988) pp. 31–50.

24 J.B. Carroll, *Language and Thought* (Englewood Cliffs, NJ: Prentice-Hall, 1964), pp. 45–46. The effects were most pronounced with a delay of one-fifth of a second.

25 W.M. Rivers, *Teaching Foreign-Language Skills*, 2d ed. (Chicago: University of Chicago Press, 1981), p. 249. See also Rivers 1983a, pp. 159–60.

26 For a sample of informal English speech, see W.M. Rivers and M.S. Temperley, *A Practical Guide to the Teaching of English as a Second or Foreign Language* (Oxford: Oxford University Press, 1978), p. 65.

27 Krashen (1982a), p. 16.

28 Anderson (1983).

29 Krashen (1985), p. 2.

30 Ibid, p. 4.

31 Terrell (1977), p. 26.

32 For a discussion of whether a second language is learned in the same way as the first, see W.M. Rivers, *Communicating Naturally in a Second Language: Theory and Practice in Language Teaching* (Cambridge: Cambridge University Press, 1983a), pp. 9–10, 87–93, 156–58.

33 J.J. Asher, "The Extinction of Second-Language Learning in American Schools: an Intervention Model," in H. Winitz, ed., *The Comprehension Approach to Foreign Language Instruction* (Rowley, Mass.; Newbury, 1981) and Krashen and Terrell (1983).

34 C. Trevarthen, "Conversations with a Two-month Old," *New Scientist,* May 2, 1974, pp. 230–235, quoted in T.E. Weeks, *Born to Talk* (Rowley, Mass.: Newbury, 1979), p. 41.

35 R.H. Weir, "Some Questions on the Child's Learning of Phonology," in F. Smith and G.A. Miller, eds., *The Genesis of Language; A Psycholinguistic Approach* (Cambridge, Mass.: MIT Press, 1966), pp. 155–57).

36 R.H. Weir, *Language in the Crib* (The Hague: Mouton, 1962).

37 Krashen and Terrell (1983), pp. 77–79.

38 G. Wells et al., *Learning through Interaction: The Study of Language Development* (Cambridge: Cambridge University Press, 1981), pp. 46–47.

39 M. Swain and S. Lapkin, "Canadian Immersion and Adult Second Language Teaching: What's the Connection?" *Modern Language Journal* 73 (1989):150–59, call this "functionally restricted input." Language learners, they say, "are unlikely to learn what they neither hear nor read" (p. 155).

40 Asher in Winitz, ed. (1981), p. 65.

41 D.I. Slobin, *Psycholinguistics*, 2d ed. (Glenview, Ill.: Scott Foresman, 1979), p. 37.

42 Configurational and local sign cues are discussed in J.M. Carroll, M.K. Tanenhaus, and T.G. Bever, "The Perception of Relations: The Interaction of Structural, Functional, and Contextual Factors in the Segmentation of Sentences," in W.J.M. Levelt and G.B. Flores d'Arcais, eds., *Studies in the Perception of Language* (New York: John Wiley and Sons, 1978), pp.187–218.

43 Semantic networks are discussed in relation to vocabulary in W.M. Rivers, "Recognition, Retention, Retrieval: The three R's of Vocabulary Use," in P. Hashemipour and R. Maldonado, eds., *Festschrift for T.D. Terrell* (New York: McGraw-Hill, in press).

44 Carroll, Tanenhaus, and Bever (1978).

45 For a more detailed account of listening comprehension, see Rivers (1981), pp. 151–83 (with pros and cons of massive introductory listening); "Listening," chap. 3 of Rivers and Temperley (1978); and "Linguistic and Psychological Factors in Speech Perception and their Implications for Listening and Reading Materials" in W.M. Rivers, *Speaking in Many Tongues*, 3d ed. (Cambridge: Cambridge University Press, 1983b), pp. 78–90.

46 For I.M. Schlesinger's models of speech comprehension and speech production, see *Production and Comprehension of Utterances* (Hillsdale, NJ: Lawrence Erlbaum Associates, 1977).

47 The two levels of language second-language speakers need to control are discussed in detail in "Rules, Patterns, and Creativity," in Rivers (1983a), pp. 30–39 (a revised form of an article originally published in 1968).

48 Krashen and Terrell (1983), p. 32.

49 See H.G. Furth, *Piaget and Knowledge: Theoretical Foundations* (Englewood Cliffs, NJ: Prentice-Hall, 1969), pp. 29–32.

50 For the experiments of Postovsky and Gary-Olmsted, see Rivers (1981), pp. 176–81. The Purdue Experiment, using Winitz's *Learnables,* yielded disappointing results, as reported in S.S. Corbett and W.F. Smith, "Listening Comprehension as a Base for a Multiskill Approach to Beginning Spanish: The Purdue Experiment," in Winitz, ed. (1981), pp. 223–253; and in the same book, in J.K. Swaffar and D.S. Stephens, "What Comprehension-Based Classes Look like in Theory and Practice," pp. 254–74, the University of Texas at Austin experiment is described without results.

51 McLaughlin, Rossman, and McLeod (1983), pp. 138–43.

52 In India, for instance, one meets many auto-didacts who have taught themselves English in areas where the language is rarely heard and who are able to express themselves well when in contact with English speakers.

53 R. Brecht, D. Davidson, and R. Ginsberg, "The Empirical Study of Proficiency Gain in Study Abroad Environments among American Students of Russian: Basic Research Needs and a Preliminary Analysis of Data," in A. Barchenkov and T. Garza, eds., *Proceedings of the First Soviet American Conference on Current Issues of Foreign Language Instruction* (Moscow: Visshaja shkola, 1992).

54 Schlesinger (1977).

55 T.D. Terrell, "The Role of Grammar Instruction in a Communicative Approach," *Modern Language Journal* 75 (1991):58–59.

56 Reprinted in Rivers (1981), pp. 479–99.

57 T.V. Higgs and R. Clifford, "The Push toward Communication," in T.V. Higgs, ed., *Curriculum, Competence, and the Foreign Language Teacher* (Skokie, Ill.: National Textbook Co., 1982), pp. 57–79. Quotation from p. 67, italics in the original.

58 Ibid., p. 67.

59 Ibid., p. 68.

60 Krashen (1985), p. 46.

61 Higgs and Clifford (1982), p. 68.

62 See Brecht, Davidson, and Ginsberg (1991).

63 Swain and Lapkin (1989).

64 P.M. Lightbown and N. Spada, "Focus-on-Form and Corrective Feedback in Communicative Language Teaching," *Studies in Second Language Acquisition* 12 (1990):429–46. For Krashen's comments on Swain's Comprehensible Output, Pica's study, and Lightbown and Spada's Focus-on-Form, see S.D. Krashen, "The Input Hypothesis: An Update," in J.E. Alatis, ed., *Linguistics and Language Pedagogy: The State of the Art*, Georgetown Round Table on Languages and Linguistics 1991 (Washington, DC: Georgetown University Press), pp. 409–31.

65 W. Rutherford and M. Sharwood Smith, "Consciousness Raising and Universal Grammar," in W. Rutherford and M. Sharwood Smith, eds., *Grammar and Second Language Teaching: A Book of Readings* (New York: Newbury, 1988), pp. 107–16.

66 S.D. Krashen and H.W. Seliger, "The Essential Contributions of Formal Instruction in Adult Second Language Learning," *TESOL Quarterly* 9 (1975):173–83.

67 T. Pica, "Adult Acquisition of English as a Second Language under Different Conditions of Exposure," *Language Learning* 33 (1983):465–97.

68 Krashen (1985), pp. 44–45.

69 Ibid., p. 47.

70 L. Selinker, "Interlanguage," *International Review of Applied Linguistics* 10 (1972):219–31.

71 Krashen (1985) does not concur with this view. He maintains that any apparent individual variation is "on the surface." "Deep down," he says, "the 'mental organ' for language...produces one basic product, a human language, in one fundamental way" (p. 3).

72 For a discussion of "performing rules," see W.M. Rivers, "Ten Principles of Interactive Language Learning and Teaching," chap. 19 in W.M. Rivers, ed. and contrib., *Teaching Languages in College: Curriculum and Content* (Lincolnwood, IL: National Textbook Company, 1992), pp. 372–92.

73 For the personal nature of each individual's vocabulary, see Rivers, "Recognition, Retention, Retrieval...," (in press).

74 For classroom activities in an interactive approach, see W.M. Rivers, ed. and contrib., *Interactive Language Teaching* (Cambridge: Cambridge University Press).

The Impact of Interaction on Comprehension

Teresa Pica and Richard Young, University of Pennsylvania, and Catherine Doughty, Georgetown University, USA

The study reported in this article compared the comprehension of 16 nonnative speakers (NNSs) of English on directions to a task presented by a native speaker (NS) under two input conditions: *premodified input*, in the form of an NS baseline lecturette modified by decreased complexity and increased quantity and redundancy, and *interactionally modified input*, consisting of the NS baseline lecturette without linguistic premodification, but with opportunities for interaction with the NS. It was found that comprehension was best assisted when the content of the directions was repeated and rephrased in interaction; however, reduction in linguistic complexity in the premodified input was not a significant factor in NNSs' comprehension. It was also found that NS-NNS interactional modifications in the form of comprehension and confirmation checks and clarification requests served as a mechanism for NS modification of input, either by encoding or, more frequently, by triggering repetition and rephrasing of input content, and thus played a critical role in comprehension. Results of the study support current theoretical claims regarding the role played by interactional modifications in facilitating second language comprehension. These results also provide guidelines for restructuring interaction in the classroom to serve learners' needs for comprehensible input.

In recent years, much second language research has been directed toward the study of input comprehension. This has been motivated by the belief that the learner's exposure to a target language is not in itself a sufficient condition for second language acquisition. From Corder's (1967) early claims to Krashen's (1985) current Input Hypothesis, there has been a widespread conviction that input must be comprehended by the learner if it is to assist the acquisition process.

Current second language acquisition research has tried to identify what it is that makes input comprehensible to the learner. Blau (1980), Chaudron (1983, 1985), P. Johnson (1981), Krashen (1980, 1982, 1983, 1985), and Long (1985) have considered this question from a theoretical and empirical point of view. We, too, have attempted to answer this question through a study of input comprehension in two different kinds of linguistic environment available to second language learners.

The first kind of linguistic environment is characterized by input that has been modified, or simplified, in some way before the learner sees or hears it, for example, through repetition and paraphrase of words, phrases, or sentences; restriction of vocabulary to common or familiar items; addition of boundary markers and sentence connectors; and reduction in sentence length and complexity through removal of subordinate clauses. Figure 1 provides examples of input that was modified according to a number of these characteristics for the purposes of the present study. The availability of modified input to second language learners has been established through studies of speech used by native speakers (NSs) to nonnative speakers (NNSs)—the so-called foreigner-talk studies (see Hatch, 1983, and Long, 1980, 1981, for reviews of this research). Modified input is also available within the classroom, through techniques for simplifying spoken and written language in textbooks, reading passages, and tape recordings (see Honeyfield, 1977, and Phillips & Shettlesworth, 1976, for critical perspectives on classroom input modification).

The second kind of environment for second language acquisition is characterized by opportunities for NS-NNS interaction in which both parties modify and restructure the interaction to arrive at mutual understanding. Until recently, this environment has been found mostly outside of instructional contexts, and it is especially absent in classrooms in which teachers control topic initiation and the elicitation of content and restrict students to the passive role of respondent. However, this kind of environment is becoming increasingly available within the classroom through more interactive procedures for managing classroom learning, such as conversation games, role plays, and student group and pair tasks (see, e.g., Brumfit & K. Johnson, 1979; K. Johnson & Morrow, 1981).

FIGURE 2

Examples of Modification of Selected Linguistic Features
in Input Directions for the Assembly Task

Complexity: Reduction in the number of S-nodes per T-unit per direction

Baseline: [In the center of the crossroads {right where the three meet,} put the dog in the—in the carriage] (2 S-nodes per T-unit)

Modified: [Put the dog in the middle of the three roads.] (1 S-node per T-unit)

Quantity: Increase in the number of words per direction

Baseline: Moving to the top right corner, place the two mushrooms with the three yellow dots in that grass patch down toward the road. (23 words)

Modified: Move to the top right corner. Take the two mushrooms with the three yellow dots. Put the two mushrooms on the grass. Put the two mushrooms on the grass near the road. (32 words)

Redundancy: Increase in repetition of content words per direction

Exact or partial:

Baseline: Place the two mushrooms with the three yellow dots in that grass patch down toward the road. (no repetition)

Modified: Take the two mushrooms with the three yellow dots. Put the two *mushrooms* on the grass. Put the two *mushrooms* on the *grass* near the road. (3 repetitions)

Semantic or paraphrase:

Baseline: Place the one piece with the two trees right at the edge of the water. (no repetition)

Modified: Put the two trees at the top of the water. Put the two trees *above* the water. (1 repetition)

Modifications of the interactional structure of conversations are most frequently brought about through moves first identified by Hatch (1978a, 1978b) and Long (1980, 1981, 1983). These moves, examples of which appear in Figure 2, include clarification requests and confirmation checks, by which one interlocutor seeks assistance in understanding or confirming the other's preceding utterance, and comprehension checks, through which one interlocutor seeks the other's acknowledgment that a preceding message has been understood.

Purpose of Research

The purpose of the study reported in this article was to compare the effects of these two environments for acquisition on NNSs' comprehension of input. The first environment was modeled by experimental Condition 1, in which input provided to the NNSs was modified a priori and no opportunities were allowed for interaction with the NS who provided the input. The second environment was modeled by Condition 2, in which input was not premodified linguistically but the NNSs were allowed opportunities to interact with the NS who provided the input. The NNSs could thus seek help with input they could not understand.

In focusing the study on a comparison of input and comprehension under these two conditions, we were developing a line of research which has already established that input modifications similar to those in Condition 1 promote comprehension. The studies by Blau (1980), Chaudron (1983, 1985), P. Johnson (1981), and Long (1985) noted above have shown that NNS comprehension is significantly better when the input is in the form of an a priori linguistically modified text or lecturette than when the input is presented in its original, unmodified form. What we predicted, however, was that the level of comprehension would be even greater when subjects were given opportunities to interact with the NS who provided the input.
This prediction was based on a current theory regarding the role of interaction in second language acquisition put forward by Hatch (1978a, 1978b, 1983) and Long (1980, 1981, 1983, 1985). What Hatch and Long have proposed is that in the course of interaction, learners and their interlocutors negotiate the meaning of messages by modifying and restructuring their interaction in order to reach mutual understanding. As a result of this negotiation, learners come to comprehend words and grammatical structures beyond their current level of competence and ultimately incorporate them in their own production. Thus, if comprehension of input is a necessary condition for successful second language acquisition, then interaction, or as Long has claimed more specifically, *interactional modification*, is the mechanism that brings about that comprehension.

Examples of how this input might occur can be seen in the interactions shown in Figure 2, in which the NNSs' requests for clarification and confirmation of the input they have received from the NS bring about a restructuring of the interaction and modifications of the input until understanding appears to be achieved. Since the claims regarding the importance of such restructuring of interaction had never been tested directly, the present study sought to measure what effects, if any, these modifications of interaction have on comprehension. We believed the study was, therefore, the first empirical test of the claim that interactional modifications lead to comprehension of input.

FIGURE 3

Examples of Interactional Modifications in NS-NNS Conversations	
NS	NNS
And right on the roof of the truck, place the duck. The duck.	I to take it? *Dog?*[a]
Duck.	Duck.
It's yellow and it's a small animal. It has two feet.	*I put where it?*[b]
You take the duck and put it on top of the truck. *Do you see the duck?*[c]	*Duck?*[a]
Yeah. Quack, quack, quack. That one. The one that makes that sound.	Ah yes. I see in the —in the head of him.
OK *See?*[c]	*Put what?*[b]
OK. Put him on top of the truck.	*Truck?*[a]
The bus. Where the boy is.	Ah yes.

[a] Confirmation checks: Moves by which one speaker seeks confirmation of the other's preceding utterance through repetition, with rising intonation, of what was perceived to be all or part of the preceding utterance.

[b] Clarification requests: Moves by which one speaker seeks assistance in understanding the other speaker's preceding utterance through questions (including *wh-*, polar, disjunctive, uninverted with rising intonation, or tag), statements such as *I don't understand*, or imperatives such as *Please repeat.*

[c] Comprehension checks: Moves by which one speaker attempts to determine whether the other speaker has understood a preceding message.

Research Design

The Task The study required a task which, first, would be a good measure of comprehension and, second, would provide an appropriate context for interaction. For this second reason, conventional paper-and-pencil tests of listening comprehension were rejected, and a format similar to the communication games now available for ESL teaching was adopted (see K. Johnson & Morrow, 1981).

The task required NNSs to listen to a NS give directions for choosing and placing 15 items on a small board illustrated with an outdoor scene. Individual items were two-dimensional cutouts representing a variety of plant, animal, and human figures, each of which shared at least one feature, such as shape, color, or size, with one other item. The board itself was illustrated with scenery, including figures similar to those on the cutouts, as well as landmarks such as a pond, patches of grass, a skyline, roads, vehicles, and other objects.

Each direction given by the NS included a description of the item and references to the place on the board where it was to be positioned. Comprehension was measured by the number of items which the subject selected and placed correctly. One point was given for correct selection of the item and one point for correct placement. The interactions were either video- or audiotaped, and transcriptions were made from the recordings.

TABLE 1

Comparisons of Mean Quantity, Redundancy, and Complexity in Baseline, Premodified, and Interactionally Modified Input			
Input	**Quantity**	**Redundancy**	**Complexity**
Baseline	16.47	0.20	1.20
Condition 1: premodified	33.47	7.20	1.02
Condition 2: interactionally modified	51.64	13.17	1.23
Difference between conditions 1 and 2	18.17	5.97	0.21[a]
t	2.37[b]	2.90[b]	1.91

Note: All figures for Condition 2 include baseline input. Quantity = words per subject per direction; redundancy = repetition of content words per subject per direction; complexity = S-nodes/T-unit per subject per direction.

[a] Direction of difference is opposite to that predicted.

[b] Null hypothesis rejected; $\alpha = .05$.

Two versions of the directions to the task were developed—a baseline, or linguistically unmodified, version and a linguistically modified version. The baseline version of the directions was compiled from a recording of NS-to-NS interaction on the task. The linguistically modified version of the directions was developed by taking the baseline version and simplifying it according to the criteria reviewed in Figure 1. This technique ensured that both sets of directions—the baseline and the linguistically modified versions—had similar content but differed only in the quantity, redundancy, and complexity of the language used. Table 1 provides a quantitative comparison of the linguistic features in the baseline and linguistically modified versions of the script used by the NS as input for all 15 directions.

Through a rigorous program of pretesting, the task was established as a reliable measure of listening comprehension: first, 30 linguistically modified directions to the task were tested on 10 NSs, who demonstrated 100% accuracy on all items. The same directions to the task were then tested on 25 NNSs drawn from the population of subjects who were to participate in the actual study. Item analyses were carried out, and 15 directions with a point biserial correlation of .20 or higher were selected for use under the experimental conditions of the study. Analysis of results from the directions used in the research produced a Kuder-Richardson 21 reliability coefficient of .76 for the task as a whole and a point biserial correlation coefficient of .30 or above for 13 out of the 15 directions chosen indicating that the task was a reliable and accurate test of listening comprehension.

Subjects Sixteen NNSs were selected from volunteers enrolled in preacademic, communicatively oriented, low-intermediate ESL classes. All subjects were adults and were about equally divided between European and Asian first language backgrounds. Although they had engaged in group and pair work in their classes, none of the subjects had had any previous experience of the task used in the study. Half of the subjects were assigned randomly to one of the experimental conditions, and the other half to the other experimental condition.

Data Collection Under Condition 1, premodified input, 8 subjects heard the linguistically adjusted script read by a female NS who was experienced in speaking with foreigners but not in ESL teaching. Subjects participated on a one-to-one basis with the NS, who read each direction only once and then paused, giving the NNS subject as much time as necessary to place the object on the board. Other than NS checks to see whether the next direction could be read, there was no interaction between the NS and the subject.

Under Condition 2, interactionally modified input, the same NS initially read each direction from the baseline input script. Subjects also participated on a one-to-one basis with the NS. Here, however, the 8 subjects were encouraged to seek verbal assistance from the NS if they had any difficulty in following the directions. No limit was placed on the amount of interaction that could take place. The NS also checked on whether the directions were understood or needed repeating. As in Condition 1, subjects were given as much time as necessary to place the object on the board. Unlike Condition 1, linguistic modifications were not built into the directions for Condition 2. Instead it was hypothesized that such modifications would be produced by the NS as a result of interaction with the NNSs in Condition 2.

To ensure that comprehension of the task would be based on spoken input and interaction alone, a screen was placed between the subject and the NS in both conditions, so that the NS could neither see nor physically participate in the selection and placement of items. (However, the NS and the subject could see each other's faces.)

Two major hypotheses were formulated to answer the research question: Do interactional modifications make input comprehensible? First, based on current claims from second language acquisition theory, it was predicted that the same kinds of linguistic adjustments that had been built into the modified input in Condition 1 would arise spontaneously during the interaction in Condition 2. Three experimental hypotheses were formulated based on this prediction:

1. Quantitatively more input would be available in the interactionally modified directions of Condition 2 than would be available in the premodified directions of Condition 1, as measured by the mean number of words per direction.

2. The input available in Condition 2 would be more redundant than that in Condition 1; that is, it would contain more repetitions of words naming items to be selected and places to put them in carrying out directions to the task.

3. The input available in Condition 2 would be less complex, that is, contain fewer S-nodes per T-unit than that in Condition 1.

The second major hypothesis of the study was that the subjects in Condition 2 would show greater comprehension of the directions than would the subjects in Condition 1. On the basis of this prediction three additional experimental hypotheses were formulated:

4. The mean score for selecting the correct item on the task would be higher for subjects in Condition 2 than for those in Condition 1.

5. The mean score for placing the item in the correct position on the board would also be higher for subjects in Condition 2 than for those in Condition 1.

6. The mean total score for selection and placement on the task would be higher for subjects in Condition 2 than for those in Condition 1.

Results and Discussion

The Two Major Hypotheses Results obtained in testing the first major hypothesis of the study are shown in Table 1. In terms of quantity of input, there were twice as many words per direction in Condition 1 (33.47) as a result of our own a priori modifications to the baseline data (16.47). However, approximately 18 additional words per direction were counted in the interactionally modified input in Condition 2, thus making a total of almost 52 words per subject per direction as a result of interaction. (All figures for Condition 2 in Table 1 include baseline input; thus, the quantity of input of 51.64 = the baseline of 16.47 + 35.17 additional words.)

The redundancy measure showed an even greater difference among the three kinds of input. Compared with hardly any repetitions in the baseline data, the premodified input in Condition 1 contained an average of 7 repetitions of content words per direction. However, there were 6 more repetitions of content words as a result of interaction in Condition 2, making a total of just over 13 per subject per direction. On t tests these quantity and redundancy differences were found to be significant, well below the alpha level of .05.

TABLE 2

Subjects	Mean selection score	Mean placement score	Mean combined score
Comparison of Mean Comprehension Scores of Subjects in the Two Experimental Conditions			
Condition 1: premodified	83% (12.38)	55% (8.25)	69% (20.63)
Condition 2: interactionally modified	95% (14.25)	81% (12.13)	88% (26.38)
Difference between conditions 1 and 2	12% (1.87)	26% (3.88)	19% (5.75)
t	3.37[a]	2.79[a]	3.78[a]

[a] Null hypothesis rejected; $\alpha = .05$.

Finally, we found that our own premodifications of the baseline input led to a reduction in mean complexity to just over one S-node per T-unit. However, the prediction that interaction would also lead to less complexity was not supported. Instead, interaction brought about a net increase in complexity over both baseline and premodified input.

The second major hypothesis of the study was strongly supported by our results. As shown in Table 2, scores for selection, placement, and overall comprehension were significantly higher for Condition 2 subjects than they were for subjects in Condition 1, leading to the conclusion that interactional modifications of input did, in fact, lead to significantly greater comprehension than conventional ways of simplifying input, through a priori manipulations of text.

The Effect of Interaction on Comprehension for Individual Directions
Results of the present study provided empirical evidence for the value of NS-NNS interaction in the negotiation of message meaning and for the important role which such negotiations play in input comprehension. Given these results, however, it was important to pinpoint more specifically exactly how comprehension was assisted through interaction. To do this, a more detailed analysis of results on individual directions was undertaken.

First, the effect of interaction on comprehension for each direction was measured by the difference between the mean score on that direction for the group receiving interactionally modified input and the corresponding score of the group receiving premodified input. It was found that of the 13 directions with positive point biserial correlation coefficients, 5 showed a high positive effect for interaction in assisting comprehension, whereas 3 showed a negligible or even negative effect for interaction.

As shown in Table 3, on Directions 15, 8, 11, 1, and 5, subjects in Condition 2 performed one and a half to three times as well as those in Condition 1. Mean scores on 4 out of 5 of these directions for subjects in Condition 2 matched or exceeded their overall mean score of 88% for all 15 directions. However, for subjects in Condition 1, scores on 4 out of these 5 directions were well below their overall mean of 69% for the 15 directions. In fact, three of the scores—on Directions 15, 8, 11—were the lowest of any under either of the experimental conditions studied. Apparently, these 5 directions were so difficult to understand that premodified input alone was not sufficient for comprehension. Instead, opportunities for interaction with the NS direction-giver played an important role in achieving comprehension.

TABLE 3

Comparison of Group Mean Comprehension Scores on Individual
Directions for Condition 1 and Condition 2

Direction	Condition 1 mean score (%)	Condition 2 mean score (%)	Condition 2 – condition 1 difference
15	31	88	57
8	36	81	45
11	50	94	44
1	60	100	40
5	69	100	31
2	63	88	25
4	69	88	19
9	56	75	19
7	81	94	13
14	81	94	13
12[a]	69	81	12
6	88	88	0
13	94	94	0
3	94	88	−6
10[a]	94	81	−13
All directions	69	88	19

[a] Directions 10 and 12 have negative point biserial correlations with
the test as a whole and hence cannot be counted on to give reliable
information about comprehension.

In contrast to this result, on three directions the subjects who received
interactionally modified input performed the same as or even, in one case,
slightly worse than the subjects who heard premodified input without interaction. Accuracy scores on Directions 6, 13, and 3 were quite high for both
groups: close to the mean overall score of 88% for subjects who had opportunities for interaction and well above the mean score of 69% for subjects who
heard premodified input only. These results indicate that both groups found
the input in Directions 6, 13, and 3 sufficiently easy to understand, whether

it was presented in an *a priori* modified form or as unmodified input but with opportunities for interaction. Based on examination of these results, it seems reasonable to conclude that modifications of interaction were most effective in achieving comprehension when the nonnative speaker had difficulty in understanding the input, but interactional modifications were superfluous when the input was easily understood.

Comparison of Input in Directions This result was then explored further in terms of the categories of input modification established for the purposes of the study, that is, quantity, redundancy, and complexity. Tables 4-6 provide comparisons of the input available in those directions for which interaction made a difference in NNSs' comprehension and the input available in those directions for which interaction made no difference. Examination of the directions with the most positive effect for interaction indicated that with respect to complexity, there was hardly any difference in the input that either group received (see Table 4).

TABLE 4

Comparison of Complexity of NS Input for Directions 15, 8, 11, 1, 5 vs. Directions 6, 13, 3				
	Directions		Directions	
	15, 8, 11, 1, 5		6, 13, 3	
Input	*M*	*SD*	*M*	*SD*
Condition 1	1.00	0	1.00	0
Condition 2	1.18	0.06	1.21	0.18
Difference (2–1)	0.18		0.21	
Note: Complexity was measured by the ratio of S-nodes to T-units.				

However, as shown in Tables 5 and 6, considerable differences were found with respect to quantity and redundancy. Tables 5 and 6 compare, respectively, the mean number of words and mean number of repetitions in the directions for which interaction led to improved comprehension (15, 8, 11, 1, and 5) and in those directions for which it had no effect (6, 13, and 3). Each subject's scores for each set of directions (15, 8, 11, 1, 5 and 6, 13, 3) were averaged. The means of all subjects in Condition 1 were then totaled, as were those of subjects in Condition 2. Line 3 of each table displays the difference between the two group means, and line 4 provides a breakdown of this difference on a per subject basis.

On those directions for which interaction led to improved comprehension, there was a large difference in the amount of input given to each group (see Table 5). However, on those directions for which interaction did not have an impact on comprehension, there was a much smaller difference between the amounts of input that both groups received. To be specific, about 40 more words per subject were used on each direction in which the interactional condition brought about better comprehension than the premodified input condition. On the other hand, when interaction did not make much difference in each group's comprehension, there was an average of 11 more words per subject per direction. These latter directions were apparently easy for both groups and therefore did not require prolonged interaction with the NS for their understanding. For directions that were not easy to understand, however, opportunities for NNSs to receive more input on selection and placement of items in the task were crucial for successful comprehension.

TABLE 5

Comparison of Quantity of NS Input for Directions 15, 8, 11, 1, 5 vs. Directions 6, 13, 3				
	Directions 15,8, 11, 1, 5		Directions 6, 13, 3	
Input	M	SD	M	SD
Condition 1	279.80	59.20	253.30	39.40
Condition 2	598.80	159.00	345.00	153.40
Difference (2–1)	319.00		91.70	
Difference per subject	39.87		11.46	

Note: Complexity was measured by the total number of words per direction.

On closer examination of the data, it was found that this increase in the number of words appeared to be due to repetitions of content words, that is, lexical items naming pictures to be selected and places to put them in carrying out directions to the task. On those directions for which interaction facilitated comprehension, and which consequently required more input, there was an average increase of about 7 repetitions per subject per direction in Condition 2 over Condition 1 (see Table 6). However, on those directions for which interaction did not have an effect on comprehension, there were actually fewer repetitions in the interaction group—an average of 2 fewer per subject per direction in the interactional input in comparison with the premodified input. We inferred from this analysis that for Directions 6, 13, and 3, the baseline input required little repetition to be understood, but when the baseline input could not be understood, as in Directions 15, 8, 11, 1, and 5, an increase in the quantity of input due to repetitions was of considerable assistance.

TABLE 6

Comparison of Redundancy of NS Input for Directions 15, 8, 11, 1, 5 vs. Directions 6, 13, 3				
	Directions 15, 8, 11, 1, 5		Directions 6, 13, 3	
Input	*M*	*SD*	*M*	*SD*
Condition 1	62.40	21.74	69.30	13.63
Condition 2	115.00	46.85	51.67	6.33
Difference (2–1)	52.60		−17.63	
Difference per subject	6.58		−2.20	

Note: Redundancy was measured by the total number of repititions of content words per direction.

Taken together, these results reveal that comprehension of difficult directions was assisted by an increase in the amount of input brought about by repetitions of content words relevant to selection and placement of task items. However, a decrease in the complexity of the input did not appear to be a critical factor in comprehension. Indeed, as has been shown over all directions, interaction resulted in input that was more complex than input that was modified according to conventional criteria of linguistic simplification.

This result is especially important because most current methods of simplifying input, especially readability formulas and structural grading applied to written ESL materials, concentrate on facilitating comprehension by shortening sentences and removing embedded clauses. This procedure, while intuitively appealing, since it corresponds to conventional ideas of foreigner talk, may actually impede rather than aid understanding. Reducing the number of words may eliminate redundancy, whereas removal of embedded clauses may serve no useful purpose at all.

The Role of Interactional Adjustments in Assisting Comprehension One final examination was conducted on the interactional modifications used in those directions that showed the most positive effects for interaction. Table 7 indicates that there were more interactional adjustments in those directions for which interaction made a difference in comprehension, but the wide variation in the numbers of these adjustments in Directions 6, 13, and 3 made us reluctant to conclude that this difference was a significant one.

TABLE 7

Comparison of Modifications in NS–NNS Interaction				
Interactional	Directions 15, 8, 11, 1, 5		Directions 6, 13, 3	
modification	M	SD	M	SD
For all subjects in condition 2	49.00	6.13	33.00	22.13
Mean per subject	6.13		4.13	

Note: Interactional modifications were measured by the total number of clarification requests, confirmation checks, and comprehension checks.

However, in light of theoretical claims made by Long (1980, 1981, 1983, 1985) that it is not interaction per se that aids comprehension, but rather modifications to the structure of the interaction by moves to check or to seek help with comprehension, the interactional data were examined more closely in an effort to pinpoint the role the interactional modification moves played in assisting comprehension. In this regard, it was believed that these moves may have been the mechanism that triggered the increase in repetitions and hence overall quantity of input, which helped subjects to comprehend the more difficult directions.

As shown in Figure 4, a total of 575 repetitions of content words were found in the NS input on those directions for which interaction proved to be critical to comprehension. Of these repetitions, 81, or 14%, were encoded either within the NS's checks on the NNS's comprehension or within her follow-up responses to comprehension checks brought about by requests for help by the NNS. Again, a further 50% of the repetitions of content words were triggered by interactional moves on the part of the NNS. Exactly half, or 289, of the repetitions were made in direct response to NNS requests for clarification or confirmation.

FIGURE 4

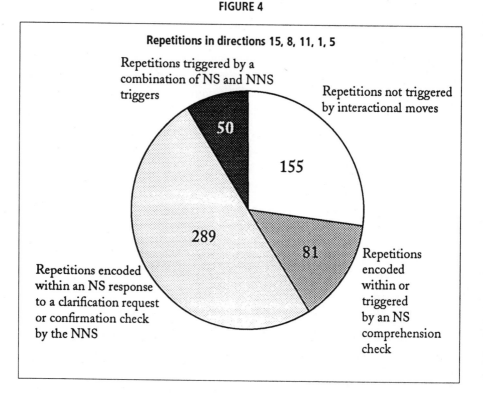

Repetitions in directions 15, 8, 11, 1, 5

Repetitions triggered by a combination of NS and NNS triggers — 50

Repetitions not triggered by interactional moves — 155

Repetitions encoded within an NS response to a clarification request or confirmation check by the NNS — 289

Repetitions encoded within or triggered by an NS comprehension check — 81

There were also a number of instances in the data in which a comprehension check on the part of the NS was followed by a clarification request by the NNS. Similarly, appeals by the NNS that were followed by a confirmation check or clarification request from the NS were also found. The data include 50 repetitions produced under these circumstances, accounting for 9% of the total. In these cases, it was often difficult to pinpoint exactly which move—the initial or the immediately preceding one—was more directly responsible for the following repetition. Therefore, we want to emphasize that although our analysis showed that 50% of the modification moves that triggered a repetition appeared to be initiated by the NNS and only 14% of these moves were initiated by the NS, this proportion is far from rigid.

Naturally, when seeking help with directions on the task, the NNSs frequently repeated content words, but these were not included in our tally of repetitions, since we were interested only in the input from the NS. We were not sure of the exact role that NNS repetitions played in the process of comprehension. However, their frequent presence in NNS interactional modification moves suggests that they may have served as yet another signal for the NS to repeat words and thus, indirectly, may have acted as aids to the comprehension of the directions to our task.

Altogether, a total of 420, or 73%, of all repetitions in the interactions on Directions 15, 8, 11, 1, and 5 were triggered by interactional modification moves initiated either by the NS or by the NNS, leaving only 27% that were apparently not triggered by some sort of interactional modification move. It thus seems likely that the positive effect for the interactions that occurred on these directions was due primarily to the large number of repetitions that the input in those interactions contained.

Although Figure 4 separates the analysis of interactional modification moves into those initiated by the NS versus those initiated by the NNS, it is important to bear in mind that neither participant was acting in isolation. It was difficult to determine who (or what) actually initiated the interactional modification move itself. Since participants could see each other's faces, it is possible that the NS was motivated to check the NNS's comprehension because of looks of confusion or frustration on the subject's face or because of other nonlinguistic behaviors of which we have no trace in our recordings.

It is also possible that the relatively long periods of time that the NS allowed the subjects in the interactional condition for selection and placement of task items gave those subjects more time to process the input and seek to clarify or confirm its meaning. The question of time leads us to speculate whether comprehension is an instantaneous phenomenon or whether it is built up slowly over a series of input segments. What we saw on the videotapes was a hand moving to select or place an item, and this movement itself may have reflected a buildup of comprehension over time rather than instantaneous comprehension followed by an action based on that comprehension.

Apart from these reservations about our findings, we feel that we have enough evidence to infer that interactional modifications do in fact serve as an important stimulus or vehicle for the repetition of input, which our own study and many studies before us (e.g., Chaudron, 1983; Long, 1985) have shown to be crucial to comprehension.

Conclusions

We feel that the results of our research are important in three ways. First, they provide additional support to research that has focused on identifying which features make input comprehensible to second language acquirers. To restate our results, redundancy in input was found to be an important factor in comprehension, whereas grammatical complexity of the input seemed to make little difference. The quantity of the input also appeared to be important, but primarily as a vehicle for redundancy.

Second, these results provide empirical support for what, up to now, have been only theoretical claims about the importance of interactional modifications in aiding comprehension of input. Interaction had a facilitating effect overall on comprehension, but when interaction had the greatest effect, this appeared to be accomplished through interactional modifications in the form of confirmation and comprehension checks and clarification requests that brought about the greater number of repetitions necessary for comprehension.

Finally, our results have implications for classroom teaching. Our own previous research (Doughty & Pica, 1986; Pica & Doughty, 1985a, 1985b, in press), as well as that of Long and Sato (1983) and Pica and Long (1986), has revealed that very few moves to modify interaction for the purpose of achieving comprehension occur in the classroom, even in those classrooms considered to be highly communicatively oriented or those geared toward the promotion of skills and strategies for comprehension. Our current findings suggest that it is possible for teachers to assist understanding of input through adjustments in quantity and redundancy of teacher talk, made without requests for clarification or confirmation from their students, and that with certain kinds of input, these adjustments may be sufficient for learners' comprehension. However, our research results also indicate that an increase in the redundancy of teacher talk is not, of itself, enough to ensure comprehension; rather, teachers should check on how well their students have understood and should constantly encourage them to initiate requests for clarification of meaning or to check with the teacher that they have understood correctly.

Facilitating input comprehension in classroom settings thus requires a teacher-student relationship and patterns of classroom interaction that are radically different from the pattern of teacher elicitation, student response, and teacher feedback that classroom research has identified as typical of teacher and student discourse (Mehan, 1979; Sinclair & Coulthard, 1975). Facilitating input comprehension in the classroom requires elicitations from teachers that seek to check on learners' understanding and not merely on the form of their spoken production. It also requires contributions from learners that are geared toward understanding input and not simply toward providing formally correct speech.

Our findings also suggest that if classroom input is to become optimally comprehensible, it should no longer be the teacher's sole prerogative to ask questions; the scope and purpose of questions should extend beyond mere student display and teacher evaluation. All participants in classroom interaction should ask questions, and those questions should serve to clarify and confirm input, thereby making it comprehensible.

This study helps to define which approaches to language instruction provide an environment that is rich in potentially comprehensible input. Other things being equal, those classrooms that encourage spoken interaction among participants, so that both teachers and students feel confident to initiate discussion of unclear points, will help to make input comprehensible. However, it should be noted that there are other ways of making input comprehensible that do not involve spoken interaction, such as consulting a dictionary, reviewing material as homework, or consulting with classmates or the teacher outside of class time. Further research is needed before the relative merits of these different means of obtaining comprehensible input can be compared.

Moreover, we cannot conclude that this study endorses any particular teaching method, since in-class oral interaction is a part of most instructional practices. However, in the absence of spoken interaction or of other ways of making input comprehensible, the present study indicates that pre-modification of input by the teacher and curriculum designers in the form of carefully graded syllabuses and simplified reading texts and tape recordings is of limited utility. Instead, results of the study suggest that if oral interaction between students and teacher is encouraged, even *ungraded* syllabuses and materials may provide input that will become comprehensible. Perhaps the most significant pedagogical implication to be drawn is that any teacher or method that facilitates a realignment of the traditional roles of teacher and student so that students can take greater initiative or assume more responsibility for their own learning is likely to encourage in-class oral interaction, which in turn can increase comprehension of input.

In light of these implications for classroom instruction, however we have a number of practical concerns about teacher-student interaction and interactional modification. We are worried about those students whose styles of classroom participation make them reluctant to question their teacher, to speak out voluntarily, or to respond to general classroom solicitations. Here, we are thinking of those Asian students, identified by Sato (1982) who were far less interactive than their Hispanic peers during teacher-fronted classroom interaction. Certainly the findings of Allwright (1980) and Day (1984) suggest that voluntary participation is not necessarily a key variable in successful classroom second language acquisition, and student self-reports gathered by Politzer and McGroarty (1985) have shown that good language learner behaviors of this kind, again, do not always correlate with factors of second language proficiency.

Because of these concerns, we are presently engaged in further research that, we hope, will begin to shed light on our questions and that will provide more details on the interactional processes that have been shown to play such an important role in comprehension. Right now, the importance of interactional modifications in facilitating the comprehension of input enjoys strong theoretical support. This is a theory that makes a good deal of sense to us. We hope that through our study of input, interaction, and comprehension, we have provided the theory with a long-overdue empirical base.

References

Allwright, R. (1980). Turns, topics, and tasks: Patterns of participation in language teaching and learning. In D. Larsen-Freeman (Ed.), *Discourse analysis and second language acquisition* (pp. 165–187). Rowley, MA: Newbury.

Blau, E.K. (1980). The effect of syntax on readability for ESL students in Puerto Rico. *TESOL Quarterly, 16,* 517–528.

Brumfit, C., & Johnson, K. (Eds.). (1979). *The communicative approach to language teaching.* Oxford: Oxford University Press.

Chaudron, C. (1983). Simplification of input: Topic restatements and their effects on L2 Learners' recognition and recall. *TESOL Quarterly, 17,* 437–458.

Chaudron, C. (1985). Intake: On models and methods for discovering learners' processing of input. *Studies in Second Language Acquisition, 7,* 1–14.

Corder, S. P. (1967). The significance of learners' errors. *International Review of Applied Linguistics, 5,* 161–170.

Day, R. (1984). Student participation in ESL classroom or some imperfections in practice. *Language Learning, 34,* 69–102.

Doughty, C., & Pica, T. (1986). "Information gap" tasks: Do they facilitate second language acquisition? *TESOL Quarterly, 20,* 305–325.

Hatch, E. (1978a). Acquisition of syntax in a second language. In J. C. Richards (Ed.), *Understanding second & foreign language learning: Issues & approaches* (pp. 34–69). Rowley, MA: Newbury.

Hatch, E. (1978b). Discourse analysis and second language acquisition. In E. Hatch (Ed.), *Second language acquisition: A book of readings* (pp. 401–435). Rowley, MA: Newbury.

Hatch, E. (1983). *Psycholinguistics: A second language perspective.* Rowley, MA: Newbury.

Honeyfield, J. (1977). Simplification. *TESOL Quarterly, 11,* 431–441.

Johnson, K., & Morrow, K. (Eds.). (1981). *Communication in the classroom.* London: Longman.

Johnson, P. (1981). Effects on reading comprehension of language complexity and cultural background of a text. *TESOL Quarterly, 15,* 169–181 .

Krashen, S. (1980). The input hypothesis. In J. Alatis (Ed.), *Current issues in bilingual education* (pp. 144–158). Washington, DC: Georgetown University Press.

Krashen, S. (1982). *Principles and practice in second language acquisition.* Oxford: Pergamon.

Krashen, S. (1983). Newmark's "ignorance hypothesis" and current second language acquisition theory. In S. Gass & L. Selinker (Eds.), *Language transfer in language learning* (pp. 135–153). Rowley, MA: Newbury.

Krashen, S. (1985). *The input hypothesis.* London: Longman.

Long, M. H. (1980). *Input, interaction, and second language acquisition.* Unpublished doctoral dissertation, University of California, Los Angeles.

Long, M. H. (1981). Input, interaction, and second language acquisition. In H. Winitz (Ed.), *Annals of the New York Academy of Sciences: Native Language and Foreign Language Acquisition, 379,* 259–278.

Long M. H. (1983). Linguistic and conversational adjustments to nonnative speakers. *Studies in Second Language Acquisition 5,* 177–193.

Long, M. H. (1985). Input and second language acquisition theory. In S. Gass & C. Madden (Eds.), *Input in second language acquisition* (pp. 377–393). Rowley, MA: Newbury.

Long, M. H., & Siato, C. J. (1983). Classroom foreigner talk discourse: Forms and functions of teachers' questions. In H. Seliger & M. H. Long (Eds.), *Classroom oriented research in second language acquisition* (pp. 268–285). Rowley, MA: Newbury.

Mehan, H. (1979). *Learning lessons: Social organization in the classroom.* Cambridge: Cambridge University Press.

Phillips, M., & Shettlesworth, C. (1976). Questions in the design and use of English for specialized purposes. In G. Nickel (Ed.), *Proceedings of the Fourth International Congress of Applied Linguistics* (Vol. 1, pp. 249–264). Stuttgart: Hochschul Verlag.

Pica, T., & Doughty, C. (1985a). Input and interaction in the communicative classroom: Teacher-fronted vs. group activities. In S. Gass & C. Madden (Eds.), *Input in second language acquisition* (pp. 115–132). Rowley, MA: Newbury.

Pica, T., & Doughty, C. (1985b). The role of group work in classroom second language acquisition. *Studies in Second Language Acquisition, 7,* 233–238.

Pica, T., & Doughty, C. (in press). Effects of task and participation pattern on classroom interaction. In J. Fine (Ed.), *Second language discourse.* Norwood, NJ: Ablex.

Pica, T. & Long, M. H. (1986). The linguistic and conversational performance of experienced and inexperienced teachers. In R. Day (Ed.), *Talking to learn: Conversation in second language acquisition* (pp. 85–98) Rowley, MA: Newbury.

Politzer, R., & McGroarty, M. (1985). An exploratory study of learning behaviors and their relationship to gains in linguistic and communicative competence. *TESOL Quarterly, 19,* 103–124.

Sato, C. J. (1982). Ethnic styles in classroom discourse. In M. Hines & W. Rutherford (Eds.), *On TESOL '81* (pp. 11–24). Washington, DC: TESOL.

Sinclair, J., & Coulthard, M. (1975). *Towards an analysis of discourse.* London: Oxford University Press.

Part 2   Some Hypotheses Examined

Introduction
to Part 2:
Some Hypotheses
Examined

In this section, three contributors (one from the USA, one from the UK, and one from Sweden) concentrate on different aspects of Krashen's theory of second-language acquisition. As suggested earlier, there is a degree of overlap with the preceding section, and various of the points raised here are also taken up in later contributions. They concern specifically three of the basic hypotheses, those concerning *Acquisition/Learning*, the *Natural Order* and the operation of the *Monitor*.

Our first contributor, Carlos Yorio, notes the coincidence of the appearance of "communicative" language teaching and Krashen's *Acquisition/Learning Hypothesis*, which in general he accepts, while claiming that learning should play a more important role than Krashen allows, especially in adult second-language development, citing self-study as a case in which conscious learning strategies lead to acquisition. From observation of his own use of English as a second language, Yorio sees the possibility of developing advanced monitoring strategies and notes that the use of the Monitor is not necessarily associated with "repair"; extensive monitoring need not have an adverse effect and should be considered desirable. Looking at "fossilized" learners, Yorio queries the oversimplification of Krashen's belief that comprehensible input *automatically* leads to acquisition and that acquisition is more important than learning, regardless of the second-language environment or of the precise achievement goals. Immersion programs lead not only to fluency but to fossilized inaccuracy. Acquisition and learning should be regarded as part of the same continuum and not as opposing forces.

In the second article in this section, **Rod Ellis** sets out to examine how the *Natural Order Hypothesis* stands up in the context of what is known about variability in the output of second language learners. Krashen's Monitor Model, Ellis points out, depends to a large extent on research that purports to show that there is a "natural order" in second language acquisition, but this claim is based on performance data, and studies of contextual variability indicate that second-language performance varies according to task. The order of acquisition is a reflection of the kind of performance elicited from learners and different tasks produce different orders. Therefore, it makes little sense to talk of a single "natural" order. Krashen recognizes that performance can vary, and he accounts for this in terms of whether the learner draws on "acquired" or "learned" knowledge. Ellis challenges whether such a dichotomy can adequately account for second-language variability and argues that the learner's competence should be viewed as a variable system. In such a framework it is no longer possible to defend the concept of a "natural" order or to posit totally different systems for "acquisition" and "learning." Citing Schumann's view that second language acquisition theories should be seen as both art and science, Ellis concludes that the Monitor Model is good art but bad science.

Finally, **Peter af Trampe** takes a psycholinguist's look at the basic *Acquisition/Learning Hypothesis*, though different from that taken in the earlier contribution by Yorio. Examining what is meant by "rule" in Krashen's contention that learned rules never themselves become sub-conscious and are available only for use as a Monitor, af Trampe finds that the concept of rule is in fact never defined and that Krashen appears to employ the term to denote two quite discrete types of rule—*rules of language* and *rules of grammar*—the former subconscious and the latter articulated by linguists in an attempt to describe them. Despite the contemporary emphasis on the primacy of the *spoken language,* it is in fact *written language* that forms the basis for rules of grammar. (af Trampe points out, incidentally, that not enough is as yet known about the precise difference between spoken and written language and that this is an area much in need of research.) While not denying the function of the Monitor as Krashen describes it, af Trampe questions its actual usefulness above the primitive level of mnemonic devices and its role as "attention focusser," since the differences between spoken and written language throw some doubt on the precise suitability of consciously learned rules of grammar as reference blueprints for rules of language. Though af Trampe makes his point in low key, it does seem to be one that has been little treated and calls for an answer.

The Case for Learning[1]

Carlos Yorio,
Late, of the City
University of New York,
USA

Stephen D. Krashen's hypothesis that L2 learners can take in L2 input in two different ways, which he calls *acquisition* and *learning*,[2] has been extensively discussed by himself, by supporters, and by detractors. The literature covering this controversial hypothesis will not be discussed here. I will, in fact, accept Krashen's distinction between *acquisition* and *learning* because there appears to be enough evidence to support the existence of learning (and communicative) strategies that seem to be much more conscious than others, that seem to be used primarily in certain situations and not in others, that seem to be exploited more extensively by some people than by others, and that appear to explain some second language phenomena in an intuitively satisfying fashion.

This great intuitive appeal has made Krashen's *acquisition/learning* hypothesis one of the most widely accepted aspects of his theory among language teachers and methodologists. Not very many theoretical hypotheses or insights find their way into practice so easily as this one has. Whether the distinction between *acquisition* and *learning* caused a change in attitude toward "communicative" language teaching in North America or whether it provided timely "theoretical justification" for an unrelated methodological movement is not entirely clear. Both causes may have played a role. One way or the other, Krashen's views on the primacy of *acquisition* over *learning* in the general teaching/learning field have made a considerable impact and will probably continue to influence practitioners' views.

It is the purpose of this paper to examine one aspect of the *acquisition/learning* hypothesis: the role of *learning* as a learning/communication strategy. I will claim that *learning* plays (or could play) a much more significant role both in the learning process and in L2 pedagogy than Krashen believes. I will further claim that even maximal exploitation of *acquisition* strategies may not be sufficient for successful adult second language development.

Krashen's Views on Learning

Krashen's views on the characteristics of *learning* have been discussed extensively by himself and others. Although there may have been some changes in the terminology in some more recent versions of Krashen's views, the essence remains unchanged.

Learning Means Conscious Linguistic Processing Studying linguistic rules in books or in classrooms and consciously applying them in linguistic situations constitutes *learning*. According to Krashen, learning can only operate through the Monitor. The Monitor is a device that is responsible for conscious linguistic processing: "The linguistic knowledge that one gains through monitoring can be used to consciously formulate sentences and to correct one's own speech and writing" (Dulay, Burt, and Krashen, 1982: 59). Krashen has repeatedly stated that *learning/the Monitor* can only play a secondary or peripheral role in adult L2 acquisition. For Krashen, it is *acquisition*, the unconscious internalization of linguistic rules, that is essential to the L2 process. Furthermore, in his view only *acquisition* can initiate communication. He has also stated that *learning* (a learned system) cannot lead to *acquisition* (an acquired system) (Krashen, 1982).

The Case of Self-Study

In a paper presented at the 1979 TESOL convention in Boston, Jeremy Marks (1979) described two situations in which he claims that conscious (in fact, *very* conscious) learning strategies led to communication and later to acquisition.

It must be said at this point that Marks was a student of linguistics, a fact that, though significant, does not invalidate his claims. This very issue will be discussed later.

In the first situation, Marks decided that he was going to learn Portuguese from his housekeeper. Her almost nonexistent, incomprehensible English made communication difficult and created much misunderstanding. Using techniques that he had learned in his field-methods class, he started eliciting lexical items from her. With the help of a Portuguese grammar book, he started to construct little sentences to say to her. After several months of this very conscious, highly monitored language learning situation, Marks and his housekeeper were able to discuss household chores and other uncomplicated issues in Portuguese.

The second situation that Marks describes relates to his attempts to communicate and learn Italian with the aid of a Berlitz phrase book while traveling in Italy. In addition, Marks consciously used his knowledge of Portuguese when phrases or lexical items were not available. He also noted that he started to compare the two languages in an attempt to keep them apart. Although this experience lasted only three weeks, it appears to have been highly successful, particularly in terms of communication.

Marks' paper clearly demonstrates that highly conscious L2 intake can be successful as a language learning and as a communicative strategy. As Marks puts it, "We have evidence to indicate that utterance initiation can happen in learning. This is not the ludicrous claim that all utterance initiation happens in learning, only that, when acquisition is not sufficiently developed, learning, if sufficiently developed itself, can take over" (1979: 41). Marks was consciously manipulating and analyzing the L2 input and it is obvious that he was using his linguistic training to do it. In the two situations that he describes, however, his goal was communicative rather than academic. Marks concludes: "Since learned material can perform every function that acquired material can, it should be accorded as high a status. The very existence of self-teaching demonstrates this" (1979: 43).

Although I will not claim that Marks was an "average L2 learner," it is clear that highly conscious learning and successful communication are not incompatible. If "average learners" were taught to develop linguistic awareness and to use it appropriately, there is no reason to believe that they would be anything but successful both as learners and communicators.

The Case of the Super Monitors[3]

The degree of awareness of second language learners toward the input they receive and the output they produce is both a theoretical and practical question. On the one hand, it bears upon Krashen's theoretical claims relating to *learning* and the Monitor, mentioned above. On the other hand, the degree of awareness and the amount of monitoring that second language learners/users do, or are capable of doing, has relevance for teaching since, depending on whether monitoring enhances or hinders successful performance, it is a skill that teachers will want to develop or stifle in second language classes.

In "Confessions of a Second Language Speaker/Learner" (Yorio, 1978) I reported on an introspective[4] study of monitoring in second language performance. Although I had always been conscious of my successes, failures, and shortcomings as a user of English, my second language, I had never attempted to observe my own language performance in a systematic way.

Encouraged by the success of the methodology used by the Schumanns and the insights revealed in their diary study (Schumann & Schumann, 1977) I set out to record individual examples of performance self-awareness: every time that I "caught myself" monitoring my linguistic output in English, I made a note of the specific linguistic items that had triggered the Monitor and the circumstances in which this had taken place. I kept this informal diary for about six months.

Awareness is defined here as the conscious focusing on linguistic form in my own performance or the performance of others in the context of a real communicative situation. Awareness, in this sense, is broader than Monitoring (as Krashen defines it) in that it can occur in a wide variety of circumstances—formal and informal—in my own performance and that of others. It happens in speaking, listening, reading, and writing, and even in situations where communication is one sided (e.g., watching television). It can occur whether or not I am focusing on form; in fact, it occurs mostly in situations where I am *not* focusing on form. In all cases, it is a certain linguistic item (a word, a sound, a grammatical pattern, etc.) that seems to "trigger the switch" from meaning to form. In certain situations (for example, when giving a lecture) a thought flashes through my mind: "I shouldn't do this; I'll lose my train of thought." But this does not seem to happen.

Another characteristic of awareness, as used here, is the fact that it is not necessarily related to error and is, in consequence, distinct from "repair."

E. Bialystok (personal communication) has indicated that native speakers also do this. Two points need to be made here. First, the fact that it *is* possible to develop "advanced monitoring" strategies in a second language that are similar to those of native speakers. Second, a large number of the linguistic items that I am consistently aware of and monitor are related to Spanish phonological and syntactic "interference." This whole area is obviously unrelated to L1 monitoring/awareness.

The range of linguistic items that I monitor is quite extensive: vowels and vowel sequences, particularly those vowels that exhibit contrasts different from Spanish (i/I, æ/ʌ, u/ʊ, etc.); consonants (s/z, v/b, š/ž); phonological rules (vowel length before voiced consonants, nasals in final position, vowel reduction, secondary stress in polysyllabic words, etc.; morphology (past tense variants t/d/Id); syntax (subjunctives, gender in pronoun reference, future perfect tense, inverted negative and positive constructions, etc.); dialect and stylistic variants, and so on.

FIGURE 5

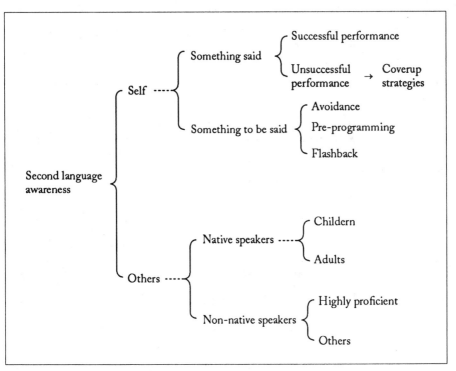

Figure 5 shows the range of situations that awaken the sense of awareness and the types of monitoring strategies used in those situations. It should be noted that this sense of awareness is not "on" all the time but is triggered by some special linguistic item that I hear in others or that I have just used or want to use.

Awareness of my own performance refers to (a) something that I have said or (b) something that I am about to say. In the first case, a successful performance (some nice turn of phrase, some complicated construction, some rare word, etc.) can produce a sense of pride in my ability to use English. I experience the same feeling when I hear other highly proficient non-native speakers (C. Paulston, H. H. Stern, etc.). When I hear myself making a mistake, however, I feel embarrassment and I immediately set out to "repair" so that my interlocutors will not think that I did not know the correct form. Quite frequently, I try to "cover up" by pretending that what I said was not what I meant.

One of the most interesting discoveries in this study was the use of conscious avoidance, planned in advance, in order to circumvent a difficult (or uncertain) form in syntax or phonology. When avoidance was not possible, pre-programming was necessary for the production of the correct output. Throughout the study, there were numerous examples of this deliberate focusing on a target, usually in phonology, and in most cases involving "troublesome" sequences (e.g., *bloodbath, blue books*, etc.). Other cases involved pronoun reference (*him/her*) or vowel lengthening (*red, sad, sag,* etc.). This pre-programming strategy is so deliberate that it often requires actual pauses, covered up as "thinking" or disguised as "searching for the right word."[5]

Flashbacks are backward rather than forward moves. They give us a good indication of the affective sources of this type of monitoring. These flashbacks are also triggered by specific linguistic items and usually involve extremely brief thoughts (or, actually, memories) of the situation in which someone corrected or pointed out an error involving the item in question.[6]

My awareness of other people's linguistic performance can, to some extent, be directly attributable to my training as a linguist and language teacher, except that I seem to be particularly aware of those items that I monitor in my own performance. A good example would be the past and past participle of the verb *run* ([ræn] and [rʌn]), which I always pre-program and which I always notice in other people's speech. It is not, then, the usual general interest of a linguist but a much narrower concern with a very clear focus.

What this study shows is that extensive monitoring does not necessarily interfere with effective communication. In the case of the "super monitor users," in fact, it enhances it by making it more accurate and by avoiding pitfalls.

Krashen has admitted that

some performers, it should be noted, can use conscious rules in casual speech with such skill that it does not interfere with communication, and can often use the Monitor for a wide range of linguistic phenomena. Our experiments have suggested that for most people, only a few rules can be consciously learned and applied in performance, only the simplest (such as bound morphology). But the "super Monitor user" may be able to control complex syntax and semantics, and may be able to apply such rules quickly and accurately. Several case histories (Yorio, 1978; Rubin, personal communication) of this sort have been brought to my attention of such performers, who typically have training or special interest in linguistics and the structure of language (Krashen, 1980: 189–190)

The issue is not whether or not these super Monitor users "typically" (Krashen's term) have a background in linguistics, but rather that extensive monitoring does not necessarily have an adverse effect on communicative performance. This is, in fact, acknowledged by Krashen, although he is unwilling to treat these cases as anything but exceptional. If, on the other hand, we believe that what the super Monitor users do is only quantitatively different from what other learners are capable of doing and that this edge is given to them by their training, which enhances their linguistic awareness, we can then try to develop these abilities in our L2 learners through classroom teaching. The development of *learning*/monitoring abilities would be something desirable rather than something detrimental and undesirable.

The Case of the Fossilized Learners

The supremacy of *acquisition* as a way of internalizing a second language is an issue that Krashen has discussed extensively for many years. It is, in fact, a pivotal notion in his theory of second language acquisition. *Acquisition*, "a sub-conscious means which is similar to child language acquisition" (Krashen, 1980: 186), is crucially related to Krashen's input hypothesis, which in essence claims that we acquire only when we understand and that we acquire structures by "going for meaning first." The implication is that if L2 learners have enough comprehensible input, fluency will develop and everything will take care of itself.

In my estimation, there isn't enough evidence to make these claims. There are many issues that have not been explored or that are being ignored: What is "enough" comprehensible input? How do "quantity" and "quality" of input relate to eventual proficiency? What is the relationship between fluency and accuracy? Are there any drawbacks or adverse effects in a pure *acquisition*-oriented L2 situation? How do *acquisition* strategies affect different language skills (speaking, listening, reading, and writing)? Is the importance of *acquisition* over *learning* justifiable in every L2 situation, regardless of ultimate achievement goals?

In my view, the evidence available does not justify Krashen's strong claims with respect to the sufficiency of comprehensible input and *acquisition* and the relative insignificance of *learning*. Some of these concerns are discussed in *Language Two* (Dulay, Burt, & Krashen, 1982) in the chapter on "The Language Environment," where it is made clear that environmental factors do affect the rate and quality of L2 achievement. However, what is interesting is that some of the evidence they cite could also be used to make a slightly different argument. The results of the Canadian French immersion programs, for example, are cited in support of the efficacy of the natural environment for language acquisition. Although it is true that children in these programs become impressive communicators in relatively short periods of time and become much more fluent than L2 students enrolled in "traditional" foreign language programs, it is also true that they develop a "special variety" of French, characterized by incorrect lexical, morphological, and syntactic forms. Furthermore, these forms do not seem to improve over time; in fact, these learners fossilize early and appear to remain fossilized (Selinker, Swain, & Dumas, 1975; Selinker & Lamendella, 1980).

What the immersion program evidence shows is that in the best of all possible *acquisition*-oriented classroom situations, comprehensible input and full emphasis on meaning result in fluency but not in accuracy. Since these learners also appear to have fossilized, it may not be possible to improve their level of accuracy if accuracy is desired. Furthermore, if these results are evident in children, what can we expect from adult learners, who are normally more self-conscious and less comfortable in communicative situations they cannot control?

The point that I am trying to make is not that immersion programs are not meritorious and that their results are not impressive. They most certainly are. The point is rather that even the most flexible second language learners—children—in a situation that maximizes *acquisition* with extended exposure to the second language with comprehensible, meaningful, and communicative input can achieve fluency but not accuracy. Swain (1985) clearly shows that grammatical acquisition cannot be accounted for solely on the basis of interactional comprehensible input and suggests that the notion of comprehensible output must be added to the theoretical construct. If accuracy is desired, as might be the situation in cases of academic or professional need, it is clear that this kind of instruction must be supplemented by other techniques more appropriate for that particular goal. Could *learning* strategies (linguistic awareness and monitoring techniques) add accuracy to fluency?

The whole issue of fossilization is very complex and one about which little focused research has been done. Only two papers that I am familiar with deal exclusively with this topic: Selinker and Lamendella (1980) and Vigil and Oller (1976). In the former, Selinker and Lamendella review the issues and research questions but refuse to espouse any definite position concerning the causes or the consequences of fossilization. Vigil and Oller, on the other hand, offer a "cybernetic model" of factors involved in the fossilization of grammatical and lexical forms.[7] In this dynamic model of interaction between learner and audience, the audience constantly gives feedback to the learner's output and, through this feedback, influences the learner's behavior. The feedback given by the audience is of two kinds: affective and cognitive. The theory is that learners will modify their grammar if the feedback they receive tells them that their output has not been successful and that unless it is modified it will not be comprehended. A combination of positive affective feedback and negative cognitive feedback will make learners continue to modify their grammar until their output is acceptable. Vigil and Oller claim that "if the corrective feedback drops below some minimal level or disappears altogether, the grammar, or the rules no longer attended by corrective feedback, will tend to fossilize. Thus, correct forms or any forms that elicit favorable feedback will tend to "fossilize" (1976: 285). For learners who *acquire* the L2, the key word is *comprehensibility*. Because these learners are always engaged in communicative interaction, negative feedback will occur only when their output is not comprehensible. Once these learners' output is understood (or understandable) by their audience, there is no further negative feedback, no further need for modification of their grammar, and, as a result, no further systematic development in their interlanguage. Vigil and Oller are not alone in believing that correction of grammatical form and negative feedback at the cognitive level are necessary conditions for a high level attainment in second language learning. Higgs and Clifford (1982) also make similar claims. They believe that when students are regularly rewarded for linguistically inaccurate but otherwise successful communication of meaning, fossilization is the most likely result.

In a recent case study (Yorio, 1985), I discovered evidence that appears to support this position. The analysis included 14 compositions (first drafts) written during the course of one semester by a native speaker of Korean (K.) enrolled as a freshman at the City University of New York. At the time of the study, K. had been in the United States for six years and had just graduated from high school, where he had taken one semester of ESL when he first entered the school. He had, in other words, been through five years of school using English as the medium of instruction and communication.

A T-unit analysis revealed that only 32% of the T units found were free of grammatical or lexical errors. A comprehensibility study using 19 judges (9 ESL teachers and 10 college professors in various disciplines), on the other hand, showed that only 2% of the T units presented any kind of "meaning difficulty." The high level of comprehensibility, the low level of grammatical accuracy, the fluency and ease with which K. handled himself both in writing and speaking, and the lengthy term of residence in an English-speaking environment show clearly that comprehensible input and an acquisition-rich environment are not sufficient to produce a communicative *and* accurate learner. K. is at present a fossilized learner who must "de-fossilize" if he is to meet the writing requirements needed for graduation from his college.[8]

The City University of New York has thousands of students like K., who can communicate but cannot graduate. Large urban centers like New York attract immigrants who "pick up" (or *acquire*) the language either in school (like K.) or at work. After years of experience with the language in communicative situations, these adult immigrants are fluent in oral-aural skills and, in other more exceptional cases, also in reading and writing (like K.). However, they are highly inaccurate in their grammar both in speech and writing. Because of their academic and professional aspirations, this level of proficiency is neither appropriate nor sufficient.

The fact that many of these learners are seniors with over 100 credits and have, in consequence, been exposed to much academic English, indicates that "academic level language input" will not be sufficient. Traditional ESL classes, which many of these learners have taken, also appear to have little or no influence on their grammatical control. Several informal experiments with special content courses (Introduction to Linguistics), writing courses using the "process" approach, and writing tutorials conducted by both native-English-speaking peers and by ESL-trained tutors also do not appear to have any immediately visible influence on these learners' language skills.

When asked what could be done to defossilize these learners, several experts, including Krashen, indicated that the answer lay in the kind of input that these learners must be exposed to—communicative, linguistically rich, and of a challenging level of difficulty (Krashen, Allwright, & D'Anglejan, personal communication). Furthermore, none of them thought that overt grammar teaching would make any significant difference.

Given the acquisitional and academic histories of these learners and our knowledge of the lack of formal accuracy in the interlanguage of immersion students, I feel that an approach that relies exclusively on *acquisition* strategies will not be successful. Traditional grammar instruction will not work either because, among other reasons, it looks at form without much consideration for meaning. It is clear that these learners have learned all they have learned in context, through meaning. It is also clear that they have reached a plateau, at a level of grammatical accuracy that is not appropriate for their academic and professional needs. In my opinion, an approach must be found that combines the *acquisition* strategies they already have with the *learning* strategies they need to develop in order to (1) understand the nature of the problem they must solve; (2) learn to focus on specific areas of difficulty through monitoring; and (3) control/edit their linguistic output.

This approach is unlike traditional approaches in that it deals with grammar at the discourse, not the sentence, level in both work done in "practice" passages and in the students' own output. In addition, it attempts to develop in the learner a linguist's attitude to the task at hand, a focused and objective attitude. Also, it is not primarily based on "error correction" by the teacher but on "error search and discovery" by the learner.

The metalinguistic awareness that these learners need to develop and that some researchers in the area of adult literacy are beginning to find important for the learners' growth (Cairns, 1985) is not unlike that of the super Monitors or the self-teachers discussed above. These learners must *learn* to look at form in addition to meaning, they must *learn* to become aware of specific problems, and they must *learn* to monitor their output.

I realize, of course, that the approach that I am advocating may not work for every learner. There are many other variables that we cannot control and that we do not even fully understand: native language development, attitudinal factors, neuro-biological constraints, etc.

The evidence that we have available about what *learning* can do suggests that it could play a much more significant role in L2 development than Krashen is willing to accept, particularly when combined with conditions favorable to *acquisition*.

Acquisition and *learning* are not incompatible; neither should they be seen as two separate, opposing forces.[9] They are, rather, like the two ends of a continuum that adult second language learners must have access to if they are to become effective *and* accurate communicators.

Notes

1 The title of this paper is partially borrowed from J. Marks' paper "Self-teaching: The case for learning" (Marks, 1979). The basic issue dealt with here, the role of learning, I have discussed with S. Krashen many times over the years. Needless to say, he does not agree with me.

2 The terms *acquisition* and *learning* are italicized when used in Krashen's sense.

3 This is a summary of a paper that I presented at the TESOL convention in Mexico City in 1978. Although the paper has been quoted from or referred to in several places, it has never been published. The term *super Monitor* was first used by Krashen in a reference to the 1978 paper (Krashen, 1980).

4 J. Lamendella (personal communication) claims that "technically" this is a retrospective rather than an introspective study.

5 E. Wheeler, a teaching assistant of mine, said that he had noticed my "pauses" and had assumed that I was thinking about what I was going to say. This type of pre-programming is not unusual for motor systems—the "concentration" of athletes is a good example. Since most of the cases recorded in my diary involved sounds or sound sequences, it would appear that these are also cases of physiological pre-tuning. S. Jagendorf (personal communication) has pointed out to me that this monitoring technique has also been used successfully with stutterers.

6 I thought this was very strange. However, many fluent bilinguals who acquired their second language as adults also claim experiences of this type.

7 We (like Vigil and Oller) are not concerned here with phonology or the issue of a "foreign accent," but rather with grammatical accuracy in speech and writing.

8 This study was replicated with another learner, a native speaker of Spanish and similar results were obtained (Kiciuk, 1985).

9 For a discussion of this polarity, see Brumfit (1984).

References

Brumfit, C. (1984). *Communicative methodology in language teaching: The roles of fluency and accuracy.* Cambridge: Cambridge University Press.

Cairns, C. E. (1985). Metalinguistic issues in literacy acquisition by adult anglophone and ESL students. *CUNY Forum, Papers in Linguistics, 11,* 21–46.

Dulay, H., Burt, M. and Krashen, S. (1982). *Language Two*. New York: Oxford University Press.

Higgs, T. V., & Clifford, R. (1982). The push toward communication. In T. Higgs (Ed.), *Curriculum, competence and the foreign language teacher* (pp. 57–79). Skokie, IL: National Textbook.

Kiciuk, M. (1985). Error analysis: A case study. Unpublished paper.

Krashen, S. (1980). Relating theory and practice in adult second language acquisition. In S. W. Felix (Ed.), *Second language development: Trends and issues* (pp. 185–204). Gunter Narr Verlag Tubingen, Germany.

Krashen, S. (1982). *Principles and practice in second language acquisition*. Oxford: Pergamon.

Marks, J. (1979). Self-teaching: The case for learning. Paper presented at the 1979 TESOL Convention in Boston, MA.

Ross, D. (1981). From theory to practice: Some critical comments on the communicative approach to language teaching. *Language Learning, 31*, 223–242.

Schumann, F. & Schumann, J. (1977). Diary of a language learner: An introspective study of second language learning. In H. D. Brown, C. A. Yorio, and R. H. Crymes (Eds.), *On TESOL 77, Teaching and learning English as a second language: Trends in research and practice* (pp. 241–249). Washington, DC: TESOL.

Selinker, L. & Lamendella, J. (1980). Fossilization in interlanguage learning. In K. Croft (Ed.), *Readings on English as a second language* (pp. 132–143). Cambridge, MA: Winthrop.

Selinker, L., Swain, M. & Dumas, G. (1975). The interlanguage hypothesis extended to children. *Language Learning, 25*, 139–152.

Swain, M. (1985). Communicative competence: Some roles of comprehensible input and comprehensible output in its development. In S. Gass and C. Madden (Eds.), *Input in second language acquisition* (pp. 235–253). Rowley, MA: Newbury.

Vigil, N. & Oller, J. (1976). Rule fossilization: A tentative model. *Language Learning, 26*, 281–295.

Yorio, C. (1978). Confessions of a second language speaker/learner. Paper presented at the 1978 TESOL Convention in Mexico City.

Yorio, C. (1985). (Many) questions and (very few) answers about fossilization in second language acquisition. Plenary address presented at the Annual Applied Linguistics Conference of the New York TESOL Association.

Variability and the Natural Order Hypothesis

Rod Ellis,
Ealing College of Higher Education, UK

Studies of second language acquisition (SLA) have generally acknowledged the pervasive presence of variability in the output of second language (L2) learners. This variability may be transitory in the sense that it can disappear as the learner's competence grows, and in such a case interlanguage development is evidenced in the gradual eradication of variable language behavior. Thus, one way of viewing SLA is as the gradual movement towards categoricality. However, in two ways, variability can also be a permanent feature of L2 use. First, it can be permanent because the L2 learner has become fossilized: rule development stops at some stage short of target language competence, so the process of eradicating variability also stops. Second, it can be permanent, because interlanguage is a natural language (Adjemian, 1976) and all natural languages display variability in at least some of their structures (Lakov, 1970). Therefore, an advanced interlanguage might be expected to include both unique variable rules (because the level of competence achieved is still not that of the native speaker) and also variable rules that occur in the target language grammar.

SLA researchers have to decide what to do about variability in their data. We can distinguish two principal approaches, depending on the view of language held. One is to find a principled way of ignoring variability. This is the approach of those researchers who operate in the Chomskyan tradition of the ideal speaker-listener in a homogeneous speech community: variability is treated as a feature of performance rather than of competence, and because the goal of research is to describe the learner's internalized grammars at different stages of development rather than the use of these grammars in production, variability can be ignored. The problem with this approach is that the only access to the learner's competence is through some kind of performance, so a decision has to be made about which type of performance best reflects the learner's competence. Not surprisingly, perhaps, researchers do not agree on what constitutes the best performance data for their research. Those operating within the homogeneous competence paradigm have preferred data that represent learners' intuitions about the L2 (e.g., data from grammatical judgment tests). The second approach is to try to account for learner variability in a principled way. This is the approach adopted by researchers working in a sociolinguistic tradition, which emphasizes the systematic way in which learner behavior is influenced by context. In other words, variability is now seen to be an integral feature of competence: there is no problem of deciding what kind of data to investigate, since all data are relevant. In fact, different data are necessary in order to study how systematic variability arises and how a variable competence is constituted.

Variability is a key issue when it comes to describing and explaining the "natural" route of SLA. The existence of this route has been hypothesized on the grounds of research that shows a standard order of development of a number of grammatical morphemes (cf. Krashen, 1977) and also a sequence of development for transitional structures such as negatives and interrogatives (cf. Ellis, 1985, chapter 3). The research data used to establish the "natural" route are, of course, *performance* data. The questions that arise concern which performance data to use and whether different performance data reveal different natural routes. These questions are particularly relevant in any consideration of Krashen's Monitor Model.

Variability in Second Language Acquisition

Variability in SLA can arise for a variety of reasons. Learners who differ in age, personality, cognitive style, and perhaps even aptitude can be expected to perform variably in a L2 (cf. Strong, 1983). However, I shall make no attempt here to consider this kind of individual variation;[1] instead, I will focus entirely on contextual variability, examining how the linguistic environment influences the language choices a L2 learner makes and also how the situational context affects L2 performance.

It is still an open question as to what extent L2 behavior (or, indeed, language behavior in general) is characterized by systematic or random variability. Sociolinguists disagree on this point. Some argue that all variability is systematic and that free variation is only apparent because the researcher has not been able to establish the factor or factors that explain its hidden regularity. Others maintain that all language systems contain some free variation, that free variation is, in fact, an essential requirement of language because it serves as a resource for later language development (cf. Ellis, 1985b), and that all language systems must have this potential. To avoid this controversy, however, I shall restrict the following account to systematic variability.

There is now substantial evidence that the use of two or more linguistic variants is determined by the linguistic environment, i.e., that the linguistic elements that precede and/or follow a structure influence the way the structure is realized, by the choice of variant a or of variant b. Linguistic environments can be ordered on a continuum from those we shall call "heavy"—favoring the use of a particular variant,—to those we shall call "light"—not favoring the use of the variant. The variants can include the target language form, or they can consist of "deviant" interlanguage forms. However, because SLA is directed at target language norms, researchers have concentrated on the use of target language variants (i.e., they have measured the "accuracy" with which these variants are performed).

Two examples will suffice to illustrate the systematic effects of the linguistic environment. Dickerson (1975) investigated variability in the speech of ten Japanese learners of English at university level, looking at the variants they used in contexts requiring (z). She found that they used a number of variants and that their choices depended on the consonants and vowels adjacent. Thus when the following sound was a vowel, the learners used the correct target language form every time; but when there was no following sound (i.e., [z] was final), they used three variants, only one of which was the target language sound. In this example, the variable structure is a phonological one. It shows that for this group of learners the "heavy" context was + VOWEL for the target language variant, while the "light" context was + ZERO.

In the second example, the variable structure is a grammatical one. Hyltenstam (1985) reported on the presence or absence of pronominal copies in the relative clauses produced by Finnish, Spanish, Greek, and Persian L2 learners of Swedish. His study showed that learners from all four language backgrounds employed pronominal copies variably (i.e., sometimes they inserted a personal pronoun into a relative clause, as in "the boy that *he* came" and sometimes they did not), but that the variation in insertion or deletion was not random. The learners' choice varied systematically according to the type of relative clause they were producing. The determining contextual factor was the position that had been relativized. Hyltenstam found that the choice of variant related to Keenan and Comrie's Accessibility Hierarchy.[2] Thus, deletion (the target language variant) occurred most frequently in contexts where the position relativized was the subject (e.g., "the boy *that* came") and least frequently where the relativized position was the object of comparison (e.g., "the boy *that* John is taller than"). In other words, the "heavy" context for the target language variant was SUBJECT and the "light" context OCOMP, with intervening positions on the continuum representing differing degrees of "weight" between these two poles. There are two significant points in Hyltenstam's results: first, the effects of linguistic context were independent of the learners' first language (L1); second, the "weight" of the linguistic environment appears to be uncorrelated with linguistic markedness, with "heavy" corresponding to "unmarked" and "light" to "marked."

The effects of *situational context* on L2 use were documented in Tarone (1983), who provides evidence that systematic variability arises as a result of learners being given different tasks to do. For example, if the learner is required to judge whether or not sentences in the L2 are grammatical, the kind of language behavior elicited can be described as "careful", but if the learner is asked to engage in free oral production, the kind of language behavior will be more "casual." Tarone reviews studies by Schmidt (1980), Fairbanks (1982), Dickerson and Dickerson (1977), Schmidt (1977), and Beebe (1980) in order to show:

1. systematic variability according to task occurs in phonology, morphology, and syntax;
2. the target language variant is used more frequently in tasks leading to more careful language;
3. an L1 variant may also be used more frequently in a task leading to more careful language, if the L1 variant has social prestige value in the mother tongue (i.e., variability is also evident in L1 transfer when certain conditions apply);
4. a "deviant" L2 variant is used more frequently in tasks leading to more casual language. This kind of variant may also be observed in pidgins and early L1 acquisition.

From subsequent studies investigating situational variability, two additional points emerge. First, greater accuracy in the use of the target language variant can occur in casual speech: for example, Tarone (1985) found that greater accuracy in the use of the article and the direct pronoun was manifest in a task expected to produce more careful language behavior. Tarone hypothesized that this occurred, contrary to expectations, because these two items served an important discourse function; that is, her subjects were more accurate in their use in a story telling task (relatively "casual") than in a grammar test (relatively "careful"), because the former required greater attention to discourse cohesiveness and the learners used the items for this purpose. Second, not all structures display variability to the same extent. Ellis (1986), for instance, found that his subjects varied systematically in their use of regular past tense forms (i.e., performed more accurately in planned than unplanned discourse) but did not do so in their use of irregular past tense forms (i.e., the accuracy of their performance in planned and unplanned discourse did not vary). This suggests that systematic variability may occur to a greater extent in structures that are regular and for which the learners can develop their intuitions.

On the basis of these studies, we might further add the following points:

5. Some structures may be performed more accurately in "casual" language behavior than in "careful" if they are required to perform an important discourse function.

6. Not all L2 structures are variable; structures that are clear and regular may be subject to greater variability.

All the studies referred up to now have used a Labovian framework — i.e., systematic variability has been investigated using data collected in different tasks designed to elicit different degrees of *attention to language*. An assumption is made that when a language learner is attending closely to the form of his utterances, he or she will supply the target language variant more frequently than when he or she is not. Thus, target language accuracy is seen to be related to attention to linguistic form. We have already seen that this assumption has had to be modified in a number of important respects (see points *3* and *4* above). It is becoming clear that the Labovian framework is not capable of explaining all instances of systematic variability in SLA.

SLA variability has also been examined using alternative theoretical frameworks. For example, Beebe and Zuengler (1983) investigated style shifting in terms of Accommodation Theory. This derived from the work of Giles and associates (e.g., Giles & Byrne, 1982) and was developed to account for how intergroup uses of language reflect social and psychological attitudes in non-ethnic communication. Accommodation Theory predicts that there will be variation as a result of how the learner relates to an interlocutor. For example, Beebe and Zuengler found that Chinese-Thai children used a greater proportion of Chinese influenced variants when speaking Thai to an ethnic Chinese interviewer than when speaking to an ethnic Thai interviewer. This occurred despite the fact that the Chinese interviewer did not use the Chinese variants in her own speech. Further evidence of this kind of accommodation has been provided by Beebe (1980) and Zuengler (1985).

Another theoretical framework that promises insights about SLA variability is provided by interactional sociolinguistics (e.g., Gumperz, 1982). According to this approach, variability arises as the result of choices that language users make in order to fulfill what they perceive to be the pragmatic requirements of an interaction. Language users need to tone down the force of their speech acts in certain circumstances, but have no need to do so in others, and hence make different selections from their repertoire according to the social meaning they want to convey. Rampton argues that these pragmatic considerations affect L2 behavior, and provides illustrative evidence to suggest that the ESL learners he studied reverted to an early, "deviant" interlanguage structure ("Me no. . . ") to reduce the force of boasts and refusals directed at fellow students or the teacher. They used this structure despite "knowing" the correct target language structure and being able to produce it without any difficulty.

Accommodation Theory and interactional sociolinguistics broaden our understanding of SLA variability. We can summarize what they tell us about variability in SLA as follows:

7. The choice of variant will in part, at least, be determined by the L2 learner's perception of his or her relationship with the interlocutor. This choice may be reflected in preference for a L1 variant or for a target language variant.
8. The choice of variant will in part, at least, be motivated by ongoing interactional factors. Learners may opt for a non-target language variant as a means of achieving a particular social effect.

It is clear that systematic variability according to task is pervasive in SLA. It is equally clear that the nature of this variability is highly complex. We are only just beginning to unravel the factors that determine it. Further research will increase our understanding of when and why learners' choices vary.

Another issue that needs attention is the relationship between the two kinds of contextual variability—that resulting from the influence of the *linguistic context* and that resulting from the influence of the *situational context*. Downes (1984), writing about language use in general, argues that the primary determinant of variability is the extralinguistic context. Probabilities can then be assigned on the basis of different linguistic environments. As an example of this, consider the variable use of third person -*s*. Fairbanks (1982) found that a Japanese learner of English supplied -*s* in tasks leading to careful language behavior but used the simple form in tasks requiring casual speech. Ellis found that a Portuguese learner of English was more accurate in supplying -*s* with pronoun subjects than with noun subjects. We can speculate that L2 learners will be more likely to use third person as correctly in formal situational contexts calling for careful language and that within such contexts greater accuracy will be manifest in utterances with pronoun subjects. Conversely, L2 learners will be least accurate in informal situational contexts when using utterances with a noun phrase subject. This is speculative, however, as there is no study investigating whether this relationship holds for SLA.

To sum up, there is a body of research to suggest that variability in the way L2 learners use the L2 is systematic. On the one hand, linguistic environment factors influence the choice of variants: the learner is more inclined to use a target language variant (and hence to perform accurately) in "heavy" contexts than in "light" ones, and markedness relations may provide an independent means of assigning "weight" to different environments. On the other hand, factors concerning situational context—as reflected in the different tasks learners are given, who their interlocutors are, and the social role the learner is performing—govern the choice of variant. Here the issues involved are complex,—how "careful" the learner's language behavior is, the social value of L1 forms that may be "borrowed" when performing in the L2, the kind of discourse the learner is engaged in, the nature of the linguistic rule, the learner's attitude to the person being spoken to, and pragmatic factors—along with, no doubt, many other factors.

The Monitor Model and SLA Variability

Krashen's Monitor Model was evolved continuously over some ten years. It is arguably the most comprehensive theory of SLA available to us, and it has had considerable influence on language pedagogy, not least because Krashen himself (1982) provided a full application of the theory to language teaching. The version on which I shall base the following account comes largely from Krashen (1985), in which a number of new elements were added to the basic model (in part to account for variability phenomena), and for this reason I refer to it as the Extended Monitor Theory (EMT). I shall consider only those aspects that deal with variability.

Krashen (1985) identified three sources of SLA variability: the monitor, inter-stage fluctuation, and the output filter. The first of these has figured in all versions of the theory and has given the theory its name. The second appears to be a development of earlier mentions about editing by "feel." The last source is a completely new development and owes much to Stevick's (1980) development of the Monitor Model. Each of these three sources will be considered separately.

The Monitor The monitor is Krashen's principal construct for explaining variability: L2 performance can be unmonitored or monitored. In the former, the learner uses "acquired" knowledge to generate utterances; in the latter, the learner calls on "learned" knowledge to modify utterances generated by "acquired" knowledge, either before or after they are articulated.

The EMT posits two conditions for the use of the monitor. There must be time available for its use, and the learner must be focusing on form (i.e., must have metalinguistic knowledge of it). However, a study by Hulstijn and Hulstijn (1984) showed that the time factor did not have any effect on the accuracy with which L2 learners of Dutch used two word-order rules. The same study did find that accuracy increased when the learners were focused on form. Therefore, Krashen acknowledges that the time factor may not be the crucial one, although he points out, correctly, that the Hulstijns' study did report that focusing on form took more time than focusing on meaning.

In order for learners to focus on form, they must "know" the rule—that is, they must possess metalinguistic knowledge that can be applied in monitoring. Krashen (1982) argues that there are constraints on the kind of rules that can be "learned." The learnability of rules is related to how simple they are. A rule can be formally simple: a rule that requires the addition of a bound morpheme (e.g., third-person -s regular past tense -ed) is simple in this sense. In contrast, rules that require permutations and movement of constituents from one part of a sentence to another (e.g., subject-verb inversion in WH questions) are difficult. A rule can also be functionally simple: an example is plural -s, where the addition of the -s morpheme conveys the simple meaning of plurality. In contrast, a functionally complex rule is where a single form distinction performs a number of different functions, such as the use of the articles in English to convey a number of different meanings. The easiest kind of rule to learn is one that is both formally and functionally simple. In his various publications Krashen emphasizes that the number of kind of rules that can normally be "learned" is limited.

Because of the constraints that exist on "learning" and on using "learned knowledge" in monitoring, Krashen (1985) argues that the gain in grammatical accuracy that results from the use of the monitor is modest. He puts it at between 7% and 50%, depending on the time available and the amount of "learned" knowledge available.[3]

Whereas Krashen is very explicit in his account of the conditions relating to the use of the monitor, he is somewhat less explicit about what actually happens when the learner is monitoring. His early accounts of the monitor suggest that it is an on-off mechanism (cf. Tarone, 1982); that is, the learner is either monitoring or not monitoring. However, Krashen (1985) appears to accept that there can be degrees of monitoring: he admits of "heavy," "light," and "no" monitor use. However, it is not clear what the distinction is between "heavy" and "light" monitoring.

The monitor can explain SLA variability in two ways. First, it can explain between-learner variability. There can be monitor over-users, monitor under-users, and optimal monitor users. More importantly for the purposes of this paper, the monitor can explain within-learner variability. Learners will perform differently, depending on whether they are using "acquired" or "learned" knowledge. Specifically, the accuracy with which certain target language rules will be manifest will depend on whether the learner is able to monitor.

Inter-Stage Fluctuation

Inter-stage fluctuation is the construct Krashen uses to explain the fact that variation in performance can take place even when the learner is using only "acquired" knowledge. Krashen appears to recognize that "acquisition" is not an all-or-nothing affair. It is possible for a linguistic feature to have been "firmly acquired"—in which case one can expect the learner to perform this feature consistently, or only "partially acquired"—in which case variability will arise even though no monitoring is involved. Features that have been only partially acquired can be accessed by "feel," when the learner is focusing on form.

The idea of editing by "feel" has remained a relatively undeveloped construct in the Monitor Model, but in the EMT it is given more prominence, because Krashen needs to cope with research that is potentially damaging to the theory—as is the Hulstijn and Hulstijn study mentioned above. They found that when they invited their subjects to focus on form, there was an improvement in their accuracy of use of the word order rules *irrespective of whether the learner had conscious knowledge of the rules* concerned. This improvement could not, therefore, be explained by the monitor. However, it can be explained by hypothesizing that the word order rules were "partially acquired" and could be used when the learners were focusing on form.

Inter-stage fluctuation, then, explains why learners vary in their choice of variants even when they are engaged in the kind of language behavior that requires "acquired" knowledge. Krashen suggests that the choice consists of the use of *i* (i.e., the "firmly acquired" form) or *i* + 1 (i.e., the "partially acquired form," which is next in line according to the natural route of development).

The Output Filter

The output filter is an entirely new construct, which we shall examine only briefly. Krashen uses it to explain why learners do not always perform to the limit of their competence, that is, why learners who have firmly "acquired" a rule do not seem able to perform it. Some learners who appear to be fossilized have in fact acquired more rules than they normally perform. Just as the input filter is a device that prevents input from reaching the Language Acquisition Device, so the output filter is a device that prevents acquired rules from being used in performance. Krashen refers to illustrative evidence from Stevick (1980), which shows that under certain conditions learners can blossom and improve the accuracy of their performance tremendously. The crucial condition, according to Krashen, is whether the learner is focused on meaning. When this takes place, the output filter is lowered and the learner is able to perform at his or her level of competence. This enables the learner to access the i+ 1—the next rule along the natural order, which is there in the learner's competence but is not always available for use.

Krashen (1985) conveniently provides a chart (see Table 8) to summarize "the differences and the similarities among the three sources of variation" that he now posits.

TABLE 8

	rise in accuracy when	rules affected
output filter	focus on meaning	apparent $i + 1$
monitor	focus on form	any learnable rule
inter-stage fluctuation	focus on form	$i + 1$ (partly acquired)

Evaluating the Monitor Model's Account of SLA Variability

The EMT offers a much more comprehensive account of variability than do earlier versions of the Monitor Model. We can ask to what extent the three sources of variability Krashen now identifies provide a satisfactory account of SLA variability.

First, does the EMT account for the effects of linguistic context on performance in an L2? Krashen seems to give no recognition whatsoever to this kind of variability. Although he acknowledges that a rule can be "partially acquired," his account of this phenomenon leads us to believe that this is true only in the sense that the learner cannot yet use the rule automatically. However, it would be possible for Krashen to extend the coverage of "inter-stage fluctuation" to include variability arising as a result of linguistic context. "Partially acquired" could mean "acquired in certain linguistic contexts but not in others." However, Krashen does not do this, and his failure to do so is surprising, given the strength of the research evidence available.

Second, how does the EMT account for the effects of situational context? In our earlier discussion of these effects we listed eight points that emerge from the research. To what extent is the EMT compatible with them?

The first point was that the situational context has a systematic effect on phonology, morphology, and syntax. Krashen limits his discussion of SLA to grammar; he has almost nothing to say about the development of L2 phonology. However, where grammar (i.e., syntax and morphology) is concerned, the EMT does predict that there will be systematic variability. However, the explanation that it provides is almost entirely psycholinguistic—that is, constructs like "automaticity" and "monitoring" are considered not in terms of the *social* conditions they relate to but in terms of *psychological* conditions. We are not told, for instance, in what kind of situations monitoring is likely to take place. Monitor theory is almost exclusively a psycholinguistic theory: the social context of SLA is ignored.

The second point was that the target language variant is used more frequently in tasks leading to more careful language. In the Labovian framework this is explained in terms of "attention to form." However, it is not a prerequisite of attention that the learner possess metalinguistic knowledge of a rule. A learner can have "intuitions" about what is correct and apply these in tasks that encourage and allow him or her to do so. Metalinguistic knowledge may be available, but it is not essential for "attending to form." The increase in accuracy during careful tasks is explained in two different ways in the EMT; first, it can result from the use of the monitor and in this case metalinguistic knowledge is required. Second, it can result from inter-stage fluctuation, when the learner focuses on form in order to edit by "feel." In this case "partially acquired" knowledge is used. However, Krashen does not explain how to distinguish empirically between monitoring and editing by "feel." Moreover, it seems very cumbersome to distinguish monitoring and editing in this way. The Labovian explanation is both more elegant and more convincing, not least because it entertains *degrees* of attention to form. Krashen also seems to be moving in this direction (i.e., by distinguishing "heavy" and "light" monitoring), but this is an aspect of the EMT that is still vague. The real problem with Krashen's explanation of the greater accuracy evident in careful tasks is the "acquisition/learning" distinction.

The third point was that a prestige L1 variant can also be used more frequently in tasks leading to careful language. Krashen's views on L1 transfer are outlined in various publications, most fully in his discussion of Newmark's Ignorance Hypothesis (Krashen, 1983). Krashen views transfer as "padding" or as "the result of falling back on old knowledge, the L1 rule, when new knowledge is lacking" (1983: 148): it constitutes a kind of "borrowing." This does not account for why the prestige L1 variants occur more frequently in careful speech. Krashen's "falling back" hypothesis would seem to predict that L1 variants will be more frequent in casual speech, when the learner has less time to access L2 knowledge. In careful speech there is more time both to access "partially acquired rules" and to monitor. To explain why monitoring does not get rid of transfer, Krashen suggests that conscious monitoring may be avoided if the repair job is too difficult. This is possible. But what Krashen does not entertain as a possibility is the idea that, for social reasons, the learner *knowingly* uses a L1 variant *in preference* to a target language variant that has been acquired. Again, it is the absence of any *social* dimension that is problematic.

The fourth point was that a deviant L2 variant is used more frequently in tasks leading to more casual language. This is predicted by the Monitor Model. In Krashen's terms, the learner uses "acquired" knowledge to participate in natural, spontaneous communication. This knowledge will consist of i; that is, the learner will perform in accordance with the stage of development he or she has reached. According to Krashen, then, "casual" language represents the true data for SLA research because it reveals the state of the learner's "acquired" knowledge. In this respect, Krashen's position differs significantly from those adopted by Tarone and Ellis, both of whom view "casual" data as only one type among many, all of which are relevant for the study of SLA.

The fifth point was that structures required to perform a language function that is important to the learner can occur with greater accuracy when the learner is focused on meaning. This runs contrary to the predictions of the Labovian model. The only way this might be explained by the EMT is in terms of the output filter, which enables the learner to perform at $i + 1$ when he or she is focused on meaning. However, Krashen's account of the output filter seems to suggest that it is the effective climate of the setting that facilitates this kind of focusing.

Variation in accuracy according to the type of discourse (e.g., narrative vs. conversation) is not entertained by the EMT.[4] What is required is a theory that acknowledges that acquisition is not an all-or-nothing affair. Learners do not so much acquire linguistic *forms*, as suggested by the EMT, as acquire the ability to perform certain language *functions* linguistically. A linguistic form may be used accurately to perform one function but inaccurately or not at all to perform another function.

The sixth point was that not all structures are subject to variability. The Monitor Model provides a convincing explanation of this point. It predicts that variable structures will be those that can be monitored,—i.e., structures that are formally and functionally simple. If degrees of monitoring are possible—as the EMT proposes—varying levels of accuracy can be expected and are, indeed, found (cf. Ellis, 1986).

Points seven and eight deal with the effect that the interlocutor has on the learner's performance and the variation that results from attending to pragmatic factors in interaction. To account for both of these, a sociolinguistic theory is required, one that recognizes the formative influence of the social context on SLA. As we have already noted, the EMT takes no account whatsoever of social factors.

To conclude, the Monitor Model, even in its extended version, is unable to explain convincingly all the patterns of variability that SLA research has revealed. This is largely for two reasons: first, the theory ignores the social context; second, the theory maintains the rigid distinction between "acquisition" and "learning." We have already commented on the first of these failings. The "acquisition/learning" dichotomy—what Krashen describes as "the non-interface position"—attracted considerable criticism (cf. Rivers, 1980; Stevick, 1980; Sharwood Smith, 1981). Early versions of the Monitor Model tried to explain variability more or less entirely in terms of whether the learner was using "acquired" or "learned" knowledge. It was the inadequacy of this that led Krashen to extend the model to allow for variability in "acquired" knowledge, by positing "interstage fluctuation" and an "output" filter. He continues to emphasize the qualitative difference of this variability from that originating from the use of the monitor. It is this which makes his three sources of variation unconvincing and the Labovian framework, despite other shortcomings, more acceptable. Yet to abandon the non-interface position would be to remove the pillar that supports the whole theory. In particular, it would have serious repercussions for the status of the Natural Order Hypothesis. It is to this that we now turn.

Variability and the Natural Order Hypothesis

The presence of variability in the learner's output is potentially problematic for the Natural Order Hypothesis. This states that the rules of the target language are acquired in a predictable order. The learner is credited with a Language Acquisition device which is then converted into L2 knowledge. The "natural" order is the result of this process. The learner progresses from stage i to stage $i + 1$ and cannot do otherwise. The main evidence for the hypothesis comes from largely cross-sectional studies that have investigated the order of acquisition of a number of English grammatical morphemes, longitudinal studies of structures involving the use of auxiliary verbs (e.g., English negatives and interrogatives), and, for German, studies of the acquisition of word order rules by migrant workers (cf. Pienemann, 1980; Meisel et al., 1981). The question that needs to be addressed is whether this hypothesis is compatible with the nature of variability in SLA.

The Natural Order Hypothesis is concerned with how knowledge is *internalized*. However, the evidence used to support it comes from learner *output*. Thus, claims are made about *acquisition* on the basis of *performance* data. We know, however, that a learner's output data is variable. So we need to examine whether claims about an invariable sequence of acquisition can be based on variable output data. In order to do this we need to consider more carefully what exactly is meant by "acquisition."

"Acquisition" might mean either of the following:

1. The first time a particular form appears in the output of a learner. This definition is proposed by Bickerton (1981).
2. The ability to use a particular form to a criterion level of accuracy. This is the definition that Brown (1973) used in L1 acquisition research and that the bulk of empirical SLA research has followed. The criterion level generally accepted is 80% or 90%.

In (2) the notion of "acquisition" is linked to that of accuracy. The more accurately a structure is performed, the more fully it has been acquired. On the basis of this kind of assumption, some researchers have proposed that the accuracy order of a set of structures reflects their order of acquisition (c.f. Dulay & Burt, 1973). This assumption has been challenged on a number of grounds (cf. Long & Sato, 1984) that need not concern us here.[5]

There may be strong grounds for (1), but, as the majority of SLA studies have been based on (2), we will consider only what the relationship is between "accuracy" order (and thus "acquisition" order) and variability. Variability in the accuracy of performance of different structures may be uniform in different styles, with the result that the accuracy order of the structures is not affected (see Table 9). Alternatively, variability may not be evident in all structures or it may not be evident in all structures to the same extent. This can result in accuracy order varying according to style (see Table 10). In this example Structure B is performed with equal accuracy on both occasions, but the other two structures are performed less accurately on the second occasion. This leads to two different orders. If accuracy order is the same as acquisition order, we would arrive at different developmental routes, depending on which performance we elicited. The research indicates that variability in SLA is not even; some structures are more variable than others. Therefore, the accuracy order can be expected to vary as suggested in the second of these two examples. This is the problem that variability poses for the Natural Order Hypothesis.[6]

TABLE 9

Structure (% Accurate)	Style A	Order (% Accurate)	Style B	Order
a	80	1	60	1
b	70	2	50	2
c	60	3	40	3

TABLE 10

Structure (% Accurate)	Style A	Order (% Accurate)	Style B	Order
a	80	1	60	2
b	70	2	70	1
c	60	3	40	3

Krashen is aware of the problem and attempts to deal with it by distinguishing unmonitored and monitored performance. The natural order will arise in unmonitored language use, when the learner is focused on meaning. A different order may arise in monitored language use. In particular, structures that are formally and functionally simple may be performed more accurately and so move up the order. Two points can be made about Krashen's explanation. The first is that the order that is taken to be "natural" is that associated with unmonitored language use. Krashen is quite explicit about this; normal language behavior draws on "acquired" knowledge and reflects the natural order. The second point is that the Monitor Model seems to predict that two orders will arise—one for unmonitored performance and a second for monitored language use.

However, research suggests that more than two orders can occur; Larsen-Freeman (1975) collected data from twenty-five adult learners of ESL using a variety of tasks—reading, writing, listening, imitating, and speaking. She found that the tasks produced different rank accuracy orders for the morphemes investigated. More than two orders were apparent. However, she did find that the orders for the two oral tasks (the ones that might be expected to be closest to unmonitored language use) were significantly correlated. Ellis (1986) found three different orders for the past-tense morphemes produced by seventeen intermediate ESL learners on three different tasks. The three tasks involved planned writing, planned speaking, and unplanned speaking. The different orders occurred because the three past-tense structures were all affected differently by the change in planning condi-tions. This is summarized in Table 11. The results, based on the study of three morphemes from the same grammatical subsystem, support the hypothesis that multiple orders will be found, not just two.

TABLE 11

Form	Task 1 % Correct Rank		Task 2 % Correct Rank		Task 3 % Correct Rank	
Past Regular	77	1=	57	2=	43	3
Past Irregular	60	3	57	2=	55	2
Past Copulative	76	1=	75	1	60	1

It might be argued that the Extended Monitor Theory does predict more than two orders. Krashen talks of "light" and "heavy" monitoring. He also suggests that accuracy can vary as a result of "inter-stage fluctuation" and the lowering of the "output" filter. But the distinction between unmonitored and monitored performance is maintained. Therefore, it would appear that we must expect different orders in unmonitored conditions—as a result of inter-stage fluctuations and the output filter—along with different orders in monitored conditions. The two sets of different orders are, of course, a reflection of accuracy levels. But accuracy levels must surely be ranged on a continuous rather than on a discontinuous scale. Therefore, it is difficult to see why the rigid distinction between unmonitored and monitored language is maintained. It is necessary only if the "acquisition/learning" dichotomy is insisted on, but to do away with it would destroy the whole theory.

A far better way of explaining the kind of task variability reported by Larsen-Freeman and Ellis would be to posit a control factor (cf. McLaughlin, 1978; Bialystok & Sharwood Smith, 1985) that determines the degree of automaticity of rules the learner has internalized. Rules that have been thoroughly acquired will be automatic and will be used accurately in all kinds of language use. Rules that are recent acquisitions will not be thoroughly controlled and so can be used accurately only when the learner has time to retrieve them. Other rules will be intermediate. This explanation is compatible with the Labovian framework, which predicts differing degrees of accuracy depending on the opportunities available to the learner for focusing on form. Rules not under full control will be performed variably, according to the extent to which the task allows the learner to focus on form.[7]

The essential difference between this explanation and what is provided by the EMT is that it is not necessary to distinguish two different kinds of knowledge, stored separately and used under different conditions. There is no single order of acquisition, and there is no order that justifies the label "natural." Different orders will arise from different kinds of language use. We can expect as many orders as there are language uses. We might wish to argue that the kind of language use associated with spontaneous oral communication in interpersonal interaction is "primary": after all, this is the kind of language use in which children engage in the process of acquiring their language, and it is the target of most language teaching. But for the educated adult L2 learner, this kind of language use is no more "natural" than, say, producing a carefully composed letter. The order of accuracy (and, therefore, acquisition) that is associated with spontaneous language use is what SLA researchers in general have chosen to examine when they want to find out how learners acquire an L2. In doing so, they have taken one type of language use to represent the whole of language acquisition. We would do well to stop talking about a "natural" order and to recognize that SLA is not a monolithic process but a highly complex and differentiated one. This is evident first and foremost in the patterns of variability to be observed in learner output.

Conclusion

In this paper I have argued that the study of variability in SLA is of central importance for model building. Variability provides windows through which to view the complexity of the language processing mechanisms involved in L2 performance. Furthermore, if we extrapolate from performance to acquisition itself (as I think we must), variability also displays the complexity of learning processes.

In the Monitor Model, Krashen acknowledges the importance of variability phenomena; indeed, the "acquisition/learning" distinction was formulated to account for them. The issue is whether the model accounts for variability phenomena efficiently. In early versions of the Monitor Model, only one primary source of variability was identified—the Monitor. In the Extended Monitor Theory, the scope of the model has been widened to permit three sources of variability. But this widening has led to a theory that is unfalsifiable: we are asked to believe that "focus on form" can take place using both "acquired" and "learned" knowledge, but we are not told how to tell which kind of knowledge is involved. Furthermore, we are told that variability in the use of "acquired" knowledge can result from both a focus on form and a focus on meaning, but we are not told how we can distinguish the two processes. The problem lies in Krashen's continued assertion of the distinctiveness of "acquired" and "learned" knowledge. The thrust of this paper is that we cannot do so. We should recognize that "acquisition" and "learning" are aspects of highly complex processes that lead to knowledge, which is differentiated continuously rather than dichotomously.

Once the "acquisition/learning" distinction is abandoned, it no longer makes sense to talk of a "natural" order of development. Rather, we can anticipate a variety of orders appearing in the performance data of L2 learners, according to the nature of the language processing involved in different types of discourse events. The performance of some linguistic features may be invariable, but from what we know of interlanguage systems, variability will be the rule rather than the exception, and this will be evident in the accuracy orders obtained in different kinds of language use. The so-called "natural" order is simply the order that emerges in one type of language use—unplanned discourse.

To cope with variability phenomena, we need a much more complex model than the Monitor Model. Edmundson (1985) pointed out one of the problems that will be encountered in developing such a model. He noted that models of SLA are constructed by proceeding linearly but that the processes of language learning do not operate in a linear fashion. Thus we are forced into offering "a linear presentation of a non-linear reality." To overcome this problem, we need to view L2 knowledge as differentiated in highly complex ways and to search for metaphors to explain how this knowledge is represented and how it is acquired. A number of such metaphors have been suggested—Edmundson himself talks of "discourse worlds" and "multi-level processing"; in a similar fashion, Selinker and Douglas (1985) talk of "discourse domains"; Bialystok and Sharwood Smith (1985) opt for the competence/performance metaphor by identifying a "knowledge factor and a control factor," both of which are subject to development; and Tarone (1983) draws on the Labovian metaphor of style shifting. All of these recognize and seek to explain the complexity of L2 knowledge and of the learning process, both of which are manifest in the variability of the learner's output. These metaphors may lack the simplicity and elegance of the metaphor Krashen offers us, but they more truly represent the reality of SLA.

Notes

1   Research involved in the ZISA project (e.g., Pienemann, 1980; Meisel et al., 1981) has made a distinction between developmental features and variable features. The former refer to features that display acquisitional regularities in all L2 learners; an example is the transitional stages that characterize the acquisition of German word-order rules. Variable features are those that display individual variation in acquisition; an example is the copula in L2 German.

2   The Accessibility Hierarchy is:
     SU > DO > IO > OB > GEN > OCOMP.
According to Keenan and Comrie, the hierarchy constitutes an implicational language universal. If a language relativizes at OCOMP, then it will also relativize in all other positions. However, a language relativizing at, say, IO will only relativize in those positions to the left on the hierarchy and not in those positions to the right.

3   A gain of 50% can hardly be realistically termed "modest." Moreover, a variation of 7%–50% is so huge that its kinetical value must be seriously open to question. (Eds.).

4   The model of SLA that conforms most with the findings that choice of variant is dependent on discourse type is that proposed by Selinker and Douglas (1985). They suggest that inter-language is internalized as a series of partially independent "discourse domains," defined as "slices of the learner's life."

5   In order to equate accuracy and acquisition orders, it is necessary to argue that acquisition involves a steady increase in accuracy. Kellerman's (1985) research suggests that this assumption is not warranted. Kellerman provides evidence of "V-shaped" behavior; on some structures L2 learners initially manifest target language correctness (as a result of positive L1 transfer), only to regress later on (as transfer is rejected) before returning to the target language form at a more advanced stage. If such behavior is widespread, it is clearly not possible to equate high accuracy levels with acquisition.

6   Lightbown (1985) pointed out that for every study that supports the natural order, there is another study that provides counter-evidence. This is exactly what is to be expected if accuracy orders are indeed variable.

7   One way in which "control" will be evidenced is in the linguistic contexts in which a rule can be used. The spread of a "new" form into increasingly "lighter" contexts is one way in which "control" advances. A fully automatic rule is one that can be used accurately in all styles and in all linguistic environments.

Rules, Consciousness, and Learning

Peter af Trampe,
University of
Stockholm, Sweden

The basic tenet of Krashen's Monitor Theory is that consciously learned rules are available only for monitoring. The theory predicts that such rules never become subconscious and the basis for utterance production. As I have pointed out in my other paper in this volume (see pp. 27–36), this is an interesting hypothesis and it ought to be tested. Actually, the hypothesis can be subsumed under a more general question—"What role, or roles, do rules and explanations play in second language learning"— that has been the subject of discussion between "naturalists" and "formalists" throughout the history of language teaching. The answer to this question, of course, is of fundamental importance for language teaching practice, which is what makes Krashen's hypothesis so interesting.

However, in order to test the Monitor hypothesis, we must make sure of what we mean by "rule." Krashen never really discusses this. He himself seems to use "rule" alternately in a general and in a very limited sense for "rules of the language" and "formal rules stated by the teacher," respectively, without being quite clear about the distinction. Perhaps his failure to clarify the rule concept is at the root of some of the misunderstandings between Krashen and his critics. Therefore, let us first look at the way "rule" is used in linguistics.

Rules of Language and Rules of Grammar

Itkonen (1976, 1978) pointed out the fundamental distinction between *rules of language* and *rules of grammar*. Rules of language are social norms that determine which sentences are correct, or grammatical, in a specific language.

A system of such rules has been internalized by the native speakers of the language, and it governs their linguistic behavior. Knowledge of the rules of language is mostly subconscious but can sometimes be made conscious.

Since the rules of language are subconscious, the exact nature of their mental representation is not known. In trying to describe the rules of language, the linguist formulates rules of grammar—i.e., generalized statements about the language that are supposed to catch the gist of the rules-of-language system. Two things should be noted here. First, as the rules of language are unobservable, we can discuss them only in terms of rules of grammar. Second, rules of grammar are "theory laden"; that is, the way they are formulated depends to a great extent upon the theory of grammar the formulator adheres to. This applies to the rules of traditional grammar and those of modern theories (e.g., generative grammar) alike.

The rules-of-language/rules-of-grammar distinction applies to linguistic theories in general. For those who are conversant with linguistics, it is, furthermore, evident that the rules of grammar may vary widely with different schools of thought. However, linguists may also differ slightly in their conception of the rules of language. Specifically, some linguists stress the social nature of language in defining the rules of language as shared social norms. Ferdinand de Saussure is the most celebrated name in this category. Other linguists emphasize the psychological nature of the rules; Chomsky, for instance, regards them as the knowledge that underlies the production and comprehension of utterances. Others go even further and think of the rules of language as the "mental programs" or "rules of use" that control linguistic behavior.

The social and psychological views are not necessarily mutually exclusive, and most linguists would probably regard them as the two sides of the same coin. Since the social norms must have mental representations and since the "executive programs" are learned from linguistic input that reflects the social norms at work, it is more economic to postulate one mental representation to cover both the norm and the program aspect of a rule of language.

Some modern theories of grammar use a formalized rule concept, where rules are schemata operating on an input to produce an output (see, for example, Wall, 1972). Depending on their formal properties, different kinds of rules (transformations, phrase-structure rules, etc.) can be distinguished. This kind of rule concept has little immediate bearing on the present discussion, so I will not enlarge upon it here, except to state that some of the formal properties of rules may have quite direct pedagogical implications. We will return to this topic later.

Apart from "rules," the concept of "strategy" is sometimes introduced. Clark and Clark (1977), for instance, talk of semantic and syntactic strategies in speech comprehension. In the literature on second language learning, "communication strategies" are the focus of interest for some researchers (for a good sample of papers on the subject, see Faerch and Kasper, 1983). It is often not very clear what is meant by a strategy or, in particular, how strategies differ from rules. As Karlsson (0000) points out, if rules are thought of as mental programs, many of the strategies that have been proposed are in fact rules, and the term *strategy* should be reserved for "non-conventional, goal-directed, global plans for context-dependent choice among options." In this sense we might propose strategies for choices, such as whether to refer to something by means of one word or a (para)phrase, or what thematic structure to impose on our message.

The Written Language Bias

Whether we take the social or the psychological view of language, one of the leading principles in twentieth century linguistics has been the primacy of spoken language. It is a fact that children normally speak before they learn to read and write. Furthermore, modern linguistics is claimed to be descriptive rather than prescriptive, and if we want to live up to this we must look for the norms reflected in speech rather than in writing, as the written language is much more influenced by prescriptive views.

In spite of the generally acclaimed principle of the primacy of *spoken* language, a good case can be made for maintaining that linguistics has been, and still is, biased towards *written* language. According to Linell (1982), linguists tend to ignore the differences between the spoken and written language systems and assume that there is one system underlying both. The written language bias in linguistics, he claims, can be evidenced in the view of language as a set of products and of linguistic structures as hierarchical systems of objects (cf. Lakoff & Johnson, 1980) and in the fact that linguistic structures are supposed to be autonomous, atemporal, and often invariant. For the purposes of the present discussion, the following quotation from Linell (1982: 60) is worth considering:

> Anyone who really pays attention to the full variability that actually characterizes spoken language may well be amazed by the fact that many of the actually occurring structures have not been described in the usual grammars, not even in modern grammars compiled by "descriptive" linguists. The most important reason for this is probably the fact that the structures in question are not accepted in written language. Hence the most natural reaction is to regard such structures as ungrammatical or deficient.

Some of the rules of the spoken language, then, might lack a counterpart among the rules of grammar if these rules are primarily based on written language. Due to differences in the conditions of spoken versus written language use, other differences can be expected as well. As Karlsson puts it, "Most norms of spoken language do not prescribe absolute correctness but rather quasicorrectness of the behaviour falling under their guidance. Quasicorrect behaviour allows for a wide latitude of realization. Spoken language norms are somewhat indeterminate ('fuzzy'), highly variable and, of course, very sensitive to context."

Rules and Consciousness

Consciousness, as a theoretical concept, is difficult to handle. For one thing, it raises the question of the nature of consciousness and touches on the dualism-versus-monism dispute about the mind-body distinction. As pointed out by McLaughlin (1978) in relation to the Monitor Model, it also causes methodological problems. To some extent consciousness is open to introspection, but in a very precarious way: when you introspect, you apply your consciousness to yourself being conscious, thereby influencing the process itself; the subconscious is by definition not open to introspection. Furthermore, consciousness can be seen as an expression of the totality of an individual's brain activity—past and present—in interaction with the environment (Rose, 1976), which makes consciousness a highly subjective experience and consequently a difficult one to operationalize in tests and experiments.

By and large, the mechanisms whereby we speak and understand are not open to conscious scrutiny. However, it is evident that the native speaker's knowledge of the language (the rules of language), though mostly unconscious, can also be partly conscious. Ryle's oft-cited distinction between "knowing how" and "knowing that" (Ryle, 1949) comes to mind. As a native speaker of Swedish, I know *how* to use the language in communicating with other speakers without necessarily knowing *that* my actions are guided by rules 1, 2, 3, etc. My knowledge is a mixture between the two. For instance, I know *how* to refer to an object in the world around me by means of the word *kopp*. I also know that *kopp* means "cup." If somebody asked me what *kopp* meant, I could tell them. For some referents I might know *how* to refer to them, without knowing *that* they are called such or such. For example, I can refer to a contraption in a car engine by using some verbal description of it, without knowing what it is called. Conversely, I might know *that* there is such and such a word, without knowing *how* to use it in the act of referring. Think, for instance, of the first time you read Lewis Carroll's "The Hunting of the Snark."

It is very likely that most of the time our conscious attention is directed at the meaning of the message. With regard to the different levels of language description, it also seems that some levels are more difficult to access than others, and it is reasonable to assume that the "further" you get from meaning, the harder it is to access that level. For instance, at the lexical level one is often aware of making a choice between words. Sometimes we even use "hedges" (Lakoff, 1975) such as "strictly speaking" and "technically" to indicate that some thought has been given to the meaning of a word (as in "technically [or strictly] speaking, a whale is not a fish"). On the other hand, at the phonetic/phonological level we are seldom consciously aware of our slips of the tongue, and even less so of the fact that we adapt to changes in the "articulatory milieu" as in compensatory articulation and reduced speech (Lindblom, 1982). Thus, we can suggest a scale for *ease of access* that looks like this:

Phonology	Morphology	Syntax	Lexicon
difficult ————————————————————— easy			

However, conscious attention can be shifted from the level of meaning towards that of form. In proofreading, for example, your attention is directed at the phonological (or, strictly speaking, graphemic) level. In psycholinguistic research a number of experimental paradigms utilize our ability to shift attention away from meaning (e.g., in "shadowing" the speech of another speaker or in "monitoring" for a particular phoneme). And, of course, the fact that we can state rules of grammar at all shows that we can render conscious what is ordinarily unconscious.

It is also plausible to assume that consciousness is a matter of degree. Clinically, there are different levels of unconsciousness, including coma, stupor, and lethargy. There are also different levels of wakefulness between deep sleep and total wakefulness. Linguistically, the tip-of-the-tongue phenomenon indicates that we can be diffusely conscious of the form of a word. In self-correction and, especially, in the detection of errors in the speech of others, we can be more or less vaguely aware that something is wrong. At a fairly high level of linguistic awareness we can locate the error, and at a higher one we can even tell why it is an error in terms of rules of grammar. We are then operating at a level that is sometimes referred to as that of *metalinguistic awareness.*

It should perhaps be stressed that meta-linguistic awareness is not an awareness possessed by linguists and language teachers only. The following is a comment from a seven-year-old on the sentence *Claire and Eleanor is a sister:* "You can't use *is* there: Claire and Eleanor *are* sisters" (Gleitman & Gleitman, 1979: 112). Comparing this comment to a rule statement such as "If a subject consists of two or more coordinated noun phrases, the verb is usually in the plural," I find that the main difference is one of generality or abstractness of expression. We cannot expect seven-year-olds to use linguistic terminology, but the lack of such terminology is no reason to deny them the possession of meta-linguistic awareness. It can be added that a child's meta-linguistic awareness and linguistic vocabulary are both expanded as a result of learning to read and having L1 lessons at school. Many foreign language beginners are consequently no meta-linguistic novices.

To sum up, our attention has been drawn to the fundamental distinction between rules of language and rules of grammar. The rules of language constitute the language user's largely unconscious knowledge of the language. However, the language user is also conscious of some aspects of his or her language use, and to some extent unconscious knowledge can be made conscious. Due to the fallibility of conscious mental processing and the relative inaccessibility of different levels, rules, or other aspects of the language, the conscious rules can be expected to reflect the rules of language only imperfectly. The systematic and generalized formulation of this conscious knowledge requires a sharpened meta-linguistic sense and a technical vocabulary for stating the rules. Such rule formulations are referred to as "rules of grammar." Now, the gap between knowing "how" to use the language and knowing "that," in the sense of consciously knowing the rules, is enormous, so the rules of grammar are in the nature of hypotheses about language and language use, and they are grounded in a theoretical framework.

Rules in the Classroom

In a "natural" environment, people do learn second languages without being presented with explicit rules of grammar. At least, some people do. It would be wrong to assume that this learning process is altogether subconscious. For instance, an adult, non-analphabetic learner can bring a lot of meta-linguistic knowledge to bear on the task of learning a new language. Furthermore, to the extent that foreign language utterances occur in the classroom, conscious and subconscious "natural learning" (i.e., learning without explicit rules of grammar) can be expected to take place there as well. In the classroom situation, however, explicit rules of grammar are normally more frequent than in "natural" situations, and our main concern here is whether, or in what ways, rules of grammar are useful.

The rules of grammar used in the classroom are not usually taken directly from the scientific grammars of the linguists. Rather, special pedagogic grammars are used. A pedagogic grammar is normally derived from scientific grammar—at least in the sense that it is written in a particular theoretical tradition. This, of course, means that whatever differences there are between theoretical grammars are likely to be reflected in the corresponding pedagogic grammars. Among other things, scientific grammars differ in the degree of autonomy they confer on language in relation to language use, and, indeed, pedagogic grammars also differ in this respect. But pedagogic grammars are different from scientific ones both in content and in form. As to content, pedagogic grammars are sometimes contrastive, which means that they only treat points of difference between L1 and L2, whereas the linguist's grammar ideally covers the whole of the language. Besides, the rules of pedagogic grammar are for obvious reasons often simplified or over-generalized. Again, as to form, a pedagogic grammar has to be adapted to its purpose and cannot use the sometimes extremely formulaic meta-language of scientific grammars. In this connection I will return to the claim I made earlier, that some of the formal properties of rules may have direct pedagogical implications. What I had in mind was exactly this adaptation of the meta-language to pedagogic use. It is important to realize that this claim applies to traditional as well as modern formalized grammars. In pedagogic grammars of Russian, for instance, the traditional term *Instrumental* is used for a particular case of nouns, etc. This term is somewhat misleading, as not only "instruments" in general but also "the actor" in passive sentences are put in the instrumental, and this, as I have had the opportunity to observe, sometimes creates confusion for the learner.

Just as there is a gap between rules of language and rules of grammar, so there is a gap between the rules of scientific grammar and those of pedagogic grammar. As already mentioned, the pedagogical qualities of the rules of grammar may also vary. The written language bias adds to these complications. Obviously, both scientific and pedagogic grammars suffer from this bias, since pedagogic grammar is rooted in scientific grammar. If the primary goal of a foreign language course is the production and comprehension of spoken language, serious questions about the usefulness of rules of grammar with a written language bias should be raised.

Incidentally, the written language bias in pedagogical grammar provides an alternative interpretation of some of the results that Krashen adduces as support for his Monitor Theory. According to Krashen, the use of consciously learned rules is most possible in the written language; so to test for monitor use, written language conditions are used. However, if the conscious rules are biased towards written language, we would expect them to be more effective under written language conditions and less effective in situations where spoken language is required. Consequently, the results of such tests may just reflect the bias of the rules of grammar that have been learned. In order to draw any conclusions about rule utilization in speaking, we should make sure that the rules that have been or are to be learned by the subjects are not biased.

When writing this, I was tempted to make the heading "Rules *of* the Classroom," because we can distinguish several manifestations of rules in the classroom situation. Not only do we have the rules of pedagogic grammar, but also the teacher's rendering of these rules, the learner's mental representation of a rule, and, finally, the rule that the learner is able to recall from memory. I think it is paramount to keep these distinctions in mind when we design experiments or other studies in order to illuminate the relationship between explicit rules and learning achievement. Suppose we devise a study where we check some learners' production in terms of accuracy. We then ask them whether they operate by "feel" or by "rule," and if by "rule," to state the rule in certain cases. The rules our subjects state could have traveled a long way. In the most complicated case we would have a chain of "rule events" like this:

> The linguist tries to get at some rule of language. → The result is a rule of scientific grammar. → This rule is adapted and converted into a rule of pedagogical grammar. → The teacher presents a version of that rule to the class. → Learner A stores a mental representation of the rule in memory. → Learner A retrieves the rule from memory and verbalizes it.

At each link in this chain of events there might be error and uncertainty. For instance, the scientific rule may show written language bias or might simply be incorrect or obsolete; the pedagogic interpretation of the rule may be oversimplified or couched in loosely defined terms; the teacher's presentation of the rule may be incorrect or imprecise; the learner's grasp of the teacher-presented rule may be faulty for various reasons; and his or her recollection of the representation of the rule will perhaps be fragmented, or even incorrect, as memories sometimes are. If sources of errors like these are not controlled to the best of the researcher's ability, few, if any, conclusions can be drawn about the usefulness of rules of grammar in foreign language/teaching.

The Role of Rules

Regardless of Krashen's claims, I maintain that the role explicit rules play in the learning process is largely unknown. Theoretically, there are many possibilities, three of which shall be mentioned here. Note that the three roles are not mutually exclusive.

The first role of rules, and the one that is probably indisputable, is that of serving as *attention focusers*. The rule directs the attention of the learner to certain aspects of the item, structure, etc. at hand. In some cases this kind of focusing is probably necessary. As any phonetician knows, there can be phonemic contrasts in a foreign language or subphonemic ones in our own that we do not "hear" unless we are somehow made aware of them. It could well be that some cases of "pidginized" and "fossilized" learner language are due to difficulties of attending to certain forms and contrasts, and that such learners would be helped by rules as attention focusers.

The second role would be as *blueprints for rules of language.* In this case we have to suppose that there is some degree of correspondence between the rules of grammar and the rules of language as mental representations. The possibility of rules of grammar in this role is denied by Krashen. He may be right, but since we know very little about the mental representation of language, judgment should be suspended until we have enough experimental data pointing one way or the other. In all probability, many—perhaps most— of the rules of pedagogical grammar are nowhere near being in close correspondence with mental schemata, but this is no reason, categorically speaking, to deny the possibility of rules in this role.

Furthermore, there is some evidence that the effect of explicit rules of grammar is different for different kinds of rules. Pica (1985) showed that formal instruction accelerated the learning of a linguistically simple construction (the English regular plural) but that it had a retarding effect on a more complex structure (the progressive *-ing)* and no effect for a high-complexity rule (the indefinite article). Strictly linguistic complexity may not be the only factor at work here. Earlier we discussed the difference between rules and strategies. Strategies are nonconventional, global, and dependent on situational context: they tend to be more "fuzzy" than the autonomous rules proper, and their dependence on context means that they have to be "lived" rather than "learned," since contexts are highly variable. One hypothesis would be, then, that the more strategy-like the rule, the more difficult it would be to couch in a formal rule statement, and consequently the less effect it would have if taught in a classroom.

The third kind of role is the one Krashen ascribes to the rules in his Monitor. In this case, the rules of grammar are *blueprints for rules of grammar*—internalized and retrieved as such. Thus they resemble various mnemonic tricks, such as the calendar rhyme for remembering the number of days in each month. If you need the number for August, you retrieve the rhyme, repeating it aloud or subvocally, and extract the information you need, more or less in the same way that you look something up in an encyclopedia. Some rules of grammar are obviously learned in this way. For instance, I can recall the following rule from my German lessons in the fifties: *"Aus, ausser, bei, gegenüber, mit, nach, zeit, von, zu* take the dative." When the need arises, I recall the mnemonic and use it for conscious monitoring, much as Krashen suggests. My suspicion is that few rules are in fact used this way, since verbatim memorization and recall of a great number of rules are difficult and the risk of error is high. Besides, the monitoring process is rather cumbersome. Thus, I find no quarrel with Krashen about rules of grammar in this role. However, I am convinced that rules can also act as attention focusers. Whether rules of grammar can be blueprints for rules of language remains an open question.

Part 3

From Theory to Practice

Introduction
to Part 3:
From Theory
to Practice

Our third section comprises six essays—three from the USA, two from the UK, and one from the Federal Republic of Germany—in which the main emphasis switches from a consideration of Krashen's theory as a whole to its implications, as a whole or in part, for application in the classroom. The section is remarkable for the wide disparity of views expressed, for the extravagance of the language sometimes used, and for the enormous gulf it reveals between assessments of the state of language teaching in recent years on different sides of the Atlantic. Traditional attitudes seem totally upset, even reversed, and developments move in opposite directions. Whereas one American contributor accepts the theory and looks for evidence to support it, another considers the theory probably untenable but finds that it works!

Opening this section, with the function also of something of a bridge between preoccupation with the theoretical and the practical, **Teresa Pica** states that in the light of the importance given to Monitor Theory both as a means of explaining unsuccessful second language acquisition in the classroom and as a basis for guidelines for effective pedagogy, it is unfortunate that until recently there have been very few studies of classroom acquirers and the classroom environment from which to draw empirical evidence in support of its claims. Therefore, Krashen has looked for support in research on adults with access both to classroom instruction and to social interaction in the wider community. Although he cites evidence from studies of subjects who received input only in the classroom, these were focused on children and adolescents, who, he admits, are not ideal candidates for a test of his claims. Most of the research he cites as evidence of the necessity of comprehensible input for the acquisition process is also not ideal; empirical work on input in a classroom content has been very limited. Recent empirical research now provides a database for study of classroom acquirers and the classroom environment and seems to call into question some of Krashen's claims. Pica describes her own research on the "natural order" of morpheme acquisition, "easy" versus "hard" to learn grammar, and input/intake distinctions. The results sometimes support and sometimes challenge Krashen's position on formal instruction and have implications beyond their application to Monitor Theory.

William T. Littlewood, the third contributor, adopts a cooly "laid-back" approach. What, he wonders, do Krashen's hypotheses mean to a tired, English, middle-aged foreign-language teacher whose classes have little interest in success and who has neither time nor energy to flog through complicated theoretical theses? Taking each hypothesis in turn, without questioning Krashen's assumptions or the evidence cited to support them, he finds that they can suggest a fresh perspective on the teacher's experience and engender a more positive view. Krashen is "the first 'applied linguist' who has not only made theoretical ideas accessible but also has shown how these ideas might be relevant to [the teacher's] practical problems." But hypotheses, he reminds us, are indeed hypotheses, not established facts. As part of a broader process of exploration, though not as the basis for a new dogma, they have a lot to offer.

Perhaps the main tenor of Reinhold Freudenstein's contribution is surprise—tinged with indignation—that Krashen is so uninformed about or dismissive of the experience of the last 25 years or so on the other side of the Atlantic. Principles of curriculum organization put forward in *The Natural Approach* as new in 1983 are almost identical with those set out by modern language experts for the Council of Europe in 1971 and subsequently adopted in various formal programs (this point is taken up later by Yalden); the "teacher talk" advocated as comprehensible input in earlier stages of language study was recommended by Lado in 1964; every other "ingredient" in the "hot pot" is derived from an earlier source. Nothing in Krashen and Terrell's "radically different" approach is in fact new. What perhaps is different is the use of a terminology that serves to present a sometimes obscure or restricted view of familiar phenomena: advocating the use of only the target language in the classroom, Krashen ignores the debate that has raged in Europe for more than 100 years, the polarization of acquisition and learning in the Monitor Hypothesis similarly ignores long-debated questions of differentiated learning, $i + 1$ input is simply the hallowed principle of moving from the familiar to the unfamiliar, the affective filter is the question of motivation, etc. Echoing Littlewood and other contributors, Freudenstein states that a hypothesis is "a suggestion put forward as a starting point for a possible explanation," not a fact, and concludes that the totality of Krashen's hypotheses does not amount to a coherent theory. Proper professional dialogue would have shown that much of what Krashen sets out as new has long been taken for granted in Europe; by polarizing acquisition and learning, Krashen impoverishes circumstances for language development (Freudenstein cites Lado as a corrective); he repeats the error of propounding one method for all language learners.

In much the same vein, Ian Dunlop (whom Freudenstein quotes) comments on the five hypotheses, stating that what is "sensible" in them is not new. Deducing that Krashen is fighting a battle against American grammar-based and audio-lingual teaching, Dunlop lists a whole series of developments in Europe and the UK of which Krashen is apparently unaware. "It is as if the discussions of the last fifteen years in "Europe had never happened," he complains, detailing research to which Krashen makes no reference. Finally, he deplores Krashen's belief that students of all ages learn languages in the same way as children learn their own native languages, since this leads to the promulgation of one "method" for everyone—a fallacy already rejected in Europe.

Bill VanPatten's highly acclaimed and entertaining article takes a look at how language teachers grapple with the problem of challenging Krashen's monitor theory and, at the same time, looks at the merits of input in language development.

The author directs his attention at the foreign language classroom where the instruction of grammar has always been an important component of the syllabus. However, meaningful imput is also an important component. Both have merit and both can be effective in the FL classroom. Looking at the beginning language learner, VanPatten tells us that research suggests that grammar instruction and error correction do little good for the learner. However, research has not shown that grammar instruction and error correction do not bring about positive results for the FL learner. VanPatten suggests modifying the Input Hypothesis to "(1) show where the hypothesis is weak and (2) modify it so that input as a variable is not neglected in the classroom." The message is clear: more research is needed to move toward, what the author calls a "global perspective on lenguage learning."

Reflecting on the current status of methods in second-language teaching, Karl J. Krahnke notes that all teachers follow some kind of method, whether it is "formalized or dictated." In this insightful and thought-provoking article, the author refers back to the days when audiolingualism and its narrow, rigid constraints dominated second-language teaching. Krahnke then proceeds to cognitive-code theory and then to Krashen's Acquisition Theory and reminds us that not even AT specifies the kind of classroom techniques or procedures to implement in the second-language classroom. The author, in a clear manner, takes us through each of the hypotheses "from the point of view of what they have and do not have to say about instruction." He concludes by giving us both positive as well as negative aspects of AT as applied to the second-language classroom.

Monitor Theory in Classroom Perspective

Teresa Pica,
University
of Pennsylvania, USA

Contrary to the good intentions of teachers and in spite of the hopes and hard work of their students, successful acquisition of a second language (L2) is not an inevitable outcome of classroom experience. From his earliest writings, Stephen D. Krashen has been sensitive to this unfortunate fact. Guided by his Monitor Theory and the research findings on which it is based, Krashen has traced many of the difficulties associated with classroom second language acquisition to the earnest but misinformed efforts of classroom participants, whose goals and activities are shaped by rule explication, oral practice, and error correction—classroom practices that are claimed to stimulate conscious learning, but get in the way of the acquisition process.

For Krashen, conditions most favorable for acquisition—provision of input containing structures slightly beyond the acquirer's current proficiency level and an environment that keeps anxiety to a minimum—are in short supply in many classrooms. Despite the many pedagogical practices that inhibit second language acquisition in the classroom, however, Krashen has emphasized throughout his work (from earlier writings—Krashen, 1976; Krashen & Seliger, 1975, 1976—to later publications—Krashen, 1981a, 1982, 1984, 1985a, 1985b) that there is nothing inherently objectionable about the classroom as a context for second language acquisition (SLA). Indeed, the classroom can provide an "acquisition-rich" environment when its activities are framed by the perspective of Monitor Theory.

In light of the importance given to Monitor Theory as both a means of explaining unsuccessful SLA in the classroom as well as a basis for providing guidelines for effective pedagogy, it is unfortunate that, until recently, there have been few studies of *classroom* acquirers and the *classroom* environment from which to draw empirical evidence in support of Krashen's claims. As a result, support for Monitor Theory came from research on adults who had access to both classroom instruction and social interaction in the wider community. (See, e.g., Dulay, Burt, & Krashen, 1982; and Krashen, 1981b, 1982, 1985a for reviews of this literature.) Although some support was available from studies whose subjects heard target input only in the classroom (e.g., Dulay & Burt, 1973; Makino, 1980), this research was focused not on adults, but rather on children and adolescents. The latter may lack facility for using formal classroom instruction for conscious learning and were therefore less than optimal candidates for a test of Krashen's claims.

In addition, to support his position about the necessity for comprehensible input in the acquisition process, most of the research available to Krashen at the time of his reviews (see, e.g., Krashen, 1980, 1985a) had been concerned with caregiver input to children developing their first language or with input to second language acquirers engaged in social interaction outside the classroom, away from teachers and textbooks. Therefore, empirical work cited by Krashen on input within the classroom context was limited to only a handful of studies (e.g., the work of Gaies, 1977; Henzl, 1973; Trager, 1978; Wiley, 1978).

In order to appreciate its relevance for second language research and pedagogy and feel a sense of confidence about its application to classroom concerns, it is important to examine Monitor Theory in terms of the *classroom* learner and the *classroom* environment. The increasing amount of empirical research directed toward these two areas certainly offers a new and enriching database through which to do so. See, e.g., books by Allwright (1988) and Chaudron (1988); edited collections of Day (1986), Faerch and Kasper (1985), Gass and Madden (1985), Hyltenstam and Pienemann (1985), Seliger and Long (1983), and Sharwood Smith (1985); individual studies by Chaudron (1977, 1983), Ellis (1984, 1985), Felix (1981), Felix and Hahn (1985), Hamayan and Tucker (1980), Higgs and Clifford (1982), Ioup (1984), Lightbown (1983a, b), Lightbown and Spada (1990), Nicholas (1984), Pienemann (1984), van Baalen (1984), White, Spada, Lightbown, and Ranta (1992); and review articles by Allwright (1983), Gaies (1983), Lightbown (1985a, b), Long (1980b, 1983a, 1988), and Long and Porter (1985). Indeed, on the basis of their research, a number of these authors (Ioup, Lightbown, Long, Pienemann, and van Baalen, among others) have already called into question many of the principles underlying Monitor Theory.

In this essay, I will review some of my own research on classroom acquirers and classroom interaction that relates to Krashen's claims about the "natural order" of morpheme accuracy, "easy" and "hard" to learn grammar, acquired vs. learned L2 knowledge, and comprehensible input in SLA. Findings from this research, some supportive of and others challenging to Krashen's theoretical perspectives on SLA, ultimately extend beyond their application to Monitor Theory. In keeping with Krashen's long-standing concern for relating acquisition theory to classroom practice, these findings also suggest practical guidelines for facilitating SLA in a classroom context.

Monitor Theory and the Classroom Acquirer

It is important to point out that Monitor Theory is not exclusively a theory of *classroom* SLA since, for Krashen, developmental sequences are similar for all acquirers, regardless of their target language environment. According to Krashen's Natural Order Hypothesis (introduced in 1977 as his "average order"), L2 acquirers, when engaged in spontaneous expression, produce a similarly occurring accuracy order of English grammatical morphemes in obligatory linguistic contexts, regardless of age, native language, or conditions of L2 exposure. Support for this hypothesis has come from numerous studies of morpheme production among L2 acquirers (reviewed in Krashen 1981b, 1982, 1985a). As noted above, the adult subjects participating in these studies resided in the target language environment. For some subjects, input from the wider community was the only linguistic environment available, while others had access to English both inside and outside the classroom. However, there were no subjects who had exclusive exposure to classroom input within settings where English was used as a foreign language. Krashen himself acknowledged a need for rounding out the morpheme studies with data from classroom acquirers, noting in fact the possibility that the morpheme orders of these subjects might deviate from the "Natural Order," an outcome brought about by pedagogical practices that promote conscious learning but inhibit acquisition (Krashen, 1981b: 55).

Controlling for target language environment (as well as proficiency level, native language, and socioeconomic class) in my own research (Pica, 1982, 1983a), I compared the morpheme production of three groups of adult acquirers engaged in spontaneous discourse with an English-speaking interlocutor. Two groups were acquiring English under conditions comparable to those of most morpheme studies: The "Untutored" group consisted of subjects whose contact with English speakers came entirely from social interaction in their professional and leisure activities. A second, "Mixed" group comprised subjects studying English in the United States whose contact came from both classroom instruction and interaction with the wider community. The third group of "Instruction Only" subjects consisted of students of English as a foreign language, living in Mexico, whose contact with English came exclusively through classroom instruction, much of which took place in a traditional format of rule explanation, production practice, and corrective feedback.

Inclusion of this third group of classroom acquirers not only expanded the database for testing the Natural Order Hypothesis but also provided it with additional empirical support: In obligatory contexts, all three groups of subjects showed a statistically similar accuracy order of morpheme production that correlated with the Natural Order at the .01 level or better. This result showed that exclusive exposure to the linguistic environment of the classroom did not alter the overall course of SLA among the instructed subjects. So powerful were their own contributions to the language learning process that classroom conditions could not suppress or reroute their path of morpheme acquisition with any degree of significance.

Despite the correspondence in the *overall* rank orders of morpheme production accuracy among the three groups, there were differences in the ranks held by plural -*s* and progressive -*ing* that distinguished the Instruction Only group from the other two groups. As shown in Table 1, in which ranks were calculated by a target-like use analysis, thereby taking into account both morpheme suppliance in obligatory contexts and morpheme oversuppliance in non-obligatory contexts (See Pica, 1983c and 1988 for more details on this measure), rank order correlations across the groups were again statistically significant and corresponded with the Natural Order at the .01 level.

However, the Instruction Only group scored at least two ranks higher than the others for plural -*s*, but two or three ranks lower than them for progressive -*ing*. Exclusive exposure to classroom instruction had apparently altered rank order accuracy for these morphemes, not enough to violate Natural Order correlations, yet enough to suggest an effect for instruction in assisting production accuracy for plural -*s* but retarding that for progressive -*ing*. This finding was in keeping with Krashen's speculations that the Natural Order might not hold for acquirers in foreign language environments, given their emphasis on "learning." Furthermore, an explanation for the result was provided by reinterpretation of another component of Monitor Theory, i.e., its distinctions between "hard" vs. "easy" to learn grammar.

Monitor Theory predicts that "hard" rules of English grammar, such as those for articles *a* and *the*, have such complex form-function relationships that they cannot be internalized through classroom instruction, but only through meaningful input that has been made comprehensible to the acquirer. "Easy" rules—i.e., those with more transparent form-function relationships, as in the case of plural -*s*—can be internalized through instruction.

However, they are stored in the learned system and made available only as a Monitor for use in editing output, given enough time and attention to message form.

TABLE 12

Grammatical Morpheme Accuracy among Instruction Only, Untutored, and Mixed ESL Acquirers: Rank Order Correlations		

Morpheme	Instruction only	Untutored	Mixed
progressive -*ing*	5	2	3
plural -*s*	2	4.5	4
singular copula	1	1	1
progressive auxiliary	7	6	7
the	3	3	2
a	4	4.5	5
past irregular	6	7	6
past regular	9	8	8
third Person singular	8	9	9

Spearman Rank Order Correlations:
  Instruction Only and Untutored: rs = .87, p < .002
  Instruction Only and Mixed: rs = .90, p < .001
  Untutored and Mixed: rs= .96, p < .001

As shown in Table 12, similar ranks were found for articles *a* and *the* among the three groups of subjects during spontaneous discourse, suggesting that formal rule instruction either had served no direct influence on the developmental course of articles acquisition or had simply acted as a stimulus for natural processes of rule internalization. On the other hand, instruction appeared to have had a mixed effect on spontaneous production of the other two morphemes, enhancing target-like use for the "easy" plural -*s* while impeding that for the more complicated progressive -*ing*.

Elsewhere, I have addressed in detail the possible role of instruction in this outcome (Pica, 1984, 1985a, b). For the purposes of this paper, however, it is important to point out that these findings can be explained within the framework of "easy" vs. "hard" to learn rules of grammar, as long as the conditions claimed to underlie this distinction are placed in a broader perspective than Krashen currently allows. For Krashen, the "easy"-"hard" distinction is conditioned by use of the Monitor. Accordingly, an effect for instruction on production accuracy for plural -*s* should be shown only in

Monitored production. However, data on the Instruction Only subjects (and all other subjects in the study) were collected through informal conversations with a speaker of English that were designed to discourage them from drawing on conscious, learned knowledge and inhibit their Monitor use. Therefore, it cannot be claimed that their increased accuracy for plural -*s* and less accurate production of progressive -*ing* demonstrated an effect for learning but not for acquisition. Based on the spontaneous production of the instructed subjects, it might be argued instead that, at least in "easy" and "hard" to learn areas of language, formal instruction had an impact on their acquisition. However, Monitor Theory, in its current articulation, cannot accommodate these results.

These findings on "easy" and "hard" to learn morphemes, while not predicted by Monitor Theory, are in fact quite consistent with other theoretical perspectives on the role of instruction in SLA, specifically that instruction may facilitate the acquisition of target language constituents by directing the acquirer's attention to their formal features, rules for distribution, and/or communicative function. See, e.g., Bialystok and Sharwood Smith (1985), Lightbown and Spada (1990), Long (1983a, 1988, 1990), Schmidt (1990), Seliger (1979), White, Spada, Lightbown, and Ranta (1991). These results are also in keeping with recent work by van Baalen (1984), in which Dutch students of English as a foreign language showed a positive effect for "easy" to learn morphology in their spontaneous expression.

In previous work (Pica, 1984, 1985a, b) I have speculated that nonsyllabic variants of morphemes might be difficult to perceive from the stream of speech and thus go unnoticed in everyday social interaction, especially if made redundant through linguistic and extralinguistic contextual features. This puts untutored acquirers at a disadvantage in their acquisition of plural -*s* and makes the contrast between them and instructed acquirers all the more striking. Since progressive -*ing* has no nonsyllabic variants, it may be easy for uninstructed acquirers to perceive its form and function from conversational input. However, introduction of -*ing* within an instructional context may make it so salient that it becomes an all-purpose verb inflection, with learners affixing it to verbs even where no morpheme is needed, a situation exacerbated by the infrequent use of -*ing* in teacher talk, thereby making its distributional rules difficult to access. (See Larsen-Freeman, 1976; Lightbown 1983; and Long & Sato, 1983 for supporting data.) What appears to happen, as will be argued below, is the form of -*ing* becomes internalized through instruction, but not the rules for its use in meaningful expression.

Moreover, what can be seen from these results is that instruction appears to have had a facilitating impact on acquisition only for morphemes whose distributional rules are relatively straightforward and without exception. Thus, acquisition of the plural -s morpheme, with its fairly limited repertoire of linguistic contexts, was aided by formal teaching. However, rules for articles *a* and *the* are so complex that they seemed to withstand the influence of instruction so that all subjects followed a similar path to their acquisition.[1] Progressive aspect, while fairly straightforward and simple in form-function parameters, may have been confusing to the instructed acquirers because its formal realization, the -*ing* form, is also employed in participle and gerundive constructions.

In addition, rules for distinguishing use of zero ending on base forms and affixation in other verb contexts may have been made needlessly difficult for the instructed acquirers, since it is rules of affixation rather than use of base forms that are emphasized in formal instruction, to the point where many classroom learners come to believe they need to put an ending on every verb they use. Although all subjects in the study produced utterances such as "I don't understanding these people," "I thinking in this holiday, I don't like to work," and "Everyday in the afternoon, I'm returning to my house," examples of such oversuppliance of -*ing* were far more numerous among those whose exposure to English had come exclusively through classroom instruction. As the only verb ending that is always syllabic, hence more perceptually salient, the form -*ing* was a likely candidate for oversuppliance in verb contexts where subjects hypothesized that an ending was needed.

In his more recent applications of Monitor Theory to classroom instruction (e.g., Krashen, 1981a, 1982; Krashen & Terrell, 1983), Krashen has argued against the teaching of formal grammar as an aid to acquisition. His position has been that grammar rules can be internalized by the learned system and called upon for purposes of editing production but will not assist the acquisition process. In keeping with Monitor Theory, results of the present research have shown that instruction in article rules appeared to have had no impact on the acquisition process. Contrary to Monitor Theory, however, this research has also shown that instruction may actually have interfered with natural processes of acquisition in the case of -*ing*. Untutored acquirers, left on their own to figure out the rules for its distribution and use from everyday conversational interaction, seemed to have had much more control over this morpheme in their spontaneous expression than instructed acquirers, who produced the -*ing* form but did so even where it was unnecessary. Moreover, production accuracy for plural -s seemed to be assisted by instruction, again during conditions which called forth acquired L2 knowledge, a result not at all expected within the framework of Monitor Theory.

Whether these results can be explained through a reinterpretation of Krashen's "easy" vs. "hard" grammar distinctions (a reinterpretation that makes room for effects of acquisition as well as for learning) or whether some other mechanism is at work, the addition of this small sample of instructed acquirers to the database for Monitor Theory has served to challenge Krashen's position regarding the scope of the impact of formal instruction on SLA. To meet this challenge more fully, research on instructed acquirers must go beyond descriptions of interlanguage production. What are needed are carefully controlled studies of specific instructional input and its effect on learner output that seek to pinpoint classroom content and procedures that either facilitate or impede acquisition. Research in this area by Doughty (1988, 1991), Gass (1982), Lightbown (1983), Lightbown and Spada (1990), Pienemann (1984), and White, Spada, Lightbown, and Ranta (1992) holds great promise, not only for testing the claims of Monitor Theory, but also a guide to more informed pedagogical programs.

Monitor Theory and Classroom Interaction

At present, descriptions of the linguistic environment of instructed acquirers have focused mainly on broad categories of classroom input and interaction, framed in pedagogical and discourse terms. Some of this research relates directly to Monitor Theory—e.g., that which has revealed differences between morpheme frequency in classroom input and that found in everyday social interaction and the "natural order" (cf. Hamayan & Tucker, 1980; Larsen-Freeman, 1976; Long & Sato, 1983). Other work holds considerable value for addressing Krashen's claims about the importance of comprehensible input to the acquisition process and his suggestions for achieving input comprehensibility. It is in light of their relevance to Monitor Theory that the following studies of L2 interaction in and out of classrooms are reviewed. As was the case with the above review of morpheme research, this material will both support and challenge Krashen's current perspectives on input comprehension and comprehensibility and ultimately serve to *broaden* the principles underlying Monitor Theory.

As has been elaborated by Krashen's Input Hypothesis (Krashen, 1980, 1985a), unfamiliar L2 input must be comprehended if it is to assist the acquisition process. Most of Krashen's current publications on SLA (especially Krashen, 1980, 1981b, 1982, 1985a) have focused on providing evidence from L1 and L2 research as to the necessity for comprehensible input in language acquisition. As noted above, this evidence has come mainly from studies of input by caregivers addressing young children and by native speakers (NSs) engaged in spontaneous discourse with non-natives (NNSs). Krashen has also sought to specify what makes unknown input comprehensible to the learner and hence available for intake. Some words or structures in the input may be comprehended, but because they are already part of the learner's current L2 knowledge, do not become intake relevant to acquisition. Still other L2 forms are too far beyond the learner's stage of interlanguage development to be internalized or assimilated as intake. According to Krashen, the best candidate for intake is input that is slightly beyond the learners current level of interlanguage in terms of its complexity and proximity to target language grammatical, phonological, and/or lexical items—a construct he labels "$i + 1$."

Criticisms have been made of "$i + 1$" as neither a construct operationalizable for empirical testing nor a commodity that can be built into materials for classroom instruction. (See, e.g., Chaudron, 1985; Gregg, 1984; and Ioup, 1984, among others.) Krashen himself has admitted that it is difficult to pinpoint its features directly. However, he counters these criticisms with the argument that "$i + 1$" is provided automatically when input is meaningful to the acquirer and focused on immediate concerns. According to Krashen, speakers engaged in meaningful communication with a L2 acquirer will adjust their input on the basis of the acquirer's interlanguage output as well as what they perceive to be the acquirer's level of comprehension. When these conditions necessary for obtaining "$i + 1$" are placed within the constraints of a classroom environment that focuses on formal rule instruction and practice, highlights structures beyond the proficiency level of some learners and below that of others, and thereby neglects meaningful communication, it is easy to understand why SLA is often so difficult to achieve in a classroom context.

A number of studies have shown that a priori adjustments to input in the form of paraphrase and repetition of linguistic constituents, simpler syntax, and commonly used words have a facilitating effect on L2 comprehension of texts or lecturettes, compared to their unadjusted counterparts. (See, e.g., Blau, 1982; Chaudron, 1983; Johnson, 1981; and Long, 1985a.) However, what Krashen has argued (initially in Krashen, 1980, and in subsequent articles) is that there is no need for pre-adjustment of input because in meaningful communication, these adjustments arise automatically, in much the same way that input adjustments in caretakers' input to young children appear to be made on the basis of their immediate concerns for communication, with neither premeditation nor pedagogical intent.

In two studies on L2 comprehension, we found considerable support for Krashen's claims. (See Pica, Doughty, & Young, 1986; Pica, Young, & Doughty, 1987; and this volume.) Both studies compared the effects of different input conditions on comprehension of directions to a task in which L2 learners had to select and place objects on an assembly board.

Under one condition, what were originally native speaker-to-native speaker (NS-NS) baseline directions were presented to our learners by a native English speaker as input that had been linguistically modified *a priori* in ways similar to those of the lecturette research described above. Our subjects listened to the directions and responded; interaction with the direction giver was not permitted.

Under the second condition, the baseline input was not adjusted *a priori*; however, subjects had opportunities to interact with the direction giver, e.g., by asking to have the directions repeated, reworded, expanded, or explained. However, in neither condition were they given help with object selection or placement because they were separated from the direction giver by a screen.

Based on selection and placement accuracy, results of this research revealed that it was during the second, interactional condition that greater comprehension of L2 input occurred. Furthermore, despite the fact that each direction in the second condition was provided initially in unadjusted, baseline form, significantly greater numbers of input modifications—i.e., repetitions, rewordings, and expansions—were produced therein.

These results were very much in keeping with Krashen's ideas that comprehensible input comes automatically during meaningful communication between a NS and a L2 acquirer. Moreover, what our research accomplished was to identify the mechanism that brought about the input modifications and that, in turn, facilitated comprehension. It appeared that interactional adjustments such as checks on comprehension and appeals for clarification and confirmation of direction content made by *both* the direction giver *and* the learners were the means by which input was adjusted until understanding was reached.[2] Moreover, those directions which showed the strongest relationship between interaction and comprehension were accompanied by more than twice as many of these adjustments, and the majority of these adjustments (close to 70 percent) were initiated by the learners themselves.

These results also provided support for Krashen's ideas as to why SLA is not always the inevitable result of classroom instruction. For Krashen, a principal explanation for this unfortunate outcome lies in the choice of classroom *content*, i.e., formal instruction on rules too abstract for learners to assimilate as acquired L2 knowledge, targeted at a level beyond or below their current level of proficiency, focused on topics unfamiliar to them or irrelevant to their immediate concerns.

Adding further support to Krashen's explanation, results of research on English as an L2 classrooms by Doughty and Pica (1986), Long and Sato (1983), Pica and Doughty (1985a, 1985b, 1987), and Pica and Long (1986) have shown that interactional features such as clarification and confirmation requests and input modifications such as repetitions and rephrasings are a scarce commodity in the classroom, far fewer in number than those found in social interaction outside the classroom context. What is curious about these results in terms of Monitor Theory is that the classroom content represented throughout these studies was not focused on formal rule instruction but rather on discussion-oriented activities, using classroom materials with an emphasis on functional use of English and decidedly off grammatical form and mechanical practice. These results suggest that it is not simply the *content* of instruction that limits the availability of comprehensible input in the classroom, but also the teacher-student relationship that plays a critical and constraining role in this area.

It is well documented in both L1 and L2 classroom research (see, for example, Chaudron, 1988; Mehan, 1979; Sinclair & Coulthard, 1975, and Long, 1980b) that classroom interaction is structured so that students can demonstrate their knowledge and skills to their teacher. In the L2 classroom, the teacher is perceived as an authority on the L2 as well as an evaluator of students' accomplishments in the L2. Students enter the classroom as subordinates, seeking the teacher's expertise to guide the progress of their learning. Therefore, decisions as to what knowledge and skills are to be displayed are seldom within the students' control, but rather are shaped and at times constrained by the teacher's questions and commands.

Because of the teacher-student role relationship, the structure of the interaction inside the classroom differs from that found in social interaction outside. Unlike the question-response patterns found in everyday conversation, with opportunities for self-selection divided equitably among participants (documented by Sacks, Schegloff, & Jefferson, 1974, among others), classroom discourse is structured so that for every student contribution, there are two teacher moves, one that elicits the contribution and a follow-up move that evaluates it. Students' responses are valued not because of the new information they bring into the classroom, but because they provide a basis for teachers to evaluate their progress in language learning. As a result, students seldom have opportunities to initiate interaction, seek clarification, or signal for help with comprehension.

This unequally distributed interactional pattern will continue to characterize the classroom as long as teacher-student roles are perceived in terms of evaluator and evaluated. Certainly, in keeping with Krashen's views, formal grammar instruction has been one way to ensure this. However, since "communicative" activities often have an equally constraining effect (see Pica & Doughty, 1985a), it is time to look toward classroom activities that engage learners in collaboration with each other as well as with their teacher.

A promising area is that offered by tasks with a two-way information-exchange requirement (described in detail in Doughty & Pica, 1986; Long, 1983c; Long & Crookes, 1992; Pica & Doughty, 1987; and Pica, Kanagy, & Falodun, in press). Here, classroom participants are given unique bits of information that must be shared in order to reach a successful conclusion. This format places teachers and students in a much more collaborative relationship than more traditional activities because no one participant enters the task holding more information than the other and each must understand the other's contribution in order to achieve a mutually acceptable outcome.

In a series of studies (Doughty & Pica, 1986; Pica & Doughty, 1985a, b) on classroom participation patterns and tasks, it was found that even in a traditional teacher-fronted format, two-way information-exchange tasks led to more interactional adjustments among classroom participants and a more even distribution of turns than did opinion-exchange and problem-solving tasks of the kind found in "communicative" textbooks. Unfortunately, these latter invited control of classroom interaction by the more linguistically sophisticated and assertive classroom participants, often to the exclusion of many of their peers.

As a former L2 teacher myself, I feel that teachers have held onto their unequal power relationship with students in the belief that this was in the best interests of their students and their goals for language learning. Unfortunately, most materials available for instructional support, no matter how "communicative" in appearance, have reinforced rather than restructured the unequal distribution of speaking privileges in the classroom. As we find increasing evidence for the importance of comprehensible input in SLA and better insights into the most efficient means for obtaining it, classroom materials and activities that emerge from this knowledge will begin to build new teacher-student relationships that are more suitable for promoting language acquisition. Positive steps in this direction have already been taken through activities offered in the Natural Approach (Krashen & Terrell, 1983).

If it is the case that adjustments in the interaction between the language learner and another speaker (be that a teacher, an acquaintance, or other acquirers) is indeed the basis for making input comprehensible (and in addition to empirical evidence from my research with Doughty and Young, there is a great deal of theoretical support for this claim in Long, 1980b, 1983b, 1985a), this finding will serve to expand the learner's own role in obtaining intake. In much of his recent work, Krashen has described the acquirer as an active listener. Production, perhaps because of its traditional association with mechanical drill and rote practice, is seen as a somewhat useful but relatively unnecessary means for obtaining comprehensible input. The results of more recent research on interaction outside the classroom (see, for example, Pica,

1987; and Pica, Holliday, Lewis, & Morgenthaler, 1989) suggest a far greater role for learners' production during interaction. Not only does interaction provide opportunities for learners to signal to interlocutors their need to have unclear input made more comprehensible, but they also receive their interlocutors' feedback on the comprehensibility of their interlanguage production. Such feedback can range from simple clarification signals or requests for repetition to target L2 models, these latter serving as additional L2 input.

According to Krashen, "'the good language learner' is an *acquirer* who, first of all, is able to obtain sufficient intake in the L2. . . . Good language learners/acquirers must do more than just be present in informal and formal environments, however. It appears to be the case that they 'go out and get' intake . . ." (Krashen, 1981a: 37; emphasis his). As far as I have been able to see, this statement appears only once in Krashen's publications. Given the important role played by the learner's production as a component of the interaction necessary for obtaining comprehensible input, Krashen's perspectives on the learner as one who "goes out and gets" intake deserve a much more prominent place in Monitor Theory.

Conclusion

Though not without controversy, Krashen's theoretical perspectives on L2 development have had enormous appeal to TESOL professionals, particularly those who seek practical solutions to the problems of teaching language in a classroom situation. Monitor Theory has assisted our understanding of classroom SLA (or lack thereof) and informed our creation of "acquisition-rich" classrooms. However, findings from research in these areas have shown that the conditions that Krashen has proposed for efficient SLA need to be expanded in several areas, through (1) inclusion of formal instruction as an aid to the acquisition of "easy" rules of grammar; (2) exclusion of instruction in more complex areas, in which it appears either to interfere with natural processes of acquisition or to have no effect at all; and (3) provision of comprehensible input not only through interesting and relevant content, but also via the interaction between teacher and student. This interaction must avoid the familiar classroom discourse structure of teacher elicitation, student response, and teacher evaluation and instead promote and sustain an equalized role relationship so that students can freely seek help in making unfamiliar input comprehensible and thereby "go out and get" intake for acquisition.

The application of L2 research results to teaching procedures has had a limited and cautious career. In contrast to the reservations of many of his colleagues (e.g., Hatch, 1978; Lightbown, 1985a; Long, 1985b; and Tarone, Swain, & Fathman, 1976), Krashen has been less reluctant to employ theoretical principles of acquisition in confronting practical classroom concerns.

He has worked from a massive empirical base, continually incorporating not only his own studies but those of many different researchers, thereby drawing from a large and varied cross-section of acquirers and acquisition environments. The growing body of research findings on classroom acquirers and the classroom environment raises questions about Monitor Theory. At the same time, however, it offers a new and important source of data for testing its claims. To support his views on the acquisition of reading and writing abilities and their application to teaching methods (Krashen, 1984, 1985a, b), Krashen has turned to research on the differing contributions of classroom instruction in these areas. Research on classroom SLA can provide a similar perspective for Monitor Theory.

Notes

1 In fact, see Pica (1983b) for examples of the complexities that article rules pose even for native English speakers.

2 See Long (1980a, 1983b) for definitions and examples of these interactional features as well as the theoretical basis for their contribution to comprehension.

References

Allwright, R. (1983). Classroom-centered research on language teaching and learning: A brief historical overview. *TESOL Quarterly, 17,* 191–204.

Allwright, R. (1988). *Interaction analysis.* London: Longman.

Bialystok, E., & Sharwood Smith, M., (1985). Interlanguage is not a state of mind: An evaluation of the construct for second language acquisition. *Applied Linguistics, 6,* 101–117.

Blau, E. K. (1982). The effect of syntax on readability for ESL students in Puerto Rico. *TESOL Quarterly, 16,* 517–528.

Chaudron, C. (1977). A descriptive model of discourse in the corrective treatment of learners' errors. *Language Learning, 27,* 29–46.

Chaudron, C. (1983). Simplification of input: Topic reinstatements and their effect on L2 learners' recognition and recall. *TESOL Quarterly, 17,* 437–458.

Chaudron, C. (1985). Intake: On models and methods for discovering learners' processing of input. *Studies in Second Language Acquisition, 7,* 1–14.

Chaudron, C. (1988). *Second language classrooms.* New York: Cambridge.

Day, R. (1986). *Talking to learn: Conversation in second language acquisition.* Rowley, MA: Newbury.

Doughty, C. (1988). *The effects of instruction on the acquisition of relative clauses in English as a second language.* Unpublished Ph.D. dissertation. University of Pennsylvania.

Doughty, C. (1991). Second language instruction does make a difference: Evidence from an empirical study of SL relativization. *Studies in Second Language Acquisition, 13,* 431–470.

Doughty, C., & Pica, T. (1986). Information-gap tasks: Do they facilitate second language acquisition? *TESOL Quarterly, 20,* 305–325.

Dulay, H., & Burt, M. (1973). Should we teach children syntax? *Language Learning, 24,* 245–258.

Dulay, H., Burt, M., & Krashen, S. (1982). *Language two*. New York: Oxford University Press.

Ellis, R. (1984). Can syntax be taught? A study of the effects of formal instruction on the acquisition of WH questions by children. *Applied Linguistics, 5,* 138–155.

Ellis, R. (1985). Teacher-pupil interaction in second language development. In S. Gass & C. Madden (Eds.), *Input and second language acquisition* (pp. 69–88). Rowley, MA: Newbury.

Faerch, C., & Kasper, G. (Eds.). (1985). Foreign language learning under classroom conditions. *Studies in Second Language Acquisition Thematic Issue, 7,* 131–267.

Felix, S. (1981). The effect of formal instruction on second language acquisition. *Language Learning, 31,* 87–112.

Felix, S., & Hahn, A. (1985). Natural processes in classroom second language learning. *Applied Linguistics, 6,* 223–238.

Gaies, S. (1977). The nature of linguistic input in formal language learning: Linguistic and communicative strategies in ESL teachers' classroom language. In H. D. Brown, C. A. Yorio, & R. H. Crymes (Eds.), *On TESOL '77*. Washington, DC: TESOL.

Gaies, S. (1983). The investigation of language classroom processes. *TESOL Quarterly, 17,* 205–217.

Gass, S. (1982). From theory to practice. In M. Hines & W. Rutherford (Eds.), *On TESOL '81*. Washington, DC: TESOL.

Gass S., & Madden, C. (Eds.). (1985). *Input in second language acquisition*. Rowley, MA: Newbury.

Gass, S., & Varonis, E. (1985a). Task variation and NNS/NNS negotiation of meaning. In S. Gass & C. Madden (Eds.), *Input in second language acquisition* (pp. 149–161). Rowley, MA: Newbury.

Gass, S., & Varonis, E. (1985b). Variation in native speaker speech modification to non-native speakers. *Studies in Second Language Acquisition, 7,* 37–58.

Gregg, K. (1984). Krashen's Monitor Theory and Occam's razor. *Applied Linguistics, 5,* 79–98.

Hamayan, E., & Tucker, G. R. (1980). Language input in the bilingual classroom and its relationship to second language achievement. *TESOL Quarterly, 14,* 453–468.

Hatch, E. (1978). Apply with caution. *Studies in Second Language Acquisition, 2,* 123–142.

Henzl, V. (1973). Linguistic register of foreign language instruction. *Language Learning, 23,* 207–222.

Higgs, T., & Clifford, R. (1982). The push toward communication. In T. Higgs (Ed.), *Curriculum, competence, and the foreign language teacher.* Skokie, IL: National Textbook.

Hyltenstam, K., & Pienemann, M. (Eds.). (1985). *Modelling and assessing second language acquisition.* Clevedon, England: Multilingual Matters.

Ioup, G. (1984). Testing the relationship of formal instruction to the input hypothesis. *TESOL Quarterly, 2,* 345–352.

Johnson, P. (1981). Effects of reading comprehension on language complexity and cultural background of a text. *TESOL Quarterly, 15,* 169–181.

Krashen, S. (1976). Formal and informal linguistic environments in language learning and language acquisition. *TESOL Quarterly, 10,* 157–168.

Krashen, S. (1977). Some issues relating to the Monitor Model. In H. D. Brown, C. A. Yorio, & R. H. Crymes (Eds.), *On TESOL '77.* Washington, DC: TESOL.

Krashen, S. (1980). The input hypothesis. In J. Alatis (Ed.), *Current issues in bilingual education.* Washington, DC: Georgetown University Press.

Krashen, S. (1981a). The fundamental pedagogical principle in second language teaching. *Studia Linguistica, 35,* 50–70.

Krashen, S. (1981b). *Second language acquisition and second language learning.* Oxford: Pergamon.

Krashen, S. (1982). *Principles and practice in second language acquisition.* Oxford: Pergamon.

Krashen, S. (1984). *Writing, research, theory, and applications.* Oxford: Pergamon.

Krashen, S. (1985a). *The input hypothesis.* London: Longman.

Krashen, S. (1985b). The power of reading. Plenary address, 19th Annual TESOL Convention. New York, April.

Krashen, S., & Seliger, H. (1975). The essential contributions of formal instruction in adult second language learning. *TESOL Quarterly, 9,* 173–198.

Krashen, S., & Seliger, H. (1976). The role of formal and informal linguistic environments in adult second language learning. *International Journal of Psycholinguistics, 3,* 15–21.

Krashen, S., & Terrell, T. (1983). *The natural approach.* Oxford: Pergamon.

Larsen-Freeman, D. (1976). ESL teacher speech as input to the ESL learner. *UCLA Workpapers in Teaching English as a Second Language, 10,* 45–49.

Lightbown, P. (1983). Exploring relationships between developmental and instructional sequences in L2 acquisition. In H. Seliger & M. Long (Eds.), *Classroom oriented research in second language acquisition* (pp. 217–245). Rowley, MA: Newbury.

Lightbown, P. (1985a). Great expectations: Second language acquisition research and classroom teaching. *Applied Linguistics, 6,* 173–178.

Lightbown, P. (1985b). Input and acquisition for second language learners in and out of classrooms. *Applied Linguistics, 6,* 263–273.

Lightbown, P., d'Anglejan, A. (1985). Some input considerations for word order in French L1 and L2 acquisition. In S. Gass & C. Madden (Eds.), *Input in second language acquisition* (pp. 415–432). Rowley, MA: Newbury.

Lightbown, P. & Spada, N. (1990). Focus-on-form and corrective feedback in communicative language teaching: Effects on second language learning. *Studies in Second Language Acquisition, 12,* 429–448.

Long, M. (1980a). *Input, interaction, and second language acquisition.* Unpublished Ph.D. dissertation, UCLA.

Long, M. (1980b). Inside the black box: Methodological issues in classroom research on language learning. *Language Learning, 30,* 1–42.

Long, M. (1983a). Does second language instruction make a difference? A review of research. *TESOL Quarterly, 17,* 359–382.

Long, M. (1983b). Linguistic and conversational adjustments to non-native speakers. *Studies in Second Language Acquisition, 5,* 177–193.

Long, M. (1983c). Native speaker/non-native speaker conversation in the second language classroom. In M. Clarke & J. Handscombe (Eds.), *On TESOL '82.* Washington, DC: TESOL.

Long, M. (1985a). Input and second language acquisition theory. In S. Gass & C. Madden (Eds.), *Input in second language acquisition* (pp. 377–393). Rowley, MA: Newbury.

Long, M. (1985b). A role for instruction in second language acquisition. In K. Hyltenstam & M. Pienemann (Eds.), *Modelling and assessing second language acquisition* (pp.77–100). Clevedon, England: Multilingual Matters.

Long, M. (1988). Instructed interlanguage development. In L. Beebe (Ed.), *Issues in second language acquisition: Multiple perspectives.* Rowley, MA: Newbury.

Long, M. (1991). The least a second language acquisition theory needs to explain. *TESOL Quarterly, 24,* 649–666.

Long, M., & Crookes, G. (1992). Three approaches to task-based syllabus design. *TESOL Quarterly, 26,* 27–56.

Long, M., & Sato, C. (1983). Classroom foreigner talk discourse: Forms and functions of teachers' questions. In H. Seliger & M. Long (Eds.), *Classroom oriented research in second language acquisition* (pp. 268–286). Rowley, MA: Newbury.

Makino, T. (1980). *Acquisition order of English morphemes by Japanese adolescents.* Tokyo: Shinozaki Shorin.

Mehan, H. (1979). *Learning lessons: Social organization in the classroom.* Cambridge: Cambridge University Press.

Nicholas, H. (1984). To be or not to be: Is that really the question? Developmental sequences and the role of copula in the acquisition of German as a second language. In R. Andersen (Ed.), *Second languages.* Rowley, MA: Newbury.

Pica, T. (1982). *Second language acquisition in different language contexts.* Unpublished Ph.D. dissertation, University of Pennsylvania.

Pica, T. (1983a). Adult acquisition of English as a second language under different conditions of exposure. *Language Learning, 33,* 465–497.

Pica, T. (1983b). The article in American English: What the textbooks don't tell us. In N. Wolfson & E. Judd (Eds.), *Sociolinguistics and second language acquisition* (pp. 222–233). Rowley, MA: Newbury.

Pica, T. (1983c). Methods of morpheme quantification: Their effect on the interpretation of second language data. *Studies in Second Language Acquisition, 6,* 69–78.

Pica, T. (1984). L1 transfer and L2 complexity as factors in syllabus design. *TESOL Quarterly, 18,* 689–704.

Pica, T. (1985a). Linguistic simplicity and learnability: Implications for language syllabus design. In K. Hyltenstam & M. Pienemann (Eds.), *Modelling and assessing second language acquisition* (pp. 137–152). Clevedon, England: Multilingual Matters.

Pica, T. (1985b). The selective impact of classroom instruction on second language acquisition. *Applied Linguistics, 6,* 214–222.

Pica, T. (1987). Interlanguage adjustments as an outcome of NS-NNS negotiated interaction. *Language Learning, 38,* 45–73.

Pica, T. (1988). Methods of morpheme research: renewing an old debate and raising new issues. *ITL Review of Applied Linguistics, 79–80,* 77–112.

Pica, T., & Doughty, C. (1985a). Input and interaction in the communicative language classroom: Teacher-fronted vs. group activities. In S. Gass & C. Madden (Eds.), *Input in second language acquisition* (pp. 115–136). Rowley, MA: Newbury.

Pica, T., & Doughty, C. (1985b). The role of group work in classroom second language acquisition. *Studies in Second Language Acquisition, 7,* 233–248.

Pica, T., & Doughty, C. (1987). Effects of task and participation pattern on classroom interaction. In J. Fine (Ed.), *Second language discourse* (pp. 41–55). Norwood, NJ: Ablex.

Pica, T., Doughty, C., & Young, R. (1986). Making input comprehensible: Do interactional modifications help? *ITL Review of Applied Linguistics, 72,* 1–25.

Pica, T., Holliday, L., Lewis, N., & Morgenthaler, L. (1989). Comprehensible output as an outcome of linguistic demands on the learner. *Studies in Second Language Acquisition, 11,* 63–90.

Pica, T., Kanagy, R., & Falodun, S. (in press). Choosing and using tasks in classroom teaching and research. In G. Crookes & S. Gass (Eds.), *Task-based learning in a second language.* United Kingdom: Multilingual Matters.

Pica, T., & Long, M. (1986). The classroom linguistic and conversational performance of experienced and inexperienced teachers. In R. Day (Ed.), *Talking to learn: Conversation in second language acquisition* (pp. 85–98). Rowley, MA: Newbury.

Pica, T., Young, R., & Doughty, C. (1987). The impact of interaction on second language comprehension. *TESOL Quarterly, 21,* 737–758.

Pienemann, M. (1984). Psychological constraints on the teachability of languages. *Studies in Second Language Acquisition, 6,* 184–214.

Sacks, H., Schegloff, E., & Jefferson, G. (1974). A simplest systematics for the organization of turn-taking in conversation. *Language, 50,* 696–735.

Sato, C. (1982). Ethnic differences in ESL classroom interaction. In M. Hines & W. Rutherford (Eds.), *On TESOL '81.* Washington, DC: TESOL.

Schmidt, R. (1990). The role of consciousness in second language acquisition. *Applied Linguistics, 11,* 129–158.

Seliger, H. (1979). On the nature and function of language rules in language teaching. *TESOL Quarterly, 13,* 359–369.

Seliger, H., & Long, M. (Eds.). (1983). *Classroom oriented research in second language acquisition.* Rowley, MA: Newbury.

Sharwood Smith, M. (1985). Who controls the learner? *Applied Linguistics Thematic Issue 6* 214–222.

Sinclair, J., & Coulthard, M. (1975). *Towards an analysis of discourse.* London: Oxford University Press.

Tarone, E., Swain, M., & Fathman, A. (1976). Some limitations to the classroom applications of current second language acquisition research. *TESOL Quarterly, 10,* 19–31.

Traeger, S. (1978). The language of teaching: Discourse analysis in beginning, intermediate, and advanced ESL classrooms. Unpublished M.A. paper, Department of Linguistics, University of Southern California.

van Baalen, T. (1984). Giving learners rules: A study into the effect of grammatical instruction with varying degrees of explicitness. *Interlanguage Studies Bulletin—Utrecht, 7,* 71–97.

White, L., Spada, N., Lightbown, P., & Ranta, L. (1992). Input enhancement and L2 question formation. *Applied Linguistics, 12,* 416–432.

Wiley, R. (1978). An investigation of foreigner talk register in and out of the classroom. Unpublished M.A. paper, Department of Linguistics, University of Southern California.

Krashen and the Captive Learner

William T. Littlewood, University College of Swansea, UK

Mrs. Walters has come home tired from the secondary school where she teaches French. She has spent the last lesson of the day with her second-year class, who are always a struggle. They aren't in the least bit interested in French or in the people who speak it—they seem to think that France is on the other side of the world. It's true that two of the children have visited France with their parents, but one went with a package tour and the other stayed at a campground full of English people. Both of them survived well enough by using English and pointing to whatever they wanted. They certainly don't see any purpose in learning to speak the way the French do. They're pleasant children in themselves and usually make some effort, because they like Mrs. Walters, but when it's last lesson—and on a Friday—they just can't keep their minds on it, however hard they try.

One of Mrs. Walters' colleagues, who has been studying for a part-time degree, has lent her a book. She reads the title: *Principles and Practice in Second Language Acquisition*, by Stephen D. Krashen. On a Friday, after her struggle with Form Two, she feels desperate enough to try anything, so she begins to read.

But what can Stephen D. Krashen's theories offer to Mrs. Walters? After all, he presents them as theories of *adult* second language acquisition, but Mrs. Walters' pupils are adolescents or younger. He has elaborated them primarily with reference to learners of a *second* language, living in a society where the language is needed for daily communication—but French, as Mrs. Walters' pupils see it, could scarcely be more "foreign" and superfluous to their daily needs. The practical implications of his ideas have been interpreted and tested mainly in relation to situations where learners are motivated and willing to engage their minds in what is taking place in the classroom. But Mrs. Walters' pupils are "captive" and reluctant learners whose minds are constantly wandering into other domains. Add to this the fact that there are so many of them—over thirty in Form Two—and that Mrs. Walters is the only person available to speak French with them, and we might well conclude that Mrs. Walters and Stephen D. Krashen are living in different worlds.

On the other hand, is it not implicit in Krashen's theories that they should also be relevant to Mrs. Walters' world? So far as the effect of age is concerned, the main thrust of the theories is that natural mechanisms are available to adults *as well as* younger learners. Therefore, the latter should be *more* implicated rather than less. As to the differences in learning situations, if natural mechanisms have psychological reality at all, this reality must be part of the mental equipment that *every* learner carries around, irrespective of his or her situation (though there may be some situations, of course, in which the mechanisms are irrelevant or more a hindrance than a help).

So what should we advise Mrs. Walters to do—to carry on reading or to choose another book? Have Stephen D. Krashen's theories, in fact, anything to offer her in her struggle to teach Form Two? That is the question this article is about.

Form Two and the Five Hypotheses

As a framework for the discussion, I will take Krashen' s "five hypotheses":
1. The Acquisition—Learning Distinction
2. The Natural Order Hypothesis
3. The Monitor Hypothesis
4. The Input Hypothesis
5. The Affective Filter Hypothesis

Since Krashen has explained these hypotheses himself in several publications, I will not do so here.[1] Nor will I get involved in a discussion about the originality of the hypotheses or the extent to which they are supported by evidence: these issues, too, have been explored in a number of places, both in the present book and elsewhere.[2] I will simply take the hypotheses as they are offered and ask how they may be useful to a teacher in Mrs. Walters' situation. How might they stimulate her to new insights and practices that are relevant to her work? How might they help her to understand and cope with her problems?

The Acquisition-Learning Distinction

The tradition within which teachers work in British secondary schools revolves very much around the assumption that language items must be selected, presented, and reinforced through intensive practice and hard work.[3] Especially in the early years, we try to control the process of learning from outside, by determining what pupils should say and providing stimuli to make them say it. This is true even within the "communicative" approach, which has entered together with Graded Objective schemes.[4] The items of language may now be more meaningful to the learners than before. However, they are still, in the main, pre-selected for the learner, into whose mind the teacher attempts to "transplant" them through controlled repetition and practice.

To a teacher working within this tradition, the idea that a foreign language can be "acquired" by spontaneous processes is a revolutionary one. Instead of taking a preconceived system and trying to teach it, we let the learners themselves develop a system by a process of natural growth. The idea has a beautiful simplicity about it that can hardly fail to be attractive to a teacher accustomed to the traditional fight against reluctance and forgetfulness. It opens up prospects of a more constructive role and relationship, based on collaboration rather than constraint. It is also nicely suited to some aspects of the current educational ethos. Learner-centered education, the development of autonomy and creativity, self-directed growth through interaction with the environment: these are ideals from which foreign language teachers have often felt themselves to be excluded by the very nature of their subject. Now, as in other subjects, it is possible to define *knowledge* in terms of what learners construct (rather than what the teacher knows) and to envision actual processes by which learners might be able to construct it.

Related to this last statement is a further attraction. Given the situation and techniques currently at our disposal, we have not yet succeeded in making foreign language learning (beyond the initial stages) accessible to children of all ability levels. We have explained this by pointing to such factors as low aptitude, poor concentration and memory, inability to grasp generalizations, and so on. These factors operate predominantly in the controlled kinds of process that, in Krashen's distinction, constitute "learning" as opposed to "acquisition." The proposal is that "acquisition" is a process within the capacity of every learner, related less to aptitude or intelligence than to attitude and other so-called "affective" factors.[5] This puts the whole issue of "mixed ability" or "less able learners" into a new perspective. We are still left to cope with problems caused by negative attitudes, of course. However, there is at least the prospect of escaping from the hopeless but widespread belief that failure is inevitable because some pupils, by their inherent qualities, are incapable of learning another language. Indeed, this belief is disproved by studies of second language acquisition in the natural environment.

Thus the notion of "acquisition" has allowed Mrs. Walters to see her role with Form Two as about to undergo a radical change. From being a "deviser of techniques to control learning" she will become a "creator of environments to facilitate acquisition." But can such a role be made effective in Mrs. Walters' classroom conditions? What *are* the conditions that enable acquisition to take place? Perhaps the later hypotheses will give some help.

The Natural Order Hypothesis

Again we must consider the tradition within which Mrs. Walters has operated so far. It is one in which items of language are taught—and expected to be learned—in an order fixed by the syllabus. If a learner is unable to conform to this predetermined plan and makes mistakes, this is an unequivocal sign of failure. As a result of learner-centered trends since the 1960s, we may now be more inclined to attribute this failure to the teacher than the learner. This change may have represented a move towards democracy but has not done much to help the foreign language teacher's morale.

For the teacher within this tradition the idea of a natural order is, again, a revolutionary one. It suggests that there is an independent dynamism for development that will inevitably lead learners along paths different from those of the traditional syllabus. This opens up a new perspective on all Mrs. Walters' efforts to combat errors. Not only did these efforts aim to achieve the impossible, in that they set themselves up against natural laws that were stronger than they were,[6] but they were also unnecessary to the development of useful language skills.

Because of their strong association with failure, errors have been a huge burden on learners and teachers alike. Therefore, a change in attitude can have a radical effect on how teaching and learning are organized and evaluated in secondary schools. The most far-reaching effect is that it can enable teachers to focus on more positive aspects of their pupils' performance in the foreign language: the tasks they can carry out, the situations in which they can interact, the meanings that they can express and understand. This new focus makes it more possible to create a constructive atmosphere in the classroom for less able learners as well as for the more gifted. Teachers can organize communication-oriented activities without fearing that the learners might make "too many mistakes" and without flinching at every wrong ending or missed agreement. All this means not only that foreign language learning can become more enjoyable and relevant to most learners' conception of what language is really for, but also that the teacher has more chance of creating conditions in which "acquisition" is likely to take place.

Mrs. Walters realizes that a more relaxed and realistic attitude towards errors does not necessarily mean that they should be ignored in every kind of learning activity. She needs to work out a coherent approach, one that takes account of the whole problem area of how instruction can influence development, how learning relates to acquisition, and how correction affects later performance. At present, she must rely to a large extent on intuition in deciding on these matters. However, perhaps more definite guidance will later emerge from the lively debate that these matters are currently stimulating among researchers and methodologists.[7]

The Monitor Hypothesis

To some of the questions raised at the end of the last section, the Monitor Hypothesis provides Mrs. Walters with possible answers.

Some of these answers have a strong intuitive appeal and lead Mrs. Walters, once again, to put her experience into a new perspective. In particular, she is given an encouraging explanation for an experience that has depressed her so often. She spends a long time explaining, practicing, and revising some new piece of language until the pupils can produce it perfectly, but as soon as they have occasion to use it in a composition or role play, they get it wrong. She no longer needs to conclude simply that she "hasn't taught it properly": the Monitor Hypothesis gives her a new insight into why material that has been "learned" may not be available for more spontaneous language use. Of course, this insight is related to what she read earlier about errors being a normal part of communicative development. Again, she can take a less negative attitude towards her experience, realize the limits on how her teaching can influence performance, and concentrate on more positive matters.

The new perspective also gives her a useful, though simple, way of categorizing the activities that take place in her classroom. It makes her realize how few "unmonitored" activities—involving focus on meanings—she has been organizing in her classroom and using in her tests. She is now in a better position to adjust the balance in her teaching and assessment in order to give a greater role to those "unmonitored" activities that are not only her goal but also, apparently, the main facilitators of "acquisition."

She is happy, especially with her less able learners, to move away from the old emphasis on "monitored" activities, since these are the ones that demand the conscious processes (learning rules, memorizing endings, and so on) these learners find particularly difficult. If these processes can be given a less dominant role, foreign language learning should become both more pleasant and more accessible to the learners in her classes.

However, there is one idea that Mrs. Walters finds intuitively unconvincing. This is that "monitored" and "unmonitored" activities constitute two separate categories, drawing on two separate knowledge systems, rather than being at two ends of a continuum. There seems to be no reason or evidence for seeing them as so distinct. Her experience makes her believe, too, that there is more interflow between the systems than this—for example, that items which have first been learned consciously have eventually become available for spontaneous use. This is a very crucial issue for her classroom approach, since it will determine the amount of time that she will devote to traditional activities such as giving explanations and conducting controlled practice. Again, this is an issue that we cannot resolve, but we can point to some interesting discussions, many of which support her intuitions.[8]

The Input Hypothesis

Mrs. Walters reads that this hypothesis and the next one sum up what Krashen considers to be the "true causes of second language acquisition." Here, then, she is coming to the crucial facts for her as a practitioner: what should she actually do to make acquisition take place?

The first of Krashen's answers seems almost ludicrously simple. She should expose her pupils to plenty of French that they can understand and find interesting. Structurally, it should be at a slightly more advanced level than their present knowledge but need not be finely graded. There is no need to compel pupils to produce French themselves: let this ability develop naturally over the course of time.

This presents Mrs. Walters with yet another departure from the tradition she has received. She has been trained into a strongly production-oriented methodology. Drills, question-and-answer practice, describing pictures, and a range of other productive activities have formed the backbone of her approach. The emphasis has been on language use as a performance skill that can be mastered only through intensive, overt practice.

With the large classes that Mrs. Walters teaches, this notion that oral production is essential to learning has not been easy to accommodate. After almost every lesson there has been some sense of not having quite "reached the target," because she has felt that the children have not spoken as much as they ought to have done. It has been an impossible task, of course. A simple calculation shows how little each individual child can speak, on average, during a typical week, even when some of the time is devoted to pair work. As such, the tension has been inherent in the situation, but no less real because of that.

Now the suggestion is being made that all this tension is unnecessary, because the real process of acquisition takes place while learners are exposed to "comprehensible input" through listening or reading. The implications of this suggestion for Mrs. Walters' classroom methodology are considerable. Freed from the pressure to organize constant opportunities for production at all costs, she can allow herself to exploit more fully the advantages of receptive activities. Among these advantages we might mention the following: it is easier to arrange successful experiences for children of varying abilities; it is easier to provide materials that capture the learners' interest through their subject matter; it is easier to maintain a focus on the communication of meanings; above all, it is possible to go some way towards solving the dilemma of a situation in which there is only one competent speaker of the foreign language for a group of thirty learners.

Mrs. Walters would probably agree with those who doubt whether production plays quite such an inessential role as Krashen suggests.[9] Therefore, she will continue to reserve an important place for productive activities. She is happy, however, to be able to give listening and reading a greater place in her methodology.

The Affective Filter Hypothesis

The previous four hypotheses have all held a measure of good news for Mrs. Walters. They have revealed to her the following:

1. a different and more creative way of internalizing language;
2. a fresh perspective on errors that sees them as a sign of learning rather than bad teaching;
3. a new way of categorizing activities and explaining why the effects of her teaching often seem so short-lived;
4. a methodological upgrading of receptive activities that suits nicely the constraints of her situation.

Now comes some bad news: none of this can take place unless her pupils can lower their "affective filter." But a high "affective filter" is one of the most striking features of her situation with Form Two. The pupils do not want to learn French: she has to press it upon them in a constant struggle to overcome boredom and apathy.

However, if Mrs. Walters takes the fifth hypothesis in conjunction with the previous four, the situation seems less hopeless. She can now envision ways of organizing her classroom so that the pupils have more scope for being themselves and using the language for real expression, in groups as well as with the teacher. She will be able to let them use the language more freely without feeling obliged to correct every mistake that occurs (this constant expectation of being corrected has contributed a lot to Form Two's dislike of French). She will have more chances to capture their interest by providing language input materials that are more exciting and relevant for them. In a number of ways, then, the previous hypotheses point toward a more natural and human environment for learning, with less anxiety and more scope for positive experiences. Mrs. Walters feels that she has more chance than before to create and sustain favorable attitudes and to foster a real motivation to participate in the learning experiences that she offers.[10]

Conclusion

In the previous section I have suggested a number of ways in which reading Krashen can provide teachers of "reluctant learners" in secondary schools with useful and relevant ideas. Above all, these ideas can suggest fresh perspectives on experience and, in many respects, help teachers towards a more positive view of the task before them. We might add that these ideas are particularly appropriate to the context provided in Great Britain by the new GCSE examination criteria, since they, too, encourage an increased emphasis on the actual use of language and a more positive approach to evaluation.[11]

In the course of the discussion, I have adopted a mainly non-critical attitude towards the ideas that Krashen proposes and have not questioned the assumptions or evidence that underlie them. This has been intentional, since I have wanted to appraise the potential value of the ideas for a reader who is less interested in examining their theoretical justification than in the useful insights they might offer for coping with classroom realities. It is one of Krashen's major achievements that he has been able to speak to such a wide readership; for many teachers, he is the first "applied linguist" who has not only made theoretical ideas accessible but also shown how these ideas might be relevant to their practical problems.

In considering the practical implications of Krashen's hypotheses, there are obviously some major unresolved issues. Two of the most important of these are (a) the relationship between "acquisition" and "learning" (are they really as separate as Krashen suggests?) and (b) the role of active production in the learning process (is this role really as non-essential as Krashen suggests?). Krashen's views are hypothetical and not based on sufficiently firm evidence to warrant the practical conclusion that they point toward: that teachers can abandon, without detriment to their learners' progress, those activities which involve conscious learning or controlled production.[12]

It is as well to finish, then, by bearing in mind that Krashen's "five hypotheses" are just that: *hypotheses* about learning, rather than established facts. They can help teachers to develop, in turn, a set of hypotheses about what might *stimulate* more effective learning in the classroom. This second set of hypotheses then has to be submitted, by teachers themselves, to what is ultimately the only valid test: whether it enables learners to make better progress. Provided that Krashen's ideas are accepted as part of a broader process of exploration, such as that just described, rather than as the basis for a new dogma, they have a lot to offer to the teacher of foreign languages in the secondary school.

Notes

1   See, for example, Krashen (1981, 1982, 1985) and Krashen and Terrell (1983).

2   For example, see Ellis (1985), Gregg (1984), Littlewood (1984) and McLaughlin (1978).

3   An interesting book that reflects this assumption within a "communicative" orientation is Rowlinson (1985).

4   A useful survey of graded objectives is Page (1983).

5   See, for example, Gardner (1985: 128, 148) and Genesee (1976).

6   Lightbown (1985) highlights this point clearly.

7   See, for example, the discussions in Ellis (1985b), Felix (1981), Lightbown (1983), Long (1983a), and Pienemann (1985).

8   For example, Bialystok and Sharwood Smith (1985), Littlewood (1984b), Rivers (1980), and Stevick (1980).

9   Ellis (1985b) is one who argues that production plays an important role. Gibbons (1985) provides interesting counter-evidence to the claim that children normally go through an extensive "silent period." The function of interaction (rather than just "input") as a stimulus for learning is discussed by Hatch (1978) and Long (1983b).

10 The need for this in the British context is stressed by Rowlinson (1985) and is embodied in teaching materials such as the French course by Buckby (1980–1985).

11 This emerges clearly from the training handbook by Jones (1986).

12 This conclusion is suggested by Krashen and Terrell (1983). For a detailed questioning of the theoretical basis from which such conclusions are drawn, see Gregg (1984).

The Natural Approach and Language Teaching in Europe

Reinhold Freudenstein, University of Marburg, Federal Republic of Germany

If you showed the following examples of curriculum organization and classroom activities to someone who has been familiar with European foreign-language teaching and learning since the early sixties, the person would have no difficulty in attributing each item to a certain period or school in the development of teaching strategies within the last twenty-five years. Let us assume for a moment that this person had never heard of Krashen and his Natural Approach. In this case he or she would most certainly insist that the various examples could never belong to just one coherent theory, saying instead that they originated from different, contradictory, educational and methodological principles and thus could never work when used together. However, all the examples illustrate the Natural Approach and its implications in the classroom.

Curriculum Organization

Krashen's approach is designed to develop personal communication skills. Communication goals are expressed by Krashen in terms of situations, functions, and topics, examples of which are shown in the following:

> Students in the classroom
> TOPICS
> 1. Personal identification (name, address, telephone number, age, sex, nationality, date of birth, marital status)
> 2. Description of school environment (identification, description and location of people and objects in the classroom, description and location of buildings) (Krashen & Terrell, 1983: 67)

This curriculum design is almost identical with a concept drawn up by a group of Council of Europe experts established in 1971 to investigate the feasibility of a European unit/credit scheme for foreign language learning by adults (Van Ek & Alexander, 1975) and further developed in connection with a European language certificate program for adults that specified its learning objectives in the form of speech intentions (functions), general concepts, and topics. Here is the part that corresponds to Krashen's example above:

B.1. People
1.1. Name; address; family status; sex; date and place of birth; age.
1.2. Nationality; mother tongue.
1.3. Education and training . . .

B.3. Places
3.1. Type, size, and location of place
3.2. Public services; buildings, facilities . . .
(International Certificate Conference, 1984: 29f)

Specifications of this kind became very popular once language learning was no longer regarded as merely a contribution towards general education or as a key to foreign literature. The ability to communicate was the new overall objective from the early sixties onwards (Lado, 1964). Communicative competence in everyday situations had become more important than the teaching of academic learning skills.

Classroom Activities

For early production exercises, Krashen supports comprehensible input by the teacher, which he calls "teacher-talk":

Is there a woman in the picture? (Yes). Is there a man in the picture? (No). Is the woman old or young? (Young). Yes, she's young, but very ugly. (Class responds: No, pretty). That's right, she's not ugly, she's pretty. What is she wearing? (Dress). Yes, she's wearing a dress. What color is the dress? (Blue). Right, she's wearing a blue dress. And what do you see behind her? (Tree). Yes, there are trees. Are they tall? (Yes). And beside here is a _____ (dog). Yes, a large dog is standing to her right. (Krashen & Terrell, 1983: 79)

Actually, there is no basic difference between this exercise and the one reported by Lado in connection with an improvised pattern practice chart:

The teacher points to the first picture and says, *It's a train.* The class repeats, *It's a train.* The teacher points to the next picture and says, *It's a ship.* The class repeats. The third picture will elicit, *It's an orange,* when the teacher points to it. . . . Questions and affirmative short answers can follow: *Is it a train? Yes, it is.* Affirmative and negative short answers can be practiced by pointing to the wrong picture now and then, e.g. pointing to the train and saying, *Is it a ship?* to elicit, *No, it isn't. It's a train.* (Lado, 1964: 198f)

A trainee teacher who performed like this in a demonstration class today would most certainly fail the examination. And yet Krashen states that he refers to "activities, as opposed to audiolingual drill. . . . For acquisition to take place, the topics used in each activity must be intrinsically interesting or meaningful, so that the students' attention is focused on the content of the utterances instead of the form" (Krashen & Terrell, 1983: 97). But this goal can only be achieved if students' answers are not predetermined (as they are in both preceding examples). If the answer to a question is known beforehand to both the person who asks it and the one who is going to answer it, then this activity simply cannot be meaningful. For this reason "teacher-talk" exercises à la Krashen have become increasingly unpopular and are no longer so extensively used in newer language learning materials. They are referred to as being old-fashioned, mechanistic, and therefore out-of-date.

Krashen's approach is obviously open to every method propagated since foreign-language teaching was first based on scientific foundations. He advocates audiolingual strategies; he is in favor of audiovisual learning aids; he does not reject alternative methods. He wants to involve the students individually in the learning process; they should be able to make personal statements and express wishes and desires, as in the following open dialogue:

Student 1:   Are you hungry?
Student 2:   _____.
Student 1:   I think I'll order a _____. How about you?
Student 2:   I'd prefer _____.
(Krashen & Terrell, 1983: 100)

To make students say what they would like to say, and not what they are expected to produce, has been a regular component in all European language courses since the communicative orientation. Even courses that are based on a strict grammatical progression have always provided exercises in which the content of a statement has to be—and can only be—decided upon by the speaker, as in the following example:

Tell your neighbor about your life:
My name is _____.

I live in _____.
I have _____ children, _____ and _____ girls.
I work _____ hours a day.
I like _____.
I speak _____. (Jacoby & Kleine, 1978: 67)

The next example is also taken from an earlier textbook for adults. This exercise is designed for beginners, too. It proves that the notion of the students' personal involvement in the language-learning process from the very beginning is by no means a new one. The "classic" example is the restaurant situation:

Customer: Can I have the menu, please?
Waiter: What would you like to start with?
Customer: I'd like _____, please.
Waiter: And what would you like to follow?
Customer: I'd like _____ with _____.
Waiter: And what about dessert, sir/madam?
(Bliemel, Fitzpatrick & Quetz, 1976: 81)

This form of guided dialogue is not reserved for adult learners only. A course for children (starting to learn English at the age of ten) offers "Models for Saying and Doing" *(Gesprachs-und Handlungsmuster)* from the very first lesson. This kind of learning strategy provides the student with the linguistic material (structures and vocabulary) for self-expression, leaving the content up to him or her. Here is an example from the third year of learning:

—Are there things you're $\left\{\begin{array}{l}\text{afraid}\\\text{frightened}\end{array}\right\}$ of?

Hm? I don't like. . . .

Oh yes, I'm $\left\{\begin{array}{l}\text{afraid}\\\text{frightened}\end{array}\right\}$ of. . . .

—Well, I can't think of any.

—No, not really. There really aren't any.

(*YES*, 1979: 24)

This list of examples could easily be extended, including evaluation and testing strategies. A thorough analysis shows that there is not a single item of curriculum organization, classroom activity or testing mode in the Natural Approach that could be labeled innovative or "a radically different approach to language instruction" (Krashen & Terrell, 1983: 2). One must agree with the British language expert who has said the following about what Krashen has written: "What's true isn't new, and what's new isn't true" (Dunlop, 1985: 4; this volume).

"New" Elements

What, then, actually are the new elements that have made Krashen so popular on the professional scene, particularly in the United States, in spite of the fact that so many of his ideas lost popularity in Europe some time ago? Undoubtedly one of the factors is his terminology. The most striking example is the distinction between "learning" and "acquisition." Normally, we think of naturally "acquiring" our mother tongue only, while tutored "learning" is connected with (foreign) languages in addition to the mother tongue. Krashen's theory transfers acquisition strategies into the foreign language classroom: he believes in something like "tutored acquisition." However, this involves several controversial issues that Krashen does not discuss in detail. One of these is the order for the presentation of language skills, in which Krashen borrows the audiolingual doctrine of comprehension before production—a claim that is not undisputed, since it has become clear that the development of various language skills is directly dependent on different learning objectives and individual learning qualifications. Then there is the problem of having the teacher use the target language only. This has been a focal point of interest in Europe for more than a century, with constantly changing arguments for and against the use of the mother tongue in the foreign-language classroom. Krashen does not examine these arguments as one would have expected him to in light of the historical importance of the problem: he simply adds his point of view to the long list of arguments. Thus the use of "acquisition" is in no way connected with new elements in the teaching or learning process. It is nothing but a new technical term that—in the way Krashen uses it—has simply replaced "learning."

Another attractive term is "monitor." Here again Krashen uses long-established pedagogical principles but at the same time limits their application to very special cases: "Our 'formal knowledge' of a second language, the rules we learned in class and from texts, is not responsible for fluency, but only has the function of checking and making repairs on the output of the acquired system" (Krashen & Terrell, 1983: 30). While this might well be the case with some learners, it cannot be accepted as a general rule. Teaching practice over the years has shown that the role of grammar must be interpreted in a much more differentiated way. This view is supported by recent research. A "rule" can be simple or complicated; it can be presented in an easily comprehensible or in a complicated and confusing manner; it can be short and precise or long-winded; it can be motivating or boring; and most of all it will always be learned by different people in different ways (Zimmermann & Wissner-Kurzawa, 1985). Only if these and other aspects are seriously considered in the context of grammar teaching and learning can one realistically speculate about the contribution of conscious factors to the learning of foreign or second languages.

There are other newly coined terms that Krashen uses to denote well-known phenomena, always with a restricted field of validity. What used to be the "favorable attitude" towards foreign cultures, their speakers and their teachers, and fellow students is in Krashen's terminology a low "affective filter." The presentation of words and structures, phrases and sentences has become the "input," and the corresponding term for saying something is "output." The standard procedure of presenting new material on the basis of what is already known is offered with the help of a formula that looks like the result of scientific research: $i + 1$. In reality, however, it signifies nothing but intelligent guesswork that is most probably correct.

Next to the terminology, Krashen's impact on the professional scene seems to be based on his attempt to present the Natural Approach and its elements as a coherent theory that leaves no questions unanswered. But the model is a theoretical one, and its five components are only hypothetical assumptions. However, a hypothesis is not a fact: it is an idea that is used to explain something. It is a suggestion put forward as a starting point for a possible explanation. What should follow is extensive empirical research, but here Krashen fails to provide convincing data based upon practical tests. Research is necessary to support or to reject his hypotheses, and until it has been conducted, his theory remains a mixture of facts, experience, hopes, and speculations, a methodological stew—a hodge-podge approach that presents a little bit of everything in the hope of offering something to everyone.

The Lack of Professional Dialogue

Krashen's work and its reception outside Europe are perfect examples of the fact that the professional dialogue between the United States and Europe in the past has largely taken place in a kind of a one-way street only, a street from the West to the East. If there had also been an acceptance of ideas in the opposite direction, Krashen might well have developed his theory in a different way. Had Krashen understood the typically European method of always trying to combine educational innovation with traditional elements that have proved to be reliable, successful, and suitable for modification, he might have been less convinced that replacing something old and common by something (in his eyes) entirely new was the right way forward. A glance at his bibliographies shows that hardly any European authors of importance are listed; one must assume that Krashen is simply not familiar with European foreign- and second-language developments.

There are three fundamental, crucial issues that are involved in the missing professional dialogue:

1. Many of Krashen's statements concern matters that have long been taken for granted in Europe. They are so well-known that they can hardly be regarded as aspects belonging particularly to the Natural Approach. Some examples are formal grammar instruction does not have a central place in the curriculum, but it does have an important role to play; children in second or foreign language programs will not be interested in the same topics that adult students are interested in; grammar exercises are not used for real communication; and if students encounter too much new vocabulary and structure in an activity, they will not participate in conversation (Krashen & Terrell, 1983: 45, 61, 98f). Anyone familiar with language teaching in Europe is familiar with these tenets and would either accept or reject them; they would never be put forward in the guise of a "new" theory.

2. In the past, new directions in foreign language teaching have always been sought in approaches and methods that stressed the system of *teaching* as the sole and universal center of success. This accounts for the replacement of the grammar-translation method by the direct method, the direct method by a "compromise" (audiolingual plus cognitive) method, and this, in turn, by audiolingual and audiovisual methods leading into strategies that stress communicative competence. Krashen's Natural Approach follows this tradition; he actually admits to having "rediscovered" the natural, direct method (Krashen & Terrell, 1983: 17). He advocates a method that he wants to see applied to all learners of another language, rather than recommending individual learning strategies suitable for students of different origin or age, and with different learning objectives.

3. In a well-publicized interview, Lado pointed out that language instruction should tap all the learning powers of students. Thus he put the *individual* at the center of the learning process, not a particular method. His recommendations for future research are a guide to the way in which language teaching approaches, strategies, and methods can really be advanced:

> Research on the discourse level of language in addition to and not in place of the linguistic level, and an unrestricted approach to teaching that appeals to all the learning powers of the student can produce another forward leap in our professional ideas and practices. The discourse level includes function, intentions, roles and appropriate usage. All the previous knowledge of the students and all teaching resources of the teacher should be brought to bear on

learning. This includes the first and other languages already known, samples of the new language in context, practice in context, speaking, listening, reading, writing, and translation when necessary, analogy, association, induction, deduction, classification, as well as affective factors that motivate the students and facilitate assimilation, and intentional practice in context to develop facility. Facility makes possible the use of the language to pursue individual interests such as preparation for and practice of a technical or professional career, enjoyment of literature, study of culture, travel, or simply the pleasure of social conversation across cultures. (Lado, 1985: 169)

This, rather than the re-invention of the wheel under another name, is a perspective from which we can expect genuine advances in our professional knowledge.

Conclusion

I do not want to advocate judgments that any one person or any one direction in the language-teaching profession is right or wrong. Over the centuries, millions of people have learned foreign languages regardless of the methods they had been exposed to—or even in spite of them! But we should surely learn from these experiences and acknowledge a simple and basic fact: languages can be learned for communication purposes in many ways, since there is no single approach or method that is ideal or unique. Each and every student is an individual with his or her own preferences, requirements, experiences, and wishes. More important than the methods are the students to whom they are applied, and here only one principle is decisive: does the method work or not? The Natural Approach might work with some students, but it is not the final solution for the many problems with which we have to deal in language learning—or language acquisition.

The True
and the New

Ian Dunlop,
English Language
Centre, Hove, UK

Some time ago the BBC and IATEFL arranged a seminar on how children learn language.[1] The first speaker described child acquisition of language and then said that he thought people learned a foreign language in the same way as children learn their own language. This worried me a great deal because ever since 1968 I have found Lenneberg's biological theory of language (Lenneberg, 1967) a compelling one, for several reasons:

- it explains why one should always consider different age levels when talking about teaching methods and approaches;
- it means that we should not talk about learning a foreign language in the same way as a child acquires his or her first language;
- it gives a theoretical background for the oft-mentioned fact that there is a difference in the way children learn a foreign language before puberty and after puberty and therefore in the way they should be taught at different ages (cf. Abercrombie, as quoted in Allen, 1965: 189);
- Lenneberg's theory of the Language Acquisition Device (LAD) explains how children at a very early age could put in order a language system at a time when they had not yet developed the intellectual ability to analyze and deduce.

An example from my own experience: my younger son, who was born in Sweden, made friends with an elderly Swedish lady who knew no English, and when he was about three years old I heard him say to her: *Kom lat oss builda* — "Come on, let's build" (something with my bricks), which sounds fine, except that in Swedish *to build* is *bygga;* so what he had done was to take the English verb (because he didn't know the Swedish) and add on the correct ending for the Swedish infinitive (i.e., he added -*a* to the stem of the verb and turned *build* into *builda*).

This is a considerable analytical and deductive feat, and even a child of mine doesn't have the intellectual development to achieve this at the age of three. Lenneberg's theory explains it by saying that we have an automatic aid to help us learn language between the ages of approximately two and puberty, and that this Language Acquisition Device (LAD) quickly declines in effectiveness after puberty.[2] Naturally, Lenneberg is talking about first language acquisition, but he also says about learning a foreign language that "automatic acquisition from mere exposure to a given language seems to disappear after puberty, and foreign languages have to be learned through a conscious and laboured effort" (1967: 176). Before puberty we have a Language Acquisition Device that enables us (as long as we hear the language around us) to acquire language automatically; after puberty we still have the capacity to learn a foreign language, but language learning is not automatic, as it was in early childhood.

However, this view has been challenged by Krashen in his acquisition-learning hypotheses (Krashen & Terrell, 1983). Krashen states that "the acquisition-learning hypothesis claims that adults can still acquire a second language, that the ability to 'pick-up' languages does not disappear at puberty, as some have claimed, but it is still with us as adults" (1983: 26). In addition, "adults can access the same natural 'language acquisition device' as children use" (Krashen, 1982). And, finally, "adult acquisition processes are posited to be similar to child language acquisition" (Krashen & Terrell, 1983). My uneasiness about Krashen is in his use of words such as *posited*. What does he mean by "are posited to be similar"? Obviously, "posited" can only mean that this is Krashen's assumption. And what does he mean by "similar"? Does Krashen really mean that adults learn a foreign language *in the same way* that pre-pubescent children do? I do not mean *in a similar way;* I mean *in the same way*. I do not find him clear on this point. Does Krashen believe that an adult can subconsciously structure language as a pre-pubescent child can do? He seems to think so.

His Input Hypothesis states simply that "we acquire (not learn) language by understanding input that is a little beyond our current level of (acquired) competence" (Krashen & Terrell, 1983). It is the teacher's job to provide comprehensible input that is a little above the level of the student's present level in, for example, English. The student will then acquire more English through "context and extralinguistic information [e.g., through visual aids] . . . . The input hypothesis thus claims that we use meaning to acquire language" (Krashen & Terrell, 1983).

There is also the Natural Order Hypothesis, which states that "grammatical structures are acquired in a predictable order. . . . The order of acquisition for second language is not exactly the same as the order of acquisition for first language, but there are some clear similarities" (Krashen & Terrell, 1983). Therefore, Krashen believes that there is no point in a graded course of grammar, since the student will learn when he or she is "ready" to learn a particular structure—which can be at different times for different people. Krashen also believes that the natural order only works with adults when their attention is focused on communication. We should also note that he says that "theoretically, speaking is not necessary for language acquisition" and that speech will come as a result of language acquisition (Krashen & Terrell, 1983).

Thus Krashen says that adults learn a foreign language in much the same way as children learn their first language, which is by acquisition, not conscious learning; it is through listening to comprehensible input that the student acquires the foreign language; it is the teacher's task to provide this comprehensible input, which should be at a level slightly above the student's present level of competence in the language; grammatical structures should not be deliberately planned and sequenced into this input, as there is a natural order in which students will learn structures and they will therefore learn a new structure when they are ready for it, but not before; conscious learning (i.e. through using rules, with the students trying to monitor their own correctness) has a very limited use in foreign language learning.

Many native speakers of the language they teach will have had the experience of living abroad as teachers and will also have had the experience of "picking up" a foreign language in the country of origin. They all know that they were able to pick up words and phrases, some of the pronunciation, and perhaps even the intonation (if they had enough "immersion"); they also picked up a smattering of the grammar and so usually acquired good fluency and poor accuracy, thus enabling them to cope with everyday situations and conversations at a sort of intermediate level. They then probably reached a plateau in that language and did not, perhaps, wish to improve any further. Their mistakes were not irritating enough to native speakers to make them unsatisfactory social company (or they did not meet the same people often enough for their mistakes to become increasingly irritating). If, however, they did wish to improve their performance in the language, they probably noticed, as all teachers of adults do, that explanations of grammar help as long as those explanations are understandable, do explain and do not confuse, and are at the linguistic level of the student.

Krashen is right when he says that grammar explanations should not yet be acquired, learnable, portable—by which he means "what can be carried round in the students' heads" (Krashen, 1983), but what is new about that?

I quote from my own publication (Dunlop, 1970): "rules should be made explicit in terms which the pupils are able to understand and not be merely 'grammar book rules' written by linguists for linguists." Krashen's Monitor Theory says that "conscious learning has an extremely limited function in adult second language performance: it can only be used as Monitor or editor" (Krashen, 1983). The Monitor is useful to students only when the performer has enough time, the performer has to be thinking about correctness, and the performer has to know the rule. Therefore, the Monitor is most useful in writing or for a prepared speech but not, for example, in conversation.

Over-users of the Monitor will not say much or will hesitate, being afraid to make mistakes. But this is hardly a new insight. Anyone who taught in the 1950s (or indeed anyone who teaches German today) knows that many years ago we had to work out ways of increasing fluency by stopping people from worrying about mistakes in conversation. We agree with Krashen that "the optimal Monitor user is the adult second language performer who uses the Monitor when it is appropriate, when it does not get in the way of communication" (Krashen, 1983: 45).

But how did we get students in evening classes to increase their fluency and not worry too much about mistakes in conversation? We got them to relax by using first names, by smiling, by creating a friendly atmosphere. We knew that the adult student in an evening class

- feels apprehensive;
- does not know the other people in the class;
- does not know the teacher;
- is afraid of making a fool of himself/herself in front of others;
- has already done a day's work and is tired;
- wants to learn but has his/her normal life to live outside the classroom and therefore cannot devote much time between lessons to preparation;
- no longer has a child's ability to mimic sounds quickly;
- no longer has a child's memory and therefore forgets things more easily;
- (but) will remember his/her own schooldays, and if they were gruesome will be reminded of them by the classroom situation. (Dunlop, 1970)

We have known these things for years. But now Krashen produces his Affective Filter Hypothesis, which means quite simply that anxiety or lack of motivation blocks learning. This is hardly a new suggestion, although

Krashen also uses the Affective Filter Hypothesis to explain why adolescents' language behavior changes at puberty. He quotes Elkind as suggesting that Piaget's stage of formal operations may contribute to this change (Krashen, 1981). I agree—as I suggested in 1975—that it is tempting to think that as our Language Acquisition Device declines, the stage of formal operations takes over, so that analytical thinking in language learning (as in other subjects) can now be used (Dunlop, 1975).[3] However, Krashen puts forward the view that the *ability* to acquire language is blocked by the emotional problems of puberty and that therefore adolescents do not acquire language so easily. So here we are back again with the same question: does language acquisition continue as automatically after puberty as before? Krashen thinks it does, but then says the changes in adolescents' language acquiring abilities are caused by their emotional problems.

Of course, I agree that adolescents have emotional problems and problems of identity (and, indeed I have often asked the question, why make them talk at that awkward age? Why not instead concentrate on listening, reading and writing? Indeed, I often agree with Krashen, because he has said some sensible things; but usually the sensible thing is something we have known for years. I am therefore tempted to say the following about what Krashen has written: *what's true isn't new and what's new isn't true.*

It is clear from his writings that Krashen is in fact fighting a battle against American grammar-translation teaching and audiolingual teaching. If you look at the bibliographies in his books, you will not find references to European writers on TEFL, only to error analysis and linguistics. He does not refer, for example, to the VHS *Zertifikat*, the Council of Europe's *Waystage* and *Threshold Level*, the Notional-Functional Approach, or Teacher Training programs leading to the Royal Society of Arts Preparatory Certificate or Diploma in Teaching English as a Foreign Language. It is as if the discussions of the last fifteen years or so in Europe had never happened, although many of the techniques he suggests in *The Natural Approach* have been practiced all over Europe for many years. Even research work is not mentioned. On the subject of writing, for example, Krashen says that "there is, however, no published evidence relating reading and writing proficiency in second language acquirers" (Krashen, 1984). Yet IEA (The International Association for the Evaluation of Educational Achievement) published findings as long ago as 1975 (Carroll, 1975; Lewis *et al.*, 1975) giving correlations between reading and writing. Tables 13 and 14 refer to learning English in Sweden and learning French in Scotland, and are taken from surveys of languages in eighteen countries. As can be seen, there is very little correlation between recognition skills (i.e., reading and listening) and free production skills (i.e., speaking and writing compositions). However, there are higher correlations between recognition skills (i.e., reading and listening), and for both age levels the best correlations were between reading and "guided" writing (i.e., mainly a gap-filling grammar test). These results seem to support the Scherer and Wertheimer (1964) findings that pupils learn what they are taught, in the sense that no matter how good someone is at reading in a foreign language or speaking, for instance, he or she will not achieve the same level of proficiency in writing unless also given sufficient practice in that skill.

TABLE 13

SWEDEN

Population 11 (14-year-olds)

N (no. of students tested) = 2000+ for Reading, Writing, and Listening

N (Speaking) = 218

	Reading	Guided Writing	Writing: Composition
Reading	—	.81	.57
Listening	.80	.78	.55
Speaking (fluency)	.69	.66	.44

Population IV (last year of secondary education)

N = 1400+ (for Reading, Writing, and Listening)

N (for Speaking) = 204

	Reading	Guided Writing	Writing: Composition
Reading	—	.64	.41
Listening	.62	.51	.34
Speaking (fluency)	.43	.30	.24

Table 14, the study of Scottish students' abilities in French, showed the same pattern as regards the highest correlations. The IEA Studies also showed the importance of student motivation in learning languages, and Krashen agrees. He wants students to learn to communicate; he is against over-predominance of grammar; and he wants students to have comprehensible input.

TABLE 14

SCOTLAND

Population 11 (14-year-olds)

N = 800 (Reading, Writing, and Listening)

N = 230 (Speaking)

	Reading	Guided Writing	Writing: Composition
Reading	—	.87	.68
Listening	.76	.72	.61
Speaking (fluency)	.49	.49	.42

Population IV (last year of secondary education)

N = 975

N = 260 (for speaking)

	Reading	Guided Writing	Writing: Composition
Reading	—	.78	.53
Listening	.68	.64	.43
Speaking (fluency)	.62	.58	.49

The problem is that he persists in appearing to say that adults learn foreign languages in the same way as they learned their own first language as children. Therefore, he does not agree with grading structures as part of a course and says, that the Natural Approach "is in many ways the natural direct method re-discovered" (Krashen & Terrell, 1983). I have doubts about Krashen because of his seeming insistence on adults having access to the same Language Acquisition Device as pre-pubescent children. I deplore this, because if people believe it they will go back to saying, as they did twenty years ago, that students learn a foreign language in the same way as children learn their mother tongue. This will result in the same method being used to teach people of all ages, no matter their previous experience or their aims; and this, in turn, can lead to the old mistake of believing that there is only one true method for all. I feel strongly that we in Europe do not need or want to retrace those paths.

Notes

1 London, 1982.

2 Lenneberg says that "language cannot begin to develop until a certain level of physical maturation and growth has been attained. Between the ages of two and three and the early teens the possibility for primary language acquisition continues to be good; the individual appears to be most sensitive to stimuli at this time and to preserve some innate flexibility for the organisation of brain functions to carry out the complex integration of sub-processes necessary for the smooth elaboration of speech and language. After puberty, the ability for self-organisation and adjustment to the physiological demands of verbal behavior quickly declines. The brain behaves as if it had become set in its ways and primary basic language skills not acquired by that time, except articulation, usually remain deficient for life. (New words may be acquired throughout life because the basic skill of naming has been learned at the very beginning of language development). . . . the individual is seen as functioning by virtue of his own power supply, so to speak; he constructs language by himself (providing he has the raw material to do it with), and the natural history of his development provides for the mechanisms by which he will harmonize his function with that of other equally autonomously functioning individuals around him; the outer form of his language will have the outer form of the language of his community."

3 According to Dunlop, "It is tempting to think as our innate language learning capacity declines, so our ability to perform more complicated conceptual processes increases" (1975: 49).

On Babies and Bathwater: Input in Foreign Language Learning

Bill VanPatten,
University of Illinois—
Urbana–Champaign,
USA

For several years now the foreign language profession has been debating the merits of Krashen's monitor theory and its applications to foreign language teaching. Some have embraced the theory and have accepted its set of hypotheses as a sound basis from which to proceed as language teachers. Others have been critical of it. The following quotations illustrate these divergent positions quite well:

> In January 1983, following a visit to the campus by Stephen Krashen, the faculty and staff of the Spanish division began to consider developing a comprehension based approach to the teaching of Spanish to non-native speakers. The initial phase of the program involved four members of the faculty and three key decisions: 1) the decision to abandon the direct teaching of grammar as a primary focus of instruction; 2) the decision to use a large portion of classroom time to provide the student with comprehensible input; 3) the decision to allow the students to produce oral Spanish at their own rate [sic]. (Long, Pino, & Valdes, 1985: 414–415)

> One final point is that the majority of the research literature cited in support of the claims for the input hypothesis assumes a second language environment, not a FL situation involving formal, classroom instruction. . . . We must ask ourselves whether a theory that accounts for a significant range of behaviors in an immersion environment is automatically transferrable and applicable to a standard U.S. high school or university curriculum. (Higgs, 1985: 202)

With such divergent points of view to consider, the serious language teacher who attempts to keep abreast of the field of theory and its applications is faced with a crucial dilemma: to believe or not to believe in monitor theory. Should one evaluate teaching practices based on Krashen's hypotheses or not? However, by carefully examining the second citation and knowing that the title of the article from which it was culled is "The Input Hypothesis: An Inside Look," it is not monitor theory *in toto* that is really the object of criticism. Rather, it is the specific hypothesis surrounding the role of meaningful input and its relationship to the development of grammatical competence that is problematic for most of those in foreign language teaching who criticize monitor theory.

What is important to recognize is that those criticisms of monitor theory in which the input hypothesis is rejected run into a serious problem: throwing the baby out with the bathwater. In other words, teachers and researchers alike may lose sight of the very important role that input plays in language development as the push to challenge Krashen's monitor theory becomes fashionable in foreign language teaching circles. This paper is an attempt to bring input into focus and to examine the relationship between the development of grammar and traditional instruction in grammar.

In order to discuss the role of input, it is perhaps wise to state the components of monitor theory. Krashen's theory (1982) consists of five hypotheses: (1) the acquisition-learning distinction; (2) the natural order hypothesis; (3) the input hypothesis; (4) the affective filter hypothesis; and (5) the monitor hypothesis.

The hypothesis that concerns us here is the input hypothesis. Krashen claims that for acquisition (not learning) to occur, learners need to attend to meaningful, comprehensible input in the target language. If *affective variables* are favorable, then by attending to input, language can be internalized. In elaborating this hypothesis. Krashen has also made two other claims: (1) that production of the target language by the learner does not directly aid acquisition, i.e., practice in speaking does not promote acquisition of grammar or morphology; and (2) that meaningful, comprehensible input needs to contain a variety of structures and vocabulary that the learner is familiar with and not familiar with—in particular, the input has to contain items that are just a little beyond the current internalized competence of the learner This is the well-known $i + 1$ hypothesis.

The Problem

While some theoreticians have taken on Krashen for a number of points that are not important for the present discussion, what seems to be the bone of contention for many in foreign language teaching is the dubious value that the input hypothesis places on grammar instruction, forced production, and error correction: activities in which the vast majority of teachers have been engaged for years. As we see students progress and develop (generally measured by how well they do on our *discrete point grammar-centered tests*), we are reinforced in these traditional activities. And we continue to put grammar instruction in a front and center position.

For the moment, let us leave aside the matter of the adequacy of monitor theory and ask ourselves a question from an extreme position: do we want to adopt a theory or approach in foreign language learning/teaching that does *not* include meaningful input as a *major* component? Can a person internalize a non-primary language *without* access to meaningful, communcatively centered input?

To answer yes would be tantamount to the foreign language profession declaring complete independence from second language acquisition research. While SLA is generally defined as the learning of a language where the target language is spoken in the community, are we in foreign language learning where no outside speech community exists so different that we can reject or at best ignore SLA research?

To be sure, in the field of SLA itself there is much debate about monitor theory, particularly the input hypothesis as it is currently formulated (e.g., Spolsky, 1985; Gregg, 1986). Critical examination of this hypothesis will continue to spark controversy, but in the meantime there is consensus in second language circles on the following: *access to meaningful input is somehow a critical factor in successful language development.* As Hatch has recently stated, "it is clearly the case that one cannot learn a second language without any input" (1983: 84). What then of the foreign language classroom learner? The truth of the matter is that in classroom language research, the same processes involved in naturalistic second language acquisition (or better yet the results of such processes) are observed in the verbal behavior of formal learners in spite of attention to grammar and grammar practice.

Ellis has documented classroom/naturalistic comparisons in English as a second language and concludes that: "the picture which emerges from these three studies is that learners rely on natural processing mechanisms which in the long run cannot be short circuited by manipulating the linguistic environment of the classroom" (1984:40). Specifically, he found that the order of emergence of grammatical forms could not be altered by instruction and that mid and late acquired items in naturalistic language learning are also mid and late acquired items for classroom learners.

In a detailed longitudinal study of the acquisition of the two Spanish copulas ser and *estar*, I reported (VanPatten, 1985a) that the subjects demonstrated strikingly similar patterns of development in the acquisition of these verbs in spite of order of presentation, amount of practice, and overall individual differences in achievement. I concluded that "natural" processes documented in second language acquisition could not be suppressed by classroom instruction in grammar and that the subjects in my study were acquiring the Spanish copular verbs in accordance with how these natural processes interacted with the input (see VanPatten, 1988 as well). More importantly, the so-called "better students" did not outperform others in the correct use of the copulas.

As one more example, Kaplan (1983) reports a preliminary investigation of the acquisition of two past tenses in French, the *passé composé* and the *imparfait*, by adult classroom learners. These learners were enrolled in a grammar-based curriculum that carefully moved from controlled practice to "free expression." Kaplan finds that she cannot account for learner performance vis-a-vis what occurred in instruction; that is, learner output does not resemble instructional presentation and/or practice. Interestingly, she concludes that Bickerton's model of tense-aspect acquisition in pidgins and creoles is the best explanation of her data!

When considering the acquisition of grammatical structures, then, it appears that classroom language learners may behave very much like their naturalistic counterparts. However, this observation should not lead us to the conclusion that formal instruction in grammar makes absolutely no difference. The effects of such instruction, moreover, are not necessarily those expected. Eubank reports on classroom learners of German in the U.S. He investigates the acquisition of negation, which, unlike negation in Romance languages, is a bit more complicated, involving several lexical items as negators, clause structure, and word order. Eubank carefully examined his subjects' use of negation during an entire year and compared the data with those reported on naturalistic learners in Germany, the "foreign guest workers." Eubank reports that both groups begin the acquisition of negation by placing the negator in front of the sentence. The next stage is marked by the placement of the negator inside the sentence for the naturalistic learners while their classroom counterparts place the negator in external sentence final position (i.e., the mirror image of stage one). In considering explanations for these differences, Eubank concludes that the classroom learners' variation was due to the special context of the early stage classroom where insistence on complete sentences carries over into spontaneous speech. Eubank's subjects all came from classrooms where there was a heavy emphasis on linguistic accuracy and an overriding concern for students to speak in complete sentences. His subjects were apparently using negation in a manner consistent with the following: first form a complete sentence, then add on negation.[1] This strategy got them caught in an unnatural stage, as Eubank observes, and was literally delaying their acquisition of negation.[2]

Any discussion of grammar instruction also raises the question of errors and error correction. This issue has been addressed by several scholars, but in reviewing the major studies treating error correction and grammar instruction in the early stages of acquisition, I could not find one study that clearly demonstrated that error correction makes a difference (see VanPatten, 1986). However, Lalande (1984) does report significant differences between groups receiving different types of correction in German as a foreign language, but the standard deviations of his control and experimental groups deserve close attention. The standard deviation of the control group changed little from pre- to post-treatment period; there was an increase of only 1.18. On the other hand, the standard deviation of the experimental group (the one receiving the special error correction) became larger (overall increase of 5.89). One of the more plausible explanations, then, for the significant differences in that study was that a handful of learners in the experimental group improved over time. This handful of learners was able to pull up the mean score of the experimental group to make a significant difference. There was no such "pull" on the mean of the control group. Whether or not error correction helped those in the experimental group is also debatable, when one carefully examines the way in which certain variables are not accounted for in the study (e.g., aptitude, motivation, outside exposure). One factor that Lalande mentions only in passing is avoidance. Since the experimental group used a self-correction technique and had to chart errors over time, it is quite possible that the students avoided certain structures over which they knew they had no control. Also since we are dealing with a highly monitored task, it would have been illuminating had aptitude measures been taken on each subject as part of the experiment. This would have shed light on whether error correction was really helping a large group of students or merely a few as suggested by the standard deviations.[3] In sum, the numbers from Lalande's study are clear; there was a significant difference. The interpretation, however, is questionable. (For further discussion of a focus on form in language teaching, see VanPatten, 1988.)

If we stop and think for a moment about what we know from cognitive psychology and the research on attention and effort in information processing, we might find some explanation for the conclusion that most beginning language learners cannot (not merely do not) benefit from much grammar instruction and error correction. Human beings are decidedly what cognitive psychologists call "limited capacity processors." This limitation means that at any given moment, only so much attention is available to a person to process incoming and outgoing information. This attention can be divided (very generally) among those processes that are controlled and those that are automatic. Controlled processes are those tending to involve conscious awareness and use of conscious attention, such as reading a recipe and baking a cake from it. Automatic processes are those that do not involve conscious awareness, such as the striking of typewriter keys by a skilled typist. Controlled and automatic processes are not mutually exclusive and generally operate at the same time. For example, as we drive, we use conscious attention and effort (i e., a controlled process) to read street signs, decide when and how to change lanes, make decisions about the best way to go from point A to point B. At the same time, we do not use conscious attention to shift gears and interpret the color of traffic lights. But again, we must be reminded in this picture that humans are limited capacity processors, so even the most mundane task of driving a vehicle can be affected if demands are placed upon conscious attention, e.g., driving in an unknown city during peak traffic hours; driving on freeways in Los Angeles for the first time; driving through fog.

Returning to language learners, who are typical limited capacity processors, we can imagine what it is like for them to try to produce speech when it is not an imitated or elicited response such as that in a drill or formal exercise. Tremendous demands are placed on the information processing network; vocabulary is recalled, the words are strung together, it must all "sound right" and all the while learners are worrying if they understood correctly, if their pronunciation is off, if others are listening, if the listener "likes" them. Needless to say, this added worry (i.e., anxiety) also drains off attention and effort and is evident in fluent adult native speakers of a language, for example, when one gets nervous speaking in public and speaks worse than in an informal chat with friends. In the best possible scenario, the beginning language learner cannot attend to errors and error correction should we wish it.[4] *Only later, when needed vocabulary comes easily, when phrases can roll of the tongue, as it were, will error correction be of any real value.* I am not referring to errors that occur during language arts activities or during formal practice, where the amount of conscious control of the learner is limited to that "spot" or "vacancy" that the teacher wishes them to fill. In those instances, error correction may be useful, but teachers should know if this kind of activity itself relates in any way to eventual fluency and/or accuracy.

What do the kinds of studies mentioned so far tell us about input? Overcoming naturalistic processes in the classroom is difficult if not impossible. We have probably wasted much time and effort in making grammar instruction central to the classroom, for learners unknowingly seek to interact (psycholinguistically, that is) with the meaningful input that they encounter.

In a certain sense, then, regardless of any deficiencies in the input hypothesis itself, Krashen is right to focus our attention on meaningful input in the classroom. He is right to encourage us to use the foreign language purposefully; if grammar instruction is not in itself determinant, *instruction involving language use must be*. However, before we jump on the input bandwagon and throw grammatical instruction out the window with the bathwater of a grammar-based curriculum, we should acknowledge one important point: that the majority of research we have on the matter deals with beginning learners. That is, we have no research on what grammar instruction and error correction might do to learners who already have some sort of productive linguistic system. Can such attention to form improve the quality of the speech of these advanced learners? This question is crucial and needs to be addressed in foreign language research. So, while we may justifiably assume that beginning stage learners are not affected by grammar instruction to any great degree, we should not extrapolate that to more advanced classroom learners.

Modifying the Input Hypothesis

Up to this point, it has been argued that early stage classroom learners do indeed interact with input to create linguistic systems and that the processes underlying this interaction are not easily suppressed, at least not by grammar instruction and error correction. Thus, rather than simply reject the input hypothesis as wrong, a critique of the input hypothesis must (1) show where the hypothesis is weak and (2) modify it so that input as a variable is not neglected in the classroom.

White (1985) offers one such approach. Rather than reject the input hypothesis outright, she argues that Krashen is incorrect in insisting that input be comprehensible. For White, it is often incomprehensible input that leads learners to make correct hypotheses about L2 structure as they literally struggle to make meaning out of an utterance. White also argues that purely comprehensible input probably does not contain all of the data necessary for learners to construct complete grammars of the L2 so that at some point (unspecified in her discussion) negative data or explicit instruction may be crucial for some structures to work their way into the acquired system. However, she states that "Krashen's emphasis on the Input Hypothesis has been useful in drawing our attention to the role of input, and to the degree to which acquisition is dependent on the learner. It would be a pity to discard the hypothesis because of its shortcomings; rather, we should aim at a far more precise characterization of the possible interactions between learner and input."

From an information processing perspective, I have attempted to characterize the interaction between learner and input not in terms of Krashen's acquisition/learning distinction, but rather along the lines of research on information processing, thus adjusting the hypothesis somewhat to conform to what is known about human memory and information acquisition. In my essay on communicative value (VanPatten, 1985b), I argue that the relative contribution to sentence or discourse meaning that form carries interacts with the acquisition of grammatical structure vis-a-vis the continuum between controlled and automatic processes. Briefly stated, learners interact with input to abstract meaning. The more meaningful an item, the more the information processing network is likely to pay attention to it. With repeated occurrences in the input, the processing of this form will become automatic. This process occurs with many forms. As more forms become processed automatically for meaning in the input, more attention and effort are released for the controlled processing of forms that were previously "ignored" in the input. Thus, in opposition to Krashen, I posit a role for both conscious and subconscious processes in acquisition (i.e., input to intake).

Finally, Michael Long has argued in several important papers (e.g., M. Long, 1985) that the input hypothesis is basically correct, that learners acquire by attending to input. Where Long differs from Krashen, however, is that he argues for input *plus* interaction and negotiation. In other words, learners cannot merely be talked at in the hopes that they will acquire language. Instead, learners must be active conversational partners who negotiate the quality and quantity of input they receive in order to pick up language. Thus, learners help to control the input they need so as to maximize acquisition. Long's position lies in stark contrast to Krashen's assertion that learners need only receive comprehensible input.

Where do these observations on input lead us in terms of a modification of Krashen's hypothesis? Accepting the crucial thesis that acquisition results from exposure to meaningful, communicatively centered input, three essential adjustments emerge. First, the hypothesis needs to include a role for incomprehensible input as an additional trigger for the acquisition of certain structures. Second, the hypothesis should include conscious processing of incoming input and should capture the move from controlled to automatic processing of meaning at the level of input-intake in L2 development. Finally, the hypothesis should state that learners must help to control and filter the input through interaction and negotiation.

Toward A Curriculum

Proficiency has captured the attention of the foreign language profession in the last five years. The U.S. government will not give out grants unless *proficiency* is a frequently occurring word in a proposal. The ACTFL education series now has *proficiency* in the title of the last three volumes. Workshops on proficiency testing, training, curriculum development, and other areas are common at regional and national FL meetings. In short, communicative competence is out, and proficiency is in (another baby and bathwater phenomenon?). As this "Proficiency Movement" gains momentum, we run the serious risk of losing sight of some of the findings of L2 arid FL research that have been discussed in this paper. The following two quotations serve as examples. They come directly from publications on proficiency as a means of organizing curricula:

> There should be a concern for the development of linguistic accuracy from the beginning of instruction. This hypothesis is implicit in some of the discussion in previous sections relating to the structuring of communicative and personalized practice *around grammatical features*. (Omaggio, 1984: 78; emphasis added)

> As we lead students through the testing sequence, we encourage them to realize that they must first acquire linguistic building blocks and tools and then, as soon as possible, begin to use the tools to put the blocks together. (Magnan, 1985: 129; emphasis added)

Important here is the importance given to linguistic accuracy in the early stages, the implication that syllabuses need to be grammatically based and sequenced, and the explicit claim that acquisition of form must always precede use. What should we interpret from this? Are we supposed to drill structures? Are we supposed to correct learner speech consistently and constantly? How much class time should be devoted to this linguistic accuracy? And, of course, the question that comes to this reader's mind is what is the evidence that we should proceed from form to function when indeed there is sufficient evidence from both classroom and non-classroom research showing that the acquisition of form often trickles down from interactive use?

This discussion should be construed as an attempt neither to criticize the AC*TFL Proficiency Guidelines* nor to give the reader the idea that teaching for proficiency has no redeeming value(s). To be sure, as we critically examine the proficiency movement, we must be careful not to do with it what the title of the paper implies: throw out any babies with the bathwater. Still, what is of concern here is how teachers react to statements such as the ones quoted above. I am concerned that many readers will interpret such passages as carte blanche for a focus on grammar and grammatical syllabuses in beginning language instruction to which is not a step forward in the history of the profession, but a clear move backward into the past, when structural linguistics and the concept of skill getting permeated language teaching. If we are not careful with proficiency teaching and testing, we may lose those insights into non-primary language learning that we have so painstakingly worked for over the last fifteen years. I have already discussed to some degree the idea that early stage learners interact with input to create linguistic systems in the early and intermediate stages of language development. Why, then, as we construct curricula around proficiency guidelines, should we ignore these research findings?

What I would like to do now is sketch out a very rough outline of what I believe to be a curriculum that both works with the processes of second language learning (i.e., it does not ignore input processing) and at the same time encourages development in those who choose a more advanced ability, e.g., language teaching majors and business majors.

In Figure 6, this sketch for a curriculum progression is offered. As is often the case, we tend to think of classroom language learning as first year "teach all grammar," second year review, and third year review and amplification, rather than consider language learning as a continuum or progression. For this reason, I purposely avoid quantitative temporal measurements and instead use the terms *early stage, intermediate stage,* and *advanced stage* to reflect terminology from language acquisition. These stages should *not* be construed as equivalencies of first year, second year, third year.

FIGURE 6

A Suggested Outline for Curriculum Progression		
Early stage	Intermediate stage	Advanced stage
—focus on input and interaction	—focus on input/interaction; begin to focus on output	—focus on output
—reference grammar	—some explicit grammar practice	—explicit teaching of marked grammatical items
—learner interests	—focused error correction	—substantial error focus
—journal writing	—move from journals to composition writing	—composition as process
—reading	—reading comprehension via content matter	—special tracks

As is seen, the early stage curriculum is characterized by a heavy emphasis on input and interaction with input. Grammar instruction is relegated to reference material that students may use should they choose to, especially as a follow-up to communicative interaction rather than as a predecessor to the interaction. This stage may resemble the "natural approach" (Terrell, 1982), but with an addition: since we are dealing with academic environments, reading skills development (not reading for acquisitional purposes) is added. That is, learners can indeed be taught to extract meaning from texts that contain structure and vocabulary outside their competencies if taught to do so. In other words, reading is not included to provide more input or to reinforce structure and vocabulary (as most textbook readings are designed to do); rather, students are taught to read for the sake of reading itself (see Bernhardt, 1986). Writing is included as a personal experience and also as a reflection of developing oral competence. We allow writing here to mirror spoken language, as is generally the case for most beginning learners.

The intermediate stage of the curriculum would continue many natural approach activities, but would allow certain other activities to trickle in. Input and interaction are still central, but there is an emerging focus on form via some explicit grammar teaching and a very focused error correction, e.g., on early- and mid-acquired items, dependent upon individual variation. Writing as a process will cease to be a mere reflection of speaking and instead will begin to resemble composition writing, with such things as directing learners to paragraph formation, and writing introductions and conclusions (both of which will have been "previewed" in the reading skills development begun in the first year). In many ways, content language learning would make good sense here. Learners could enroll in language classes that have focused topics,—e.g., the geography of Latin America,—in which they continue to interact with input, but the emphasis is no longer on the here and now of the early stages. Their acquired and still developing reading skills could be put to work as learners read authentic materials in the target language on the course topic(s). Focused grammar attention will occur as they learn to edit compositions/essays on related topics.

The advanced stage would leave behind natural approach activities as they are currently formulated and would adopt a more focused skills development when learners' needs for language use become clearly defined. Thus, French for commerce, Spanish for legal purposes, literature courses, and the like would all work on specific skills related to their own domains. Since by this point the learners will have some productive oral ability (but more advanced listening, reading, and writing abilities), the overt teaching and practice of more marked features of a given language make sense for these features can be mapped onto a linguistic system.

Such a curriculum progression calls not only for a rethinking of what should occur in beginning language courses, but also for what should occur in more advanced classes. All too often students in advanced courses, such as literature and culture/civilization, are ignored as language learners. Once out of specific courses such as "advanced grammar" and "composition," it is generally assumed that language learning is "over" and it is time for more serious work. Such could not be further from the truth, and if we are to really make headway in terms of producing more students with functional language abilities, then opportunities for and activities in language learning must somehow be built into advanced courses as a regular component.

Conclusion

As Garrett (1986) notes, much acrimony has developed in the profession over the role of grammar instruction, and the input hypothesis has certainly sparked controversy. Yet arguments over grammar instruction have not carefully considered either existing research on the matter or the fact that most comments have implicitly dealt with early stage learners and not the "total" curriculum. Furthermore, arguments over the relative merit of monitor theory, particularly the input hypothesis, have generally resulted in a de-emphasis of input (clearly not warranted at this point). What is needed is a *better* hypothesis than we now have about learner interaction with input, not a rejection of input.

Input notwithstanding, the profession needs to move from a concern for early stage instruction and traditional concepts of first year, second year review, third year advanced grammar, etc. to a global perspective on language learning. Curriculum planners need to consider how learners get from point A to point B and eventually to point Z in language acquisition, and build curricula around these observations. Needless to say, research in the areas of intermediate and advanced stages of acquisition is crucial.

Notes

1   On the other side of the coin there is reported evidence that instruction in grammar is useful to beginning language learners. This evidence must be viewed with caution, Pica, in a frequently cited article (1983), reports that her English as a second language subjects in a strictly formal environment outperformed naturalistic and "mixed" learners on the use and suppliance of two grammatical forms: third person -s and plural -s. However, these data are inconclusive in that Pica used speakers of two radically different dialect groups of Spanish as a first language. The principal dialect of the naturalistic learners was a Caribbean dialect noted for aspiration and deletion of final -s. The formal language learners were from the Mexican Plateau and belonged to a dialect that does the exact opposite: strengthens final consonants and weakens vowels, sometimes dropping them, thus creating consonant clusters in final position that do not occur in other Spanish dialects. One very likely interpretation of Pica's results, then, is that the formal learners transferring native dialect phonology, which boosted their performance on final -s morphemes. This is quite probably what happened since there were no differences between groups on the performance of other grammatical items.

In another vein, Higgs and Clifford (1982) report that an emphasis on linguistic accuracy in the early stages is necessary in order to prevent fossilization. As l have argued elsewhere (VanPatten, 1988), there is no evidence for this in Higgs and Clifford's presentation and their conclusions on the role of grammar instruction are premature. Higgs and Clifford's "data" consist entirely of experience, as they themselves point out, and nowhere are we presented with empirical findings that can be subjected to close analysis.

Of relevance here as well is Michael Long's well-known review of the literature on the effect(s) of instruction (1983). Reviewing studies on English as a second language, Long concludes that there is an effect of instruction on language learning. This effect entails rate of acquisition of a few grammatical forms (e.g., third person -s but order of acquisition seems immutable (see VanPatten, 1984, and Wode, 1981 on natural orders and transitional stages). The items that seem to be "speeded up" by instruction are precisely those more marked and/or late acquired items, that generally can be described by "easy rules." Instruction does not seem to have much effect on early- and mid-acquired items, and in light of the discussion of Pica's data, the studies in Long's review must also be viewed with caution. However, as Long himself suggests, there is more going on in formal environments than mere grammatical practice. Thus, one cannot claim with assurance that the grammatical focus of the language class is what aids acquisition.

2   Garrett (1986) advocates a rethinking of grammar. Roughly speaking, she proposes that we replace traditional notions of it with what she calls "processing grammar," i.e., how meaning is encoded in form. This suggestion has some intuitive appeal, since learners naturally seek to map meaning to form as part of language development. However, we should be cautious with the idea of processing grammar(s) in the same way she advocates caution with traditional grammar(s). Whenever we attempt to compartmentalize language via linguistic structures, we run the risk of repeating what many cite as the ALM failure: reducing language learning to atomistic approaches to syllabuses and instruction. Furthermore, Garrett's conceptualization of processing grammar fails to deal with two major sources of difficulty in the acquisition of grammar: highly marked forms and redundant or meaningless ones. It is hard to see how grammar concepts such as arbitrary concordance can be taught or learned via processing. Until the idea of processing grammars is more fully developed, it is best not to consider its merit in the present discussion.

3   Attention must be drawn to another study on error correction in foreign language,—English as a foreign language in Japan. In this study, the authors have found that "practice in writing over time resulted in gradual increases in the mean scores [for accuracy] of all four groups . . . regardless of the method of feedback they received" (Robb, Ross, & Shortreed, 1986: 89).

4   Even experienced language learners may not fare better than naive learners. Savignon (1983) recalls an interesting episode in which she was a student in a beginning Spanish class and was on the receiving end of error correction. She remarks how she was too "flustered" to attend truly to error correction when she was in the limelight and that correction was literally lost on her.

References

Bernhardt, E. (1986). Reading in the foreign language. In B. H. Wing (Ed.), *Listening, reading, and writing: Analysis and application* (pp. 93–112). Middlebury, VT: Northeast Conference.

Dvorak, T. R. (1986). Writing in the foreign language. In B. H. Wing (Ed.), *Listening, reading, and writing: Analysis and application* (pp. 145–167). Middlebury, VT: Northeast Conference.

Eckman, F.R. (1985). Some theoretical and pedagogical implications of the markedness differential hypothesis. *Studies in Second Language Acquisition, 7*, 289–307.

Ellis, R. (1984). *Classroom second language development.* Oxford: Pergamon.

Eubank, L. (in press). The acquisition of German negation by formal learners. In B. VanPatten, T. R. Dvorak, J. F. Lee (Eds.), *Foreign language teaching: A research perspective.* Cambridge: Newbury.

Garrett, N. (1986). The problem with grammar: What kind can the language learner use? *Modern Language Journal, 70*, 133–148.

Gregg, K.R. (1986). The Input Hypothesis: Issues and implications. *TESOL Quarterly, 20*, 116–122.

Hatch, E. M. (1983). Simplified input and second language acquisition. In R. W. Andersen (Ed.), *Pidginization and creolization as language acquisition* (pp. 64–86). Rowley, MA: Newbury.

Higgs, T. V. (1985). The Input Hypothesis: An inside look. *Foreign Language Annals, 18*, 197–203.

Higgs, T. V., & Clifford, R. (1982). The push toward communication. In T. V. Higgs (Ed.), *Curriculum, competence, and the foreign language teacher* (pp. 57–80). Skokie, IL: National Textbook.

Kaplan, M. A. (1983). Developmental patterns of past tense acquisition among foreign language users of French. In B. VanPatten, T. R. Dvorak, & J. F. Lee (Eds.), *Foreign language learning: A research perspective.* Cambridge: Newbury.

Krashen, S. D. (1982). *Principals and practice in second language acquisition.* Oxford: Pergamon.

Lalande, J. F., II. (1984). Reducing composition errors: An Experiment. *Foreign Language Annals, 17*, 109–117.

Long, D. E., Pino, C. & Valdes, G. (1985). Building enrollment through curriculum change: The implementation of a comprehension based approach. *Foreign Language Annals, 18*, 413–425.

Long, M. H. (1981). Input, interaction and second language acquisition. In H. Winitz (Ed.), *Native and foreign language acquisition* (pp. 259–278). New York: New York Academy of Sciences.

Long, M. H. (1983). Does second language instruction make a difference? A review of research. *TESOL Quarterly, 17*, 359–382.

Magnan, S. S. (1985). From achievement toward proficiency through multi-sequence evaluation. In C. J. James (Ed.), *Foreign language proficiency in the classroom and beyond* (pp. 117–145). Skokie, IL: National Textbook.

Omaggio, A. C. (1984). The proficiency oriented classroom. In T. V. Higgs (Ed.), *Teaching for proficiency: The organizing principle* (pp. 43–84). Skokie, IL: National Textbook.

Pica, T. (1983). Adult acquisition of English as a second language under different conditions of exposure. *Language Learning, 33*, 465–497.

Robb, T., Ross, S. & Shortreed, I. (1986). Salience of feedback on error and its effect on EFL writing quality. *TESOL Quarterly, 20*, 83–95.

Savignon, S. J. (1983). *Communicative competence: Theory and classroom practice.* Reading, MA: Addison-Wesley.

Spolsky, B. (1985). Formulating a theory of second language acquisition. *Studies in Second Language Acquisition, 7*, 269–288.

Terrell, T. (1982). The natural approach to language teaching: An update. *Modern Language Journal, 66*, 121–132.

VanPatten, B. (1984). Morphemes and processing strategies. In F. R. Eckman, L. H. Bell, & D. Nelson (Eds.), *Universals of second language acquisition* (pp. 88–98). Rowley, MA: Newbury.

VanPatten, B. (1985a). The acquisition of *ser* and *estar* by adult classroom learners: A preliminary investigation of transitional stages of competence. *Hispania, 68*, 399–406.

VanPatten, B. (1985b). Communicative value and information processing. In P. Larson, E. L. Judd, & D. S. Messerschmitt (Eds.), *On TESOL 84* (pp. 89–99). Washington: TESOL.

VanPatten, B. (1986). Second language acquisition research and the learning/teaching of Spanish: Some findings and their implications. *Hispania, 69*, 202–216.

VanPatten, B. (1987). Adult learners' acquisition of *ser* and *estar*: Accounting for the data. In B. VanPatten, T. R. Dvorak, & J. F. Lee (Eds.), *Foreign language learning: A research perspective.* (pp. 399–406). Cambridge: Newbury.

VanPatten, B. (1988). How juries get hung: Problems with the evidence for a focus on form in teaching. *Language Learning, 38*, 243–260.

White, L. (1985). Against comprehensible input: The Input Hypothesis and the development of L2 competence. Paper presented at the LARS, Utrecht, Netherlands.

Wode, H. (1981). Language-acquisition universals: A unified view of language acquisition. In H. Winitz (Ed.), *Native and foreign language acquisition* (pp. 218–234). New York: New York Academy of Sciences.

Krashen's Acquisition Theory and Language Teaching Method

Karl Krahnke,
Colorado State
University, USA

The current state of methodology and of methodological discussion in language teaching is problematic. On the one hand, the only orthodoxy the field has known in recent decades, audiolingualism, has passed completely into history. While no equivalent orthodoxy has emerged, for some time we were (or "have been"—it is not altogether clear) offered a series of "innovative methods" (Blair, 1982), the study of which makes up the bulk of many methods courses. It is doubtful, though, that even taken together these innovative methods have had anything more than a marginal effect on actual classroom teaching.

On the other hand, strong voices are questioning the role of formalized methods altogether. Clarke's classic article on "bandwagons" (1982) suggested that formalized methods can inhibit the development of an open, individualized approach to a personal teaching style. That the article also suggested some positive, informing, and empowering roles for formalized methods is often forgotten. More recently, Pennycook (1989) and Clarke and Silberstein (1988) have raised questions about the social validity of methods, especially when they are prescribed by "experts" who are too often white male academics.

Underlying the problems raised by recent discussions of the value of formalized methods is the probability that few language teachers actually working in classrooms are tightly constrained by method not of their own choosing. While it is difficult to document this, suggestions from research (see Allwright, 1988, for one review) are that even when purporting to practice a method, teachers vary greatly in what they actually do in classrooms. In a sense, one woman's Silent Way is another man's Suggestopedia.

In such a climate, it is difficult to find a perspective from which to view the current status of method in language teaching or the effect of theory on it. But teaching a second language is not a random or haphazard act. All teaching, except the most unprincipled and chaotic, involves methodological decisions of some kind. Even the teacher who uncritically follows a routine of activities presented in a text is reflecting a complex of decisions about language teaching and learning. These decisions may be, and usually are, implicit or unconscious, but they may also reflect explicit beliefs or knowledge on the part of the teacher or materials writer. The methods are there, whether or not they are formalized or dictated.

For example, a teacher who selects vocabulary and structures from a reading passage and pre-teaches them before allowing the students to read the passage has made a decision about a classroom activity, and that decision reflects beliefs or knowledge about what reading is, how language texts are comprehended, how vocabulary is learned, the role of syntax in text comprehension, the role of vocabulary in text comprehension, learner strategies and expectations about reading in a second language, the specific abilities of the specific students in the class, and so on.

In this broader sense, any systematic teaching entails method, not necessarily either formalized or authoritarian. Method, in this sense, may be informed and principled or simply individually intuitive, and a method may be informed through research, through theory, or through analyzed or unanalyzed experience.

Thirty years of concentrated second language acquisition research has produced very little that is both conclusive and directly and positively relevant to classroom language teaching and learning (Lightbown, 1985; Ellis, 1990). Although many, myself included, had high hopes for direction from research, most fundamental pedagogical questions remain unresolved by evidence from research, just as with educational research in general. We are even beginning to see a welcome decrease in the gratuitous "application to pedagogy" sections of research articles. Even classroom-centered research has not produced a body of results that can be imported directly or indirectly into the classroom.

However, research interacts closely with theory, and the role of theory in shaping teaching method is more complex. In their well-known work, *Approaches and Methods in Language Teaching*, Richards and Rodgers (1986) distinguish approach, design, and procedure levels in the description of method. *Approach* refers to the theories of language and of learning underlying teaching methodology. *Design* refers to a number of factors, such as syllabus and objectives, roles for teachers and materials, and types of instructional activities. *Procedure* refers to the actual classroom techniques that are used in the teaching. The taxonomy helps us identify the place of theory in relation to overall language teaching method as one, divided element in a complex of considerations that can also, in a coherent method, drive many of the other elements.

The relationship between the general notions found at the approach level and the specific ones at the procedure level is not necessarily close or narrowly constraining. In the case of audiolingualism (the last clearly defined theory of learning in language teaching), the behaviorist theory of learning constrained classroom procedure rather narrowly, especially since it was accompanied by a rigid structuralist theory of language. With the constructs of reinforcement and habit formation, behaviorism dictated classroom procedures that clearly included repetitive drill on well-defined behavioral objectives with a minimum of mentalist explication or meta-knowledge.

On the other hand, the less well-defined cognitive-code theory of learning identified an end product or objective in language learning, learner-internalized rules, but did not define in a very specific way how those rules were to be established. Extensive and detailed metalinguistic explanation, followed by increasingly naturalistic practice, was one possible route to the learning of rules, but concentrated presentation (dialogs, stories, drills) and structured manipulation made up another possible route. Therefore, the two theories affected classroom practice or procedure in quite different ways.

When the theories specified at the approach level of language teaching provide specific descriptions of classroom procedure, teachers and instructional planners have little latitude in shaping classroom techniques if they adhere to the theory. When the theories are less specific, however, they may be both coherent and accurate but unable to specify very precisely what should happen in the classroom.

As I have pointed out elsewhere (Krahnke, 1985), Krashen's Acquisition Theory includes only a theory of language learning (or acquisition).[1] It does not directly address, and does not claim to address, the content of that learning or what Richards and Rodgers would call a theory of language. In addition, the constructs of Acquisition Theory are very broadly defined. As such, Acquisition Theory is a general theory of language learning/acquisition that does not specify in any precise way what classroom technique or procedure should be in any given case. To see this more clearly, the following section will review each of the hypotheses from the point of view of what they have and do not have to say about instruction.

The Acquisition/Learning distinction defines two types of language knowledge and the behavioral reflexes that they underlie. Acquisition is the knowledge leading to communicative performance, and learning is the knowledge leading to the ability to monitor. The A/L distinction also claims that one type of knowledge cannot significantly affect the other. As stated, this hypothesis has weak positive significance for classroom instruction, but the relationship is understandable only when the two types of knowledge are related to their respective causal factors, comprehensible input in the case of acquisition and metalinguistic instruction in the case of learning.

The Comprehensible Input hypothesis claims that acquisition of syntax results from an undefined quantity of experience of structures that are just beyond the present competence of the learner and that the learner experiences and comprehends in a context of meaningfulness. However, almost all aspects of CI are outside the classroom teacher's control. The teacher cannot practically determine readiness for acquisition, the degree of meaningfulness a particular language experience might have, or the degree to which it can be comprehended. Moreover, even the oft-construed negative significance of the CI hypothesis, that instruction in metalinguistic knowledge will not lead to acquisition, is erroneous, since, ultimately, any linguistic experience can serve as CI, whether it is a problem-solving exercise or a grammar lesson. What the CI hypothesis does is to suggest what kinds of experience are more likely to serve as CI in an abstract or general sense. The hypothesis cannot predetermine what will serve, since that is determined by individual learners in specific learning settings. The positive contribution of the hypothesis to instruction is that CI is more likely to be present, and acquisition to result, when the learner experiences a lot of the language (rather than a limited and simplified selection) and does so in a way that highlights the meaningful function of the new language forms. This emphasis on quantity and meaningfulness, though not new, is justified, if not explained, by the CI hypothesis.

The Monitor hypothesis operationalizes the construct of learning and provides a relatively well-defined role for the direct or primary benefits of a narrowly defined type of metalinguistic instruction. As such, it can positively provide a rationale for a limited amount of such instruction. What is undefined, however, is what secondary or indirect benefits such instruction may have, what the role of less rigidly defined, form-focused instruction (such as suggested by Higgs, 1985) might have, and how individual students might be able to use form-focused instruction as comprehensible input. The hypothesis does define a variable and useful role for monitoring, a more sophisticated definition of monitoring than popular conceptions such as "being careful to avoid mistakes" or "applying the rules you know" reflect. Overall, then, the positive contribution of the hypothesis is minimal.

The Natural Order hypothesis provides a general principle for the acquisition of some morphosyntactic phenomena, the principle being that some basic elements of morphology and syntax will be fully acquired in a generally invariant order relative to each other. When viewed against the overall task of language acquisition, however, the hypothesis says little about how vocabulary, pragmatics, phonology, and other aspects of language are acquired; little about the relationship of instruction to the order of acquisition (frequency of exposure and sequencing of instruction); and little about the well-documented individual variation in the order of acquisition. Again, the specific relevance of the hypothesis for instruction is low. Its major effect is negative, in that it makes the claim that students probably will not acquire morphosyntax in the order in which it is taught, although they may learn it in that order. So the hypothesis contributes very little to our understanding of classroom teaching and learning.

The Affective Filter hypothesis defines the facilitating and inhibiting factors in language acquisition (aptitude, motivation, anxiety). Krashen makes the claim that these factors increase or decrease the availability or usefulness of comprehensible input (and output). Once again, the constructs of the Filter are so broadly defined that it is practically impossible to determine in anything but the most general way what might raise or lower the Filter for a specific student in a specific instructional setting. The question of whether, in fact, the Filter can even be modified much at all is an empirical question not yet answered. This hypothesis, then, has a post-facto explanatory function but a weak to nonexistent directive or informing function regarding instruction. There is nothing contained in the hypothesis that can assist teachers in lowering the Filters of their students, other than the identification of the major types of affect that may be involved.

It is interesting to note that in *The Natural Approach,* the only means suggested for lowering the Filter is the use of "acquisition activities" (Krashen & Terrell, 1983: 97). I suspect that the use of such activities is neither a sure nor the only way to increase motivation and lower anxiety.

Therefore, the Affective Filter hypothesis loosely defines a teaching consideration, a consideration that can be used to explain after the fact why a specific student did or did not learn. But the hypothesis does not contribute much toward solving the problems that it identifies.

Acquisition Theory offers teachers direction through its theoretical statements themselves and through the "method" (the Natural Approach) that is based on the theoretical statements. In fact, many teachers even now consider the theory and the method based on it to be sound and useful. This seems to be least true of teachers in higher education, but in the hallways of many schools the terms "comprehensible input" and "affective filter" are more common than "topic sentence" or "verb error."

The plus side of the effect of Acquisition Theory on teaching method is that by its very generality, it allows for individual teacher interpretation and application. Each teacher can decide for himself or herself what constitutes comprehensible input in any given situation. Each teacher can decide how much form-focused instruction to include in the overall instructional mix. Each teacher can try to identify the affective factors operating in the classroom and to devise ways of minimizing their effects. Therefore, the practical, real-world effect of the theory on teaching practice is helpful to teachers in the sense that it suggests structured freedom and individual latitude rather than strict adherence.

I do an exercise in my own methods class in which I ask the students which formalized method they would most like to teach and which one they would most like to learn a language with. The perennial winner is the Natural Approach and the reason almost always given is that it is eclectic; it allows more freedom than other methods.

The negative side of Acquisition Theory's influence on method is that since it is limited to the learning side of approach, it does not help teachers strengthen their sense of what it is their students are learning or supposed to learn. I have anecdotally noted that few teachers who are strongly committed to an acquisition approach have much interest or sensitivity to the linguistic outcomes of the learning process. Admittedly, the theory suggests that these outcomes will be individual and, probably, delayed, but they still deserve attention. This lack of specific linguistic concern seems to reflect a more general lack of concern with outcomes. Acquisition Theory oriented teachers are more concerned with what they are providing their students than with what their students may or may not be doing with that input. Again, this is a broad generalization and one that is rationalized within the theory.

A common reception for methods is to regard them as resources for the eclecticism that many teachers prefer and claim to practice. If freedom and eclecticism are to be the preferred mode of operation for language teachers, the task of teacher education becomes even more difficult. How can teacher educators inform new teachers of the tradition in which they are planning to work? How can teacher educators contribute to the development of a discourse community of professionals? How can educators, to use the current jargon, empower teachers and not prescribe to them?

Unfortunately, then, Acquisition Theory tends to empower teaching method but not significantly enlighten it, and power without enlightenment is not necessarily fruitful. To paraphrase Derrida, deconstruction without a thorough knowledge of the tradition that is being deconstructed is simply chaos (Olsen & Gale, 1991: 130). Language instruction that is based on vague license with no knowledge of the context in which that license has developed and of what effects it will have also tends toward chaos.

In contrast to the methodological direction represented by Acquisition Theory and the Natural Approach, the proficiency movement (note the terminology) in foreign language teaching begins with a theory of language and a structured set of behavioral goals to which teaching can be directed, and the methods literature (e.g., Omaggio, 1986) provides methodological suggestions and "task hierarchies" (Swaffer et al. 1982) that can be used to teach toward the goals. This strikes me as a much more fruitful, enlightened enlightening, and even "empowering" way to inform method than to provide an overpowerful theory of learning that does not specify goals or outcomes at all or that provides essentially negative conclusions for teachers.

And, as much as we would like it to be positive, the essence of the Acquisition Theory/Natural Approach message seems to be that much of what teachers are familiar with doing will not be very effective (and provides "explanations" for the ineffectiveness) and that what teachers should do is some general activities aimed at generalized outcomes. While there is probably a great deal of truth to this view of teaching, in presenting it to many teachers I frequently encounter the question "How do I know if what I am trying is doing any good?" To which I find I have to respond, "Have faith." This usually elicits chuckles.

Some teachers, and some teaching enterprises, are comfortable with this undefined state of affairs. Many are not. But more importantly, the teacher who does not understand and appreciate the efforts that are still needed to prime the learning pump (provide motivation), to select and provide input in a maximally useful way, to provide feedback, and to evaluate more specific learning needs will do little more than bring street learning into the classroom.

In closing, I might add that I expect the teachers I teach to understand Krashen's Acquisition Theory. I present it not as the direct basis for what they will do in the classroom but, in addition to its descriptive value, for two other reasons. One is its value in identifying, labeling, and interrelating some of the more salient factors that appear in second language classrooms. It is useful to be able to refer to the Affective Filter and have some generalized understanding of what that entails. It is useful to talk about the proportions of comprehensible input versus instruction in form and the cognitive and behavioral outcomes expected from each of the types of input. And it is useful to be able to separate the function of Monitoring from less constrained occasions of language use. Therefore, the theory has a classificatory and descriptive function. Secondly, since the theory summarizes much of what we do know about research, it is useful in formulating plausible methods and techniques for different instructional settings, methods and techniques that, unlike many of the "pop" methods, have some sort of principled basis to them. In hypothesizing factors that operate in second language classrooms in positive and negative ways, the theory provides building blocks of practice that can be varied and manipulated. I find this approach much more educational than either a doctrinaire approach to teacher education that provides teachers with a single-explanation approach to method and a rigid set of techniques to follow or an approach that promotes unprincipled eclecticism by providing teachers with a dictionary of techniques and activities and the illusion that they are capable of uniting them into a coherent package with only their experience to guide them.

Notes

1   Although it has been variously named by others, I still find it convenient to refer to the body of Krashen's theory as "Acquisition Theory" and will do so throughout. My understanding of his work is based on his major publications regarding it (Krashen, 1981, 1982, 1985; Krashen & Terrell, 1983). No references will be made in this paper to specific publications by Krashen.

References

Allwright, D. (1988). *Observation in the language classroom*. London: Longman.

Blaire, R. W. (Ed.). (1982). *Innovative approaches to language teaching*. Rowley, MA: Newbury.

Clarke, M. A. (1982). On bandwagons, tyranny, and common sense. *TESOL Quarterly, 16*, 437–448.

Clarke, M. A., & Silberstein, S. (1988). Problems, prescriptions, and paradoxes in second language teaching. *TESOL Quarterly, 22*, 685–700.

Ellis, R. (1990). *Instructed second language acquisition*. Oxford: Basil Blackwell.

Higgs, T. V. (1985). Language acquisition and language learning: A plea for syncretism. *Modern Language Journal, 69*, 8–14.

Krahnke, K. (1985). Review of *The Natural Approach*. *TESOL Quarterly, 19*, 591–603.

Krashen, S. D. (1981). *Second language acquisition and second language learning*. Oxford: Pergamon.

Krashen, S. D. (1982). *Principles and practice in second language acquisition*. New York: Pergamon.

Krashen, S. D. (1985). *The input hypothesis: Issues and implications*. London: Longman.

Krashen, S. D., & Terrell, T. D. (1983). *The Natural Approach: Language acquisition in the classroom*. San Francisco: Alemany.

Lightbown, P. (1985). Great expectations: Second language acquisition research and classroom teaching. *Applied Linguistics, 6*, 173–189.

Olsen, G., & Gale, I. (Eds.). (1991). *(Inter)views: Cross-disciplinary perspectives on rhetoric and literacy*. Carbondale: Southern Illinois University Press.

Omaggio, A. C. (1986). *Teaching language in context: Proficiency oriented instruction.* Boston: Heinle & Heinle.

Pennycook, A. (1989). The concept of method, interested knowledge, and the politics of language teaching. *TESOL Quarterly, 23,* 589–618.

Richards, J. C., & Rodgers, T. S. (1986). *Approaches and methods in language teaching: A description and analysis.* Cambridge: Cambridge University Press.

Swaffer, J. K., Arens, K., & Morgan, M. (1982). Teacher classroom practices: Redefining method as task hierarchy. *Modern Language Journal, 61,* 325–337.

Part 4   The Panacea Fallacy

Introduction
to Part 4:
The Panacea Fallacy

In the final section of this volume our two contributors—Janice Yalden (Canada) and Christopher Brumfit (UK)—take up a point that has recurred throughout the book: it concerns the feasibility and, even more, the wisdom of adopting a universal theory of language development. More even than the details of Krashen's theory (and both agree that forcing people to think more cogently about their problems has certainly had its beneficial aspects), they question—indeed, deny—the propriety, on both academic and social grounds, of setting out a scheme that by its very plausibility positively invites abuse.

Yalden offers "more of a meditation than a response," motivated first by her concern about the relationship between theory in linguistics and theory in second language learning/teaching. Theories like those of Krashen lie outside language teaching and cannot properly be used as a basis for language teaching theory; moreover, in trying to derive a language teaching theory from the Monitor Model, Krashen and Terrell have not in fact produced anything new.

Citing the conventional portrayal of the dire state of language teaching in the USA pre-Krashen, Yalden queries Krashen's diagnosis. (If neither need nor opportunity exists, there is no revolutionary situation!) When the need for foreign language proficiency was perceived, there was indeed a tendency to seek facile innovations and shortcuts, whereas language teachers should map out their curriculum according to their own peculiar circumstances, and the only function of external theories is to inform, not to prescribe. Krashen's basic error is to draw conclusions about language teaching from research on something else. Like Freudenstein and Dunlop (see Part III), Yalden deplores the fact that Krashen and Terrell (*The Natural Approach*) make no reference to European applied linguistics, in particular to Wilkins' functional/notional approach or to the work of the council of Europe Modern Languages Project. In *The Natural Approach*, the authors have set aside, neglected, and even discredited other equally valuable work. In a sense, by its retroactive orientation it runs counter to more recent developments.

Brumfit, though well-known on both sides of the Atlantic for the breadth and humanity of his vision, bases his stance also in European language teaching. Discussing Krashen as a "social phenomenon," he is concerned primarily with his impact on teachers. Krashen's many merits include the fact that he is a serious scholar who writes clearly, refuses to isolate himself from practical teaching concerns, and is intellectually ambitious. A tendency to repetitiousness and vagueness is not important, but apparently peripheral comments do indicate a deeper problem.

For instance, Krashen's reference at the Georgetown Round Table to eclecticism as being an "intellectual obscenity" indicates a view of language teaching that calls into question the whole of his activity. Taking an analysis of Krashen's Georgetown paper as his main theme, Brumfit, like Yalden, queries Krashen's diagnosis concerning the perilous state of language teaching in the USA, finding his conclusion that this resulted from the application of the wrong theories to be totally misguided. It is Krashen's whole concept of the proper role of a theory of language teaching that is at fault. Sound practice will take account equally of research, ideas, and intuitions.

Echoing Littlewood's portrayal of reluctant learners, Brumfit calls for a more sensitive system than can be afforded by the adoption of any one prescriptive theory. Like Ellis and others, Brumfit feels that Krashen's lack of sensitivity to social contexts is a major deficiency. A theory, however cogent, can never be more than partly relevant; the lure of certainty and simple rules of thumb invite trivialization and sloganizing.

Language acquisition theory and teaching practices need to be compatible, but they cannot be identical. The mismatch between researchers' expectations and teachers' needs will be resolved only when more people are enabled (and paid) to be both researcher and teacher, and when teacher training and retraining are no longer perceived only in terms of managerial skills. The teaching profession is not a machine but a social organism; understanding must come from within, not from an externally imposed theory.

The Quest for a Universal Theory

Janice Yalden,
Carleton University,
Ottowa, Canada

There is no doubt that Stephen D. Krashen's work has made a great impact on second-language teaching in North America. It has forced reconsideration of the premises on which practice in language teaching rests. Reactions to it have been intense; there have been beneficial spinoffs at many levels of instruction (e.g., Wesche, 1984, 1985). However, the title of this collection of papers implies that Krashen, through his research in second-language acquisition, has raised questions that require responses or reactions. What I want to provide in this contribution is more of a meditation than a response. It is written from the point of view of my concern with the relation of theory in linguistics to theory of second language teaching. I shall endeavor to make two points:

1. That theory of second-language teaching operates in a manner defined by its own imperatives and that it cannot be driven by theory from outside; theories of natural first- or second-language acquisition such as Krashen's Monitor Theory lie outside the domain of language teaching; they cannot therefore be used directly as the basis for a language teaching theory.

2. That in trying to build an approach to second language teaching directly upon his Monitor Theory, Krashen and his co-author Terrell have failed to produce something distinctive; there are other approaches that are extremely similar but that are based on different premises.[1]

Let us look first at language teaching theory vis-a-vis the Monitor Theory and its applications. In recent years, several dimensions have been added to the former. Language teaching theory is seen today as drawing not on one discipline only, but on a set of disciplines. Although models differ, these basic disciplines are usually taken to be theoretical and descriptive linguistics, sociolinguistics, psycholinguistics, and education (Strevens, 1985; Stern, 1983; Richards & Rogers, 1982; Spolsky, 1978; Kaplan, 1980).[2] While one may debate the degree to which each discipline has contributed, and the value of their respective contributions, they have nevertheless all contributed. Sociolinguistics and psycholinguistics are both relatively new fields and thus relatively new contributors to second-language teaching theory. Descriptions of language and educational theories are both much older sources. It follows that when one assesses what language teaching was about at some point in the past, it is wise to do so in terms of the theory available at that time. It is equally desirable to recall the social and cultural context of the period.

Krashen and Terrell argue that the general public had in about 1949 recognized the "failure of the language teaching profession" (1983: 13) and, as a result, embraced audio-lingual methods. As evidence of this failure, they cite a survey indicating that enrollments in language courses were very low, and that as late as 1956 foreign language courses were not being provided in 56% of secondary schools in the U.S. However, one cannot help wondering whether this lack of interest in other languages in North America stemmed from the unsatisfactory psycholinguistic theory underlying teaching methods—as Krashen and Terrell imply—or from lack of need and opportunity to acquire second languages.

Krashen and Terrell state that

> It is almost a paradox that what man seems perfectly equipped to do when the need and opportunity arise—acquire the ability to communicate in another language—seems so elusive to language classes and instructors in North American education. We believe that one of the primary reasons is that educators have been misled by innovations and shortcuts. . . . The mistake the innovators have made is to assume that a conscious understanding of grammar is a prerequisite to acquiring communicative competence. (1983: 16)

There are more than a few problems with this statement. If there is neither perceived need nor opportunity available, it is not surprising that the ability to learn another language is elusive. One may well agree that there have been too many innovations and shortcuts; to make the leap from these statements to declaring that the innovators' error was to assume that a conscious understanding of grammar was a prerequisite to acquiring communicative competence is to posit intellectual attitudes that did not exist at the time. In fact, communicative competence as understood in *The Natural Approach* may not have been the goal of instruction at all prior to 1949.

It is also well to remember that there is still very little perceived need for learning second languages in North America. Krashen and Terrell themselves state that "in the United States it is not necessary to be able to communicate in another language in order to do business or travel. . . ."(1983: 65). Seen in this light, it is perhaps less paradoxical that more Americans do not communicate easily in foreign languages.

None of this means that language teaching should stand still. But the way in which it takes up contributions from the basic disciplines has altered. Rather than adopting a single "method" wholesale, language teachers map out a curriculum or at least a general approach, taking into account the most useful available theory, but not necessarily using it directly. Rather, theory from the different branches of linguistics *informs* language teaching theory. Understanding linguistic theory is useful—wholesale application is not. There is feedback from language teaching experience to theory—and possibly feedback into linguistic theory as well.

Furthermore, language teaching means working in a classroom setting. And this means planned intervention between language and learner. It is not the same as natural or untutored language acquisition. However, Krashen belongs in the tradition of linguists who are tempted to draw direct conclusions about language teaching from research on something else. This has led to some questionable statements about the Natural Approach. For example, it is stated that it is similar to other communicative approaches. This is of course true in that it draws almost entirely upon established techniques of classroom instruction, but it is also stated that what makes the Natural Approach exceptional is that the latest research in first and second language acquisition supports its tenets very strongly. Yet Krashen and Terrell state that the Natural Approach is highly flexible and is able to incorporate any of the techniques of Suggestopedia, Total Physical Response, Silent Way, or Counseling-Learning where appropriate, without depending exclusively on any of them (1983: 17).

I find this puzzling. If one can draw upon any of these techniques (and others that have been in use for many years without the benefit of a methodological label), what is the advantage of giving them a psycholinguistic substructure *a posteriori*? Is this not what occurred when behaviorist theories of language were used to support audio-lingual methodology?

Furthermore, in the present case one finds that many of the statements made about the Natural Approach could just as well be made about other communicative approaches now in existence. For instance, "the goal of the *Natural Approach* is to produce *optimal* Monitor users, performers who put conscious grammar in its proper place. . . . *If our observations about individual variation are correct, they imply that* formal grammar instruction does not have a central place in the curriculum, but it does have an important role to play" (1983: 45, italics mine). This could be rewritten as follows: "The goal of any communicative approach is to produce performers who put conscious grammar in its proper place. Formal grammar instruction does not have a central place in the curriculum, but it does have an important role to play." This statement describes not *the* Communicative Approach, but the general communicative approach to second-language teaching—an approach based upon contributions from all the basic disciplines, and not upon one to the exclusion of the others.

Another example may be in order. The authors of the Natural Approach state that "spoken fluency in second languages is not taught directly. Rather, the ability to speak fluently and easily in a second language emerges by itself, after a sufficient amount of competence has been acquired through input. It may take some time before any real spoken fluency develops" (1983: 20). One might have said the same thing about the grammar-translation method. Indeed, I can remember similar statements being made by its defenders when audio-lingual methodology was being introduced, on the grounds that spoken fluency was not a reasonable objective for classroom teaching.

What is meant by "theory" in language teaching is being looked at from new perspectives (see Stern, 1983; Brumfit, 1984). The net result is to lift the weight of linguistic theory from language teaching and abandon the attempt to do the teacher's job for him or her. This takes me back to my main point: language teaching theory is not linguistic theory. Current discussion of this issue is clearly a response to the presence of scores of methods based on various approaches to preparing the content of language courses. No one approach has yet yielded a method proven to meet all needs. Yet the search for universally applicable principles of course design and materials preparation continues, is probably unstoppable, and perhaps even beneficial since it stimulates discussion and formulation of new hypotheses for research. Krashen's theories have received a great deal of attention in this adventure— but has he been tilting at windmills?

The second point I wish to make is that many of the conclusions regarding changes required in language teaching that appear in *The Natural Approach* have been arrived at by others as well, via routes rather different from the application of the Monitor Theory. It is striking that in Krashen and Terrell's historical review of past practice (1983: 7–17), there is little or no account taken of social change as it may relate to second language learning and teaching, except for a reference to World War II. Yet changes in society elsewhere and the contributions of sociolinguistics have produced a new appreciation of the goals of second-language teaching. In particular, Krashen and Terrell make no reference at all to European applied linguistics. Changes in society in post-war Europe, together with newer theories of language as communication, have caused a complete revision of the goals of instruction in second languages. And widely known communicative approaches to second-language teaching have been developed to meet these goals.

A comparison of the general approach, goals, and teaching techniques in *The Natural Approach* and the European communicative approaches reveals numerous similarities. For example, there is a table in Finocchiaro and Brumfit, (1983: 91–92) comparing Audio-Lingual and Functional-Notional methodology. The description of Functional-Notional methodology does not differ substantially from the description of the Natural Approach. Therefore, it seems evident that since the goals of the communicative approach are what they are and since the Natural Approach is a communicative approach, cur-riculum organization and teaching techniques as represented by Krashen and Terrell cannot be said to depend uniquely on Krashen's theories of second-language acquisition.

Let me illustrate further. *The Threshold Level* (van Ek, 1980) was first published by the Council of Europe in 1975. It contains very extensive speci-fications of instructional objectives, in terms of situations, topics, language functions, general and specific notions, and language forms. Eight of the fourteen topics that appear in Chapter 8 also appear in Krashen and Terrell's list of "Goals in a Natural Approach Class" (1983: 67).[3] The latter list is in fact a mixture of topics, functions, and notions (as well as a category designed to elicit certain grammatical forms—"narrating past experiences," "childhood experiences," "adult expectations and activities"—of a kind long familiar in language teaching). The point is, once again, that they can be derived as well from Wilkins' work as from Krashen and Terrell's.

As far as methodology goes, what is gathered together in *The Natural Approach* is a cross-section of communicative techniques. It is well known that Asher's TPR techniques form the basis of the initial period of classroom work in the Natural Approach. The problem-solving activities, the work in "inferencing" strategies in reading, communicative problems in writing—no matter how these are labeled, they are all part of a general movement over the past fifteen years toward communicative techniques of second-language teaching. The pages of journals and teachers' reviews such as *English Lan-guage Teaching Journal* and *Modern English Teacher* and of textbooks in English as a second language will yield many examples. It is most gratifying to see them collected together and made available to teachers of languages other than ESL. But it should be recognized that many such techniques had been developed in the 1970s, largely as a result of the developments in English for specific purposes. And the theory that supports their use is not the Monitor Theory, but the work of linguists who belong to a different tradition, and have stressed social aspects of language in their work on language as communication far more than has Krashen.

The Natural Approach is a useful work. But in attempting to tie its communicative methodology so tightly and exclusively to Krashen's theory, the authors have set aside and neglected, if not discredited, other equally valuable work. The theory would have had an impact in any case—it was already being widely read and considered by applied linguists, language teachers, curriculum specialists and materials writers. It would surely have been preferable to allow this process to continue and to permit the theory to influence second-language teaching over the course of time. *The Natural Approach* is in fact an attempt to work out a retroactive theory of second-language teaching that runs counter to newer developments in second-language teaching theory. There is no reason to limit the fundamentals of language teaching theory to one basic discipline alone, and even though it fits into current thinking on communicative teaching, the results of so doing yield a methodology that is in no way distinctive.

Notes

1   I base my comments in this regard upon *The Natural Approach* (Krashen & Terrell, 1983).

2   See Stern (1983) for full discussion of these basic disciplines and especially for the chronology of their contributions to language teaching.

3   Compare *Threshold Level* topics 1, 2, 3, 4, 5, 7, 9, and 10 with *Natural Approach* Goals 1, 5, 4, 2, 9, 7, 10, and 8, in that order.

References

Brumfit, C. (1984). *Communicative methodology in language teaching.* Cambridge: Cambridge University Press.

Kaplan, R. (1980). *On the scope of applied linguistics.* Rowley, MA: Newbury.

Krashen, S., & Terrell, T. (1983). *The natural approach.* Oxford: Pergamon.

Richards, J., & Rogers, T. (1982). Method: Approach, design, and procedure. *TESOL Quarterly, 16*, 153–168.

Spolsky, B. (1978). *Educational linguistics.* Rowley, MA: Newbury.

Stern, H. H. (1983). *Fundamental concepts of language teaching.* Oxford: Oxford University Press.

Strevens, P. (1985). Language learning and language teaching: Towards an integrated model. LSA/TESOL Institute 1985: Forum Lecture.

Wesche, M. (1984). A promising experiment at Ottawa University. *Language and Society, 12*, 20–25.

Wesche, M. (1985). Immersion and the universities. *Canadian Modern Language Review/Revue canadienne des langues vivantes, 41*, 931–940.

The Linguist and the Language Teaching Profession: Ghost in a Machine?

Christopher Brumfit, University of Southhampton, UK

This paper is concerned with Krashen as a social phenomenon in the language teaching world. Other papers in this volume have considered strengths and weaknesses of his theoretical positions, and I have argued elsewhere about conceptual problems with some of his proposals (Brumfit, 1983). This paper addresses a more modest aspect of his work, but one that risks being neglected, for Krashen is an unusual phenomenon, whose influence in language teaching is analogous to that of Bernstein a few years ago in general education. Both are serious scholars, but the ways in which their work has been taken up and interpreted by the administrators and teachers who respond to it raise worrying issues of accountability and capacity for falsification.

However, I should start by making it clear that this discussion can only emerge from a perception located in European language teaching. I have met Krashen on a couple of occasions and have heard him speak only twice, though I have read most of his available writings and have taken part in many discussions of his work. My concern in this paper, though, is with the impact of his ideas on teachers (rather than researchers or academic commentators) particularly the impact of his writings and such performances as the BBC *Horizon* program. Krashen is an extreme example, and in many ways the most academically "respectable" example, of a general tendency to look for simple solutions to complex problems by attaching language teaching to the work of a particular publicist who is either a scholar or a successful teacher.

Let us first consider Krashen' strengths, for any attempt to assess him as a social phenomenon has to recognize that he shares with only a small number of writers on language teaching the capacity to challenge thinking outside the confines of universities and academic meetings. First, he is a scholar of great industry; few people have cited so many pertinent references in support of their hypotheses or worked so energetically to explore the implications of academic work for a language teaching theory. Second, he writes clearly, so many teachers can find his work accessible. Third, he has refused to isolate himself from practical teaching concerns; indeed he has been willing to work among and with teachers more extensively than many of his peers. Fourth, he is intellectually ambitious: the undertaking to produce a coherent model of second language learning indicates a wish to be evaluated only by the highest standards of scholarship.

Any critic of Krashen would have to concede these points. Critics should also, 1 think, acknowledge that other, superficially more irritating characteristics are understandable, given the way in which language teaching gurus currently operate. There is a great deal of repetition in his writings, but this is partly, one suspects, because good ideas bear repetition to different audiences, and most audiences demand publication as a spin-off of any lecture. And in any case, the proselytizer is bound to wish that worthwhile ideas be expressed at varying levels of sophistication to varying groups.

It is not the inevitable effects of being a popular and articulate commentator and theorist that should concern us about Krashen's role in the profession. Some of the criticisms that are casually voiced risk sounding like sour grapes rather than careful concern for the well-being of language teaching. Yet there is a real problem about presentation and attitude to teachers that is very difficult to talk about but essential to confront. Such concern may be seen more through asides than through central, published discussion. A remark at the Georgetown Round Table in 1983 to the effect that eclecticism was an "intellectual obscenity" has become legendary, but there is no indication in Krashen's published paper that any such casual bombshells had been exploded.

It would of course be easy to dismiss such a remark as being an off-the-cuff, insignificant comment with little more than amusement or phatic intention. But such a remark becomes apocryphal only because it reflects a general unease or neatly encapsulates a particular problem for the profession. The views of Krashen do indeed pose problems for the profession, not simply because of inconsistencies in the views themselves or possible deficiencies in the argumentation and exemplification (these are of course the normal currency of academic debate), but also because of the manner in which they have been both presented and taken up.

The "intellectual obscenity" remark is objectionable because it misunderstands the nature of teaching so grossly as to make teachers wonder whether someone who could say that has any understanding whatsoever of the nature of classrooms and the teacher's life. Teaching as a profession is a way of living one's life, and language teaching is part of that way. Because it is something you do, and only partially control, it is not capable of being reduced to a coherent series of hypotheses. Living is always eclectic, teaching is always eclectic, and language teaching is and always will be eclectic. Not to recognize this is to be blind to its reality; to insist on the need for intellectual consistency is one thing, but to denounce theoretical untidiness is quite another. It is particularly dangerous because it demands that teachers who are concerned with doing something complex and human should instead act as if they are, exclusively, thinkers concerned with clarifying and simplifying. The two of course interact with each other, but no service can be performed to the teaching profession by any insistence that in some sense tidiness and allegiance to one overarching theory for dealing with human beings are virtues.

It may well be felt by the reader that this makes too much of a casual remark. However, if we examine Krashen's paper at Georgetown, it is clear that there are more fundamental issues at stake. The next section of this paper will consider these issues more closely.

The Relationship Between Theory and the Preparation of Teachers: Problems with Krashen's Formulation

In this part of the paper I shall refer specifically to Krashen's paper at the Georgetown Round Table in 1983 (Krashen, 1983). This provides a convenient source for a consideration of his ideas on theory and its place for teachers, for the Round Table was concerned with "applied linguistics and the preparation of second language teachers" and the paper claimed to be developing a rationale for second language acquisition theory in the preparation of teachers.

Krashen begins this paper by asking what went wrong with the relationship between theory and the practice of teaching. Commenting that there is less applying of linguistics and more sharing of ideas that work than there used to be, he asks what caused this change. He correctly points out that methods claiming to arise directly out of academic theories did not achieve successful results and states that "the shift away from theory was thus caused by teachers' realization that theory had little to say to them. This has resulted in a rejection of all theory and in language teaching becoming a field more dependent on intuition and ideas than on research, a field prone to capricious change in method, a field in which eclecticism is considered a virtue" (Krashen, 1983: 255).

Now no one who writes in a collection such as this one need be accused of denying the importance of theoretical discussion, and it is important to echo Krashen's concern for a principled approach to language teaching.

Changes in method should not be "capricious;" teachers need theory. But that is not of course the same as the argument that language teaching, or any other teaching, is capable of the clear and predictable outcomes that need to be explored by a strongly research-based approach. There is no field of human social relations where ideas and intuitions should be denigrated, or seen as less important than research. We need all three, but the roles of each should not be confused. Krashen states that "the problem has not been theory, it has been our attempts to apply the wrong theories" (p. 256). It is the contention of this paper that this is a totally mistaken view: the problem has been far more our unwillingness to concede the limitation of theory.

At the same time it is necessary to admit the value of the exercise that Krashen has attempted to perform. Undoubtedly, we do need to produce models which claim to explain the nature of language learning and teaching. We do need to produce these as far as possible in the form of testable hypotheses, we do need to make use of as much empirical evidence as possible, through experiment, observation, and evaluation. We do need to relate evidence from other relevant disciplines to our needs as language teachers. All of these activities will help in dispelling myths, clarifying intuitions, enabling us not only to state that certain procedures "work," but some reasons "why they work." And of course it is on the basis of the latter statement that the profession will make such progress as it is capable of, for it is only by knowing why things work that we can adapt procedures to new situations and consequently address the fluctuating and unstable world of real social institutions and real learners. All this has great value. The only problem is the unstable world to which language teachers (and learners) belong and with which they must interact. Language teachers are more akin to social workers, marriage guidance counselors, career advisors, and even priests or parents than they are to lawyers, accountants, or even doctors. They are concerned with processes of development (especially when they are involved with school-level work) that are deeply embedded in the personal self-concepts and needs of learners. A small number of learners may be able to distance themselves sufficiently from other aspects of their lives to treat language learning as an abstract exercise, but these will normally be experienced adults with money and independent motivation. They are sufficiently rare phenomena for generalizations about language teaching to be able to see them as peripheral to the major concerns of a language teaching theory. Typical learners, for most teachers, will be relatively insecure, relatively unmotivated, relatively confused, and relatively uncooperative. Teachers have a responsibility to make the insecure secure, the unmotivated motivated, the confused clear thinking, the uncooperative cooperative. To do this they need skills that interact with those associated with language learning theories but that must be sensitive to students' personal and group individualities and to their constantly changing circumstances. The best teachers are able to do this, sometimes with the help of applied linguistic theories, sometimes without or in spite of such theories. But the skills required to perform a true teaching role must take us far beyond anything a theory based on a single area of the curriculum can produce. It is for this reason, primarily, that theory is wrongly seen as irrelevant; it is not actually completely irrelevant, but it is partially irrelevant, and good teachers will always recognize this, whatever educational theorists or linguists try to tell them.

Furthermore, given the diversity of ways in which individuals have successfully learned languages in the past, the theory drawn from applied linguistics is, for some teachers at least, apparently capable of being dispensed with altogether. As long as the general conditions of exposure to language, opportunity to use or interact with the language, and motivation to do this are met; the other non-linguistic skills of teachers will carry them through many teaching situations. Teachers need to be able to interact, empathize, respond, praise, and motivate before they need to know what they are doing in terms of language acquisition models. None of this is to deny the value of what Krashen does, nor of the research, even the thinking and intuitions, of himself, his rivals, and his critics. But the limits must be seen. A heavy emphasis on psycholinguistic theorizing does more harm to teaching than a heavy emphasis against, even though both positions are inadequate for the best language teaching.

Krashen continues to define theory and observes, with a hint of sympathy for the position of this paper (alas, not fully developed elsewhere), that theory cannot be our only source of information about language teaching—though he links this rather curiously with the assertion that theories are always tentative. Theories are of course only valid until they are falsified, but why this should have any implications for their value or otherwise for language teaching is unclear: it is not only theory that is provisional, it is all knowledge.

The next section of Krashen's paper usefully distinguishes between pure and applied research. However, the examples of applied research that are given provide some cause for alarm. The global questions asked—e.g., "Do students taught by method A perform better than students taught by method B?"—are examples of questions that can be answered only in a trivial sense. The concerns of the 1960s with major methodological comparisons led to extensive criticism of such all-embracing questions (see, e.g., Freedman, 1971, 1982) as it became clear that variables could not be controlled and the components of "method" either had to be trivialized or proved too complex to enforce on either teachers or students. Too theoretical a disposition leads us only to see what we can measure and to ignore what, inconveniently, we cannot—for example, the subtlety of interaction that results in one teacher being universally liked and another being merely respected.

Nonetheless, the distinction is useful, and so too is the insistence that research needs to be mediated by adequate hypothesizing directly relatable to classroom practice. It is presumably something like this that "armchair theorists" who are dismissed earlier in the paper are actually engaged in doing, unless Krashen has encountered theorists whose views on language teaching are based on something other than reading research and the experience of teaching and learning languages.

This leads Krashen to an exemplary discussion (p. 261) of the relationship between general theory and teaching methodology, concluding with the observation, frequently made but still worth repeating (and indeed the theme of these comments on Krashen), that teaching is an art as well as a science.

So it may appear that Krashen concedes the basic point, and indeed he does in principle. But the notion of teaching as an art requires more careful examination. The objections to eclecticism, the demand that we need a theory, the determined exposition of the theory to teachers, and the advocacy with Terrell of a particular "method" all tend to undervalue the "art" side and to play up the "science." It is precisely because Krashen claims to speak with authority on language teaching on the basis of a research background that the strengths of teachers become undervalued. In this respect he is of course no more than the most prominent of a number of theoreticians, but his success highlights the defects of a theory-led approach to language teaching.

The problem for anyone who operates in the international and national circuits is to prevent oneself from claiming to present a "truth" rather than one of a large number of possible hypotheses from which teachers may select according to their assessment of need, intuition, or even willingness to experiment eclectically! There is always a tendency for large institutions (and language teaching, especially English language teaching, has all the characteristics of a large institution) to prefer certainty to uncertainty. Academics have a responsibility to resist this tendency, even though publishers, understandably concerned with a clear marketing strategy, and teaching methodologists, less justifiably concerned with "simple" rules of thumb, will always push for the easily comprehensible at the expense of the truthful.

In spite of Krashen's attempts to link his scientific position to a general Popperian-type epistemology (e.g.,1982: 2), the effect on language teaching has been to breed a distrust of traditional procedures, with unclear indications of what, in terms of the hypotheses, should go in their place. If learning cannot "become" acquisition, for example, then either most language teaching in the past two thousand years has been mistaken or Krashen's formulation of the nature of learning is far away from what most teachers understand by the term in practice. But because this idea has become a slogan, it has been used in teachers' discussions to justify having no advanced planning at all, having no knowledge of language (because knowledge of language for teachers will only lead to students "learning"), and refusing to allow students to consult grammar reference books even when they so wish. All these arguments I have heard passionately advanced as central positions for language teaching on the basis of views attributed to Krashen.

Now of course we cannot hold any scholars too closely responsible for the more extreme views of their less subtle disciples. But we may ask whether scholars distance themselves sufficiently from the practical and contingent realities of classroom experience.

The difficulty is that a Popperian view of the progress of science positively demands clear cut hypotheses, because they need to be explicit enough to be falsifiable. Therefore, scholars need hypotheses to be expressed in stark and challenging forms, precisely so that they may lead to appropriate experimentation and refutation. But teaching, including language teaching, does not typically progress by confrontation and revolution. When these do occur, the social structure suffers and the necessary confidence between the masses of learners and the large numbers of teachers is destroyed. In periods of major political upheaval, when teachers represent a politically coercive force, such loss of confidence may be necessary or unavoidable. But teaching methodologies for specific subjects should be attacked this strongly only when the intention is political rather than narrowly pedagogic. Pedagogic confrontation of this kind will distort professional expertise because of the insensitivity of the cutting edge for research being applied to the living tissue of social and personal needs. It is this living tissue that is the concern of the teaching profession, and few people who have not been teachers for several years at least will appreciate its quality. Indeed, there are many who have taught for extended periods who remain unaware of the clumsiness of their professional activity.

Unless the limitations of a research or theoretical perspective are recognized, there will continue to be a mismatch between the perceptions of practitioners and the expectations of researchers from outside. However carefully Krashen tries to write about the role of "ideas and intuitions" (1982: 4–5), there will be a weakness unless it is acknowledged that teachers do not simply have "ideas" but—at best—coherent positions that are in principle incapable of being subjected to empirical tests in terms of any one discipline but that provide them with an integrated basis for effective and sensitive teaching.

Toward an Interactive Base for Teaching Theory

The language teaching profession is not a well-ordered machine waiting for life to be injected through a series of theoretical pronouncements from external disciplines. And all study of matters relating to teaching is external by definition. Second language acquisition theory needs to be compatible with the practice of teaching, as much as teaching needs to be compatible with second language acquisition theory. But neither can usefully identify with the other, for their intentions are, and must remain, different. The intention of research is to understand; the intention of teaching is to facilitate learning. Those who are good at the latter will not necessarily have the skills to evaluate the former, while those who are trained in research will not have the experience to be able to understand the teaching process unless they have also had substantial experience in being an ordinary teacher.

Teachers do not have time to survey authoritatively the research literature on which commentators like Krashen base their hypotheses, and only rarely will they have the expertise to evaluate it. They will necessarily be dependent on the opinions of the commentators. But they are even more dependent on researchers not moving beyond their own expertise, for researchers carry status, have easier access to publishers and conferences, and can thus persuade the teaching profession more readily than fellow teachers can. It is easy to despise the informal, generally unacademic, predominantly interactive skills of teachers, when set against those required of researchers, but this is to confuse teaching skills with those of research. While we all want teachers, like any other professionals, to make intelligent appraisals of their role and its effectiveness, it is unreasonable to deny them prime expertise in the activity at which they spend most of their time.

But a position such as this only partially resolves the problem of mismatch between researchers' expectations and teachers' needs. There are of course many teachers whose "methodology" is reduced to nothing more effective than coping strategies, whether because of overwork, overstrong tradition, heavy bureaucratic control, or sheer human weakness. We still need criteria for improvement and means of distinguishing the good teachers from the rest, the positive aspects of methodology from the negative, the helpful learner environments from the obstructive.

Such improvement will only come if two administrative changes occur. First, the divide between teachers and researchers, theorists and commentators needs to be crossed by having more and more people who operate sometimes as teachers, sometimes as writers and researchers. But such people must be able genuinely to cross the boundaries; at the moment there is plenty of loose research done by teachers and plenty of loose teaching done by people whose prime concern is research or discussion. Only when funding agencies allow teachers to research into their own or others' teaching, not as token teachers but as genuine researchers, with a full-time (even if temporary) commitment will the divide be crossed effectively.

The second change that is necessary is for openness of argument to be encouraged between teachers and theorists. What teachers desperately lack is range: most are aware of work in their own time in their own place. Problems that are urgent and contingent occupy them from hour to hour. Academics and others with interests in the teaching profession are able to make comparisons, refer to experiences in other places and times, and think about their implications. The movement in Britain to encourage in-service training as a pulling oneself up by one's own bootstraps is as dangerous as a movement (more common in the U.S., perhaps) to follow the advice of a guru and believe in the catch phrases of scholarship. Either extreme leads to arrogance, which performs a disservice to teaching and learning. If Krashen's career illustrates some of the risks of dependence on scholarship for a rich and subtle mode of human interaction like teaching, current policies for making teacher education precisely practical at the local level entail the opposite risk. Curiously, both approaches suffer from the same defect: they are essentially managerial, for they presume that a limited set of trainable skills or a clear set of principles can be incorporated simply into the complexity and mishmash of real lives that constitute any class. Both models sound impressive to the manipulative mind of a bureaucrat, but both are fundamentally and literally inhumane. The parts of education that can be made more "efficient" are relatively unimportant in the process of teaching learning. Of course teachers need to manage themselves efficiently, and of course they need to think clearly about what they do, but what they do arises out of what they are, and what they are only they will truly understand. It is when teachers are encouraged to reflect on their own work, and research into their own work, with the same standards of rigor that are demanded of doctors or lawyers (to give two other professional examples) that the temptation to call upon outside researchers to resolve their problems will be rendered unnecessary. Teachers who can be both genuine teachers and scholarly investigators of their own condition need far more support than they have traditionally been given.

The teaching profession is not a machine but a social organism, all the parts of which interact intimately together. The process of understanding must come from within. Insofar as current practices in teaching methodology lead to judgments on what teachers should do coming from outside the teaching profession itself, they will distort the progress of the profession. Insofar as Krashen is representative of this tendency, his work entails risks that we should be unwilling to accept.

References

Brumfit, C. J. (1983). Some problems with Krashen's concepts "acquisition" and "learning." *Nottingham Linguistic Circular, 12,* 95–105.

Freedman, E. S. (1971). The road from Pennsylvania—where next in language teaching experimentation? *Audiovisual Language Journal, 9,* 33–38.

Freedman, E. S. (1982). Experimentation into foreign language teaching methodology: The research findings. *System, 110,* 119–133.

Krashen, S. D. (1982). *Principles and practice in second language acquisition.* Oxford: Pergamon.

Krashen, S. D. (1983). Second language acquisition theory and the preparation of teachers: Toward a rationale. In J. E. Alatis, H. H. Stern, & P. Strevens (Eds.), *Applied linguistics and the preparation of second language teachers: Toward a rationale* (pp. 255–263). Washington, D. C.: Georgetown University Press.

Appendix   Topics for Discussion

Monitor Theory: Application and Ethics
Peter af Trampe

1. How, by whom, and on what grounds do you think a theory of second language learning is judged as good or bad?

2. What can we do to safeguard against the application of bad theories and misapplication of good ones?

3. Suppose you find some regular pattern of learning (e.g., a certain acquisition order for a number of morphemes) across language learners. What different explanations could there be for the appearance of such a pattern?

4. What cues could you as a teacher (or, for that matter, interlocutor) use to assess the state of an FL learner's competence in the foreign language? Discuss also the kind and precision of information that each type of cue yields.

5. Krashen arid Terrell stress that language input to the learner should be comprehensible arid interesting. However, this goal is not all that easy to achieve. List some of the problems, and discuss what could be done to solve them.

Krashen's Theory, Acquisition Theory, and Theory
Kevin Gregg

1. In what ways is Krashen's use of the LAD insufficiently incorporated into his theory of second language acquisition?

2. Gregg tells us that Krashen offers us an acquisition theory, not a pedagogical theory. Discuss the differences between these two types of theories. Is one more applicable to L2A than the other?

3. Make a list of the kinds of errors (phonological, morphologic, syntactic) that native speakers make but are not possible for non-natives. What implications do these errors have for a theory of second language acquisition?

4. Comment on Krashen's claim that "adults can access the same natural 'language acquisition desire' that children use."

5. In your classroom, do you teach structures in a "predictable order?" Why or why not?

The Anti-Pedagogical Aspects
of Krashen's Theory of Second Language Acquisition
Waldemar Marton

1. Do you think that teaching theory and practice should:

   a. totally disregard the natural processes of first and second language acquisition on the assumption that they cannot be replicated in the classroom anyway?
   b. try to imitate and recreate these processes in classroom learning as much as possible, with a minimum of pedagogical interference?
   c. adopt these processes as the underlying basis but at the same time strive to improve on them and make them more efficient by various typically pedagogical devices?

   Justify your position, and criticize the two other solutions.

2. Krashen's prescription for remedial teaching is simply to provide a lot of comprehensible input containing frequent occurrences of troublesome items. Describe another solution that would be more sophisticated from the pedagogical point of view.

3. What pedagogical dangers do you see in an attempt to replicate the natural acquisitional process in an acquisition-poor environment, e.g., in the conditions of a non-intensive course in a foreign-language context?

4. Do you agree that the notion of the three basic language teaching strategies presented in this paper constitutes a universal framework, in terms of which all the language teaching methods and procedures can be classified? List three language teaching methods that have been found to work, and try to classify each of them as receptive, communicative, or reconstructive (or, at least, as predominantly receptive,etc.).

5. List three procedures or techniques that have been used in language teaching but that would be probably rejected by the majority of language educators today. Explain why they should be rejected.

Comprehension and Production: The Interactive Duo
Wilga M. Rivers

1. Discuss ways in which the subconscious command of one's native or mother language assists the language learner in acquiring the second language.

2. Krashen hypothesizes that fluency in a second language comes from what we "pick up," i.e., what we acquire in natural communicative situations. The rules learned in the classroom, he posits, are not responsible for fluency. What implications does this have for the language classroom and the texts that are published for the teaching of a second language?

3. Given the constraints of classroom contact hours in high school as well as college, how realistic is it to delay production of student speech?

4. In what ways will focusing on semantic rather than syntactic clues help students to retain meaning and thus become better language listeners?

5. Rivers states that comprehending a new language "is a lengthy and demanding process." Why is this so?

The Impact of Interaction of Comprehension
Teresa Pica, Richard Young, and Catherine Doughty

1. Discuss the two modes for acquisition in NNs' comprehension of input. Which do you think gives students the most help in negotiating meaning?

2. Relate Krashen's "i + 1" to the research done by Hatch and Long, two researchers mentioned in this article.

3. The authors rejected conventional paper-and-pencil tests of listening comprehension and instead choose communication games to elicit responses from the student group. Why do you think they did this?

4. Why do you think that a decrease in the complexity of the input did not affect comprehension?

5. Select an ESL or foreign language textbook, and discuss the ways in which the textbook writer has premodified the input. How would you alter the text to support the authors' claim that ungraded syllabuses and materials may provide input that will become comprehensible"?

The Case for Learning
Carlos Yorio

1. Discuss ways in which L2 learners can increase their proficiency by developing more sophisticated learning/monitoring abilities.

2. Cite examples from Yorio's paper to show that relying on acquisition strategies is not enough to ensure success in L2.

3. How would you individualize a language class for students with serious fossilized forms that impede communication?

4. In the author's acquisition of English as a second language, he made discoveries about techniques he used for "repair." Think of other strategies that you use or have used in repairing your own output of a second language.

5. In your own experience in acquiring a second language, what structures did you monitor? Why were these structures monitored more heavily and not others?

Variability and the Natural Order Hypothesis
Rod Ellis

1. How do we determine what acquisition has taken place? The introduction to this paper discusses which type of performance provides the best indicator of what acquisition has taken place. This is an important question both for the SLA researcher and the language teacher. Reread the paragraph that outlines the basic options, and then discuss which option you think is most relevant for the language teacher.

2. Give examples of the following types of variability from either your own use of languages or from classroom L2 learners you have taught:

   a) Free variation
   b) Contextual variation according to linguistic environment
   c) Contextual variation according to situational context

3. The paper criticizes the Monitor Model's account of variability in SLA on the grounds that it lacks a "social dimension." Explain why a "social dimension" is important for understanding SLA and how it can account for variability.

4. The paper argues that "there is no single order of acquisition. . . . Different orders will arise from different kinds of language use." Summarize the arguments and evidence used to make this claim. What implications does this claim have for language teaching?

5. This distinction between "acquisition" and "learning" is the cornerstone of the Monitor Model. In what way does an understanding of variability challenge the distinction? What alternative is suggested, and how useful do you find this for language teaching?

Rules, Consciousness, and Learning
Peter af Trampe

1. To what extent do you think that the teaching materials that you are familiar with show the written language bias? Try to find evidence for this bias in some materials and grammars that you work with.

2. List and discuss the usefulness of various techniques used by teachers to direct learners' conscious attention towards a particular form, contrast, structure, etc. in the FL.

3. In the "Rules in the Classroom" section a chain of "rule events" is briefly described. Recapitulate this section and discuss in more detail what may cause distortions between successive events (i.e., between different manifestations of the original rule of language).

4. Discuss the different roles that rules may play in the classroom and what effect this may have on the learning process.

5. How would you go about testing the hypothesis that rules presented in the classroom cannot serve as blueprints for (conscious or subconscious) rules of language?

Monitor Theory in Classroom Perspective
Teresa Pica

1. For the language that you teach, make a list of "easy" and "hard" rules. Which rules are most likely acquired in a formal classroom setting, and which can be acquired from conversational input?

2. In what ways does the ongoing research project of Pica, Doughty, and Young support Krashen's theory of comprehensible input?

3. Can you think of ways in which your language classroom can be made less pedagogically oriented and more real-world oriented?

4. Design some information-gap tasks for your second language learners. Follow their progress in order to determine if less teacher-oriented activity leads to greater communicative success.

5. Why do you think so much criticism has been made of "i +1"? Do you feel the criticism is justified? Why or why not?

Krashen and the Captive Learner
William T. Littlewood

1. Imagine a teacher who has been trained, like Mrs. Walters, to be a "deviser of techniques to control learning." What new knowledge and skills will become necessary when she decides to broaden this role and become also a "creator of environments to facilitate acquisition"?

2. In the light of your views about learning and acquisition, draw up a coherent set of guidelines that would help a teacher work out his or her approach to dealing with learners' errors.

3. List some of the common activity types that you organize in the classroom. Try to categorize them into "monitored" and "unmonitored" activities. To what extent do you feel satisfied that two separate categories of activity can be distinguished in this way? Or is it a question of a particular activity being "more or less" monitored?

4. It is easy to see that natural acquisition processes take place in natural environments. However, it is not easy to decide what elements in the environment are crucially important for triggering these processes. In your view, what features are likely to be crucial for enabling natural acquisition to take place? Do these features include any that, in your view, cannot be reproduced in the classroom situation?

5. What factors do you see as contributing towards a "high affective filter"? If possible, categorize these factors according to whether they have their source in (a) the individual learner's psychological make up; (b) the nature of the classroom situation; (c) the effects of certain teaching methods; or (d) the wider sociocultural setting in which learning takes place. In what ways can a teacher attempt to change these factors and thus help to lower the learners' affective filters?

The Natural Approach and Language Teaching in Europe
Reinhold Freudenstein

1. Try to identify classroom activities of the "Natural Approach" that are new and unique.

2. Krashen advocates the use of the target language only in foreign language instruction. Can you think of situations in which the use of the mother tongue is necessary or helpful?

3. Try to name at least five European language experts who have influenced American foreign and second language studies during the last ten years, and characterize their contributions.

4. What does the application of the "$i + 1$" formula in concrete teaching situations really mean?

5. What is more important in foreign and second language teaching and learning the teaching method or individual learning preferences? Why?

The True and the New
Ian Dunlop

1. Why does Lenneberg's biological theory of language appeal to the author?

2. How does Krashen differ from Lenneberg in his views on language acquisition?

3. What examples does the author give of Krashen being "true but not new"?

4. In the IEA tables, what does Listening correlate best with in both the English and French studies and at both age levels?

5. With what does the author agree with Krashen, and on what points does he take issue with him?

On Babies and Bathwater: Input in Foreign Language Learning
Bill VanPatten

1. Of Krashen's five hypotheses, why do you think criticism has focused primarily on the Input Hypothesis? Relate any experiences you may have had as either a teacher or a learner of a second language to the function of comprehensible input in accelerating the acquisition of a second language.

2. Discuss how a teacher's insistence on linguistic accuracy of a particular language structure might interfere with a student's acquisition of that structure. Can you provide examples from your own classroom experiences as either a teacher or a learner of a second language?

3. What demands are placed on the second language learner when asked to produce spontaneous speech? Relate your response to VanPatten's contention that language learners are "typical limited capacity processors."

4. Why is error correction of little value for the beginning language student? If you are a second language teacher, think about errors you correct and what, if any, benefits are derived by the student from your corrections.

5. Discuss the three adjustments to Krashen's Input Hypothesis suggested by VanPatten. Are all three valid? Would you make additions?

Krashen's Acquisition Theory and Language Teaching Method
Karl J. Krahnke

1. Write some classroom activities for your second language classroom that will provide your students with a maximum amount of comprehensible input.

2. Describe some of the methods courses you were required to take to teach a second language. Which ones have provided you with teaching techniques that have been indispensable to your classroom?

3. What types of basic communicative skills are most appropriate for your students? Does AT account for these skills?

4. Comment on the author's claim that research provides very little to the second-language teacher.

5. Discuss the kinds of acquisition activities you have incorporated into your classroom. Have they increased motivation and lowered anxiety?

The Quest for a Universal Theory
Janice Yalden

1. Can language teaching expect the same kind of input from each of the basic disciplines identified in Yalden's article? How might input from each be used?

2. List some possible contributions to language teaching from other disciplines/areas of knowledge.

3. To what extent do non-linguistic factors determine the goals of language learning?

4. How might a change in the goals of a second language course affect the methodology used in it?

5. The expressions *language for communication* and *language as communication* have appeared frequently in discussions of applied linguistics and language teaching in recent years. Locate and compare several definitions of these expressions. What else can language be?

The Linguist and the Language Teaching Profession: Ghost in a Machine?
Christopher Brumfit

1. To what extent are academic scholars responsible for the beliefs of their followers? Is it their responsibility to distance themselves from simplistic interpretations?

2. Are there other ways of understanding classrooms than teaching in them? Can we "understand" something we have experienced only briefly?

3. What does it mean to say that teachers "are more akin to social workers ... than to lawyers, accountants, or even doctors"? What distinguishes teaching from other professions?

4. Can we evaluate methodology? How much does it depend on intangible factors such as teacher and student personalities, social climate, and administrative support? Are factors like these measurable?

5. Are language teachers different in crucial ways from teachers of other subjects? Does it make sense to have a language acquisition theory for teaching, independent of a general educational theory?

Due to publisher's error, the following bibliographies were inadvertently omitted from the printed version of *Beyond the Monitor Model: Comments on Current Theory and Practice in Second Language Acquisition*, Ronald M. Barasch and C. Vaughan James, editors.

This bibliography accompanies "Monitor Theory: Application and Ethics" by Peter af Trampe, and should appear following page 36.

References

Berenstein, B. (1971). *Class Codes and Control*, Volume 1. Theoretical Studies towards a Sociology of Language. London: Routledge & Kegan Paul.

Brumfit, C.J., & Johnson, K. (Eds.). (1979). *The Communicative Approach to Language Teaching*. Oxford: OUP.

Burling, R. (1982). *Sounding Right*. Rowley: Newbury House Publishers.

Candlin, C.N. (Ed.). (1981). *The Communicative Teaching of English*. Harlow: Longman.

Carey, S. (1978). The Child as a Word Learner. In Halle, M., J. Bresnan & G.A. Miller (Eds.), *Linguistic Theory and Psychological Reality*. Cambridge, Mass.: The MIT Press.

Clark, H.H., & Clark, E.C. (1977). *Psychology and Language*, New York: Harcourt, Brace Jovanovich, Inc.

Gregg, K.R. (1984). Krashen's Monitor and Occam's Razor. *Applied Linguistics*, 5:2, 79-100.

Hakuta, K. (1976). Prefabricated Patterns and the emergence of structure in second language acquisition. *Language Learning 24*, 287-98.

Hatch, Marcussen E. (1983). *Psycholinguistics*. Rowley, Mass.: Newbury House Publishers, Inc.

Hawkins, E. (1981). *Modern Languages in the Curriculum*. Cambridge: CUP.

Hesse, M.G. (Ed.). (1975). *Approaches to Teaching Foreign Languages*. Amsterdam: North Holland Publishing Co.

Hulstijn, J.H. (1982). *Monitor Use by Adult Second Language Learners*. Dissertation, University of Amsterdam.

Krashen, S.D. (1978). The Monitor Model for Second Language Acquisition. In R.C. Gingras (Ed.), *Second Language Acquisition & Foreign Language Teaching*. Washington: Center for Applied Linguistics.

Krashen, S.D. (1981.) *Second Language Acquisition and Second Language Learning*. Oxford: Pergamon Press.

Krashen, S.D. (1982). Accounting for Child-Adult Differences in Second Language Rate and Attainment. In S.D. Krashen, R.C. Scarella & M.H. Long (Eds.), *Child-Adult Differences in Second Language Acquisition*. Rowley, Mass.: Newbury House.

Krashen, S.D., & Terrell, T.D. (1983). *The Natural Approach*. Oxford: Pergamon Press.

Labov, W. (1966). *The Social Stratification of English in New York City*. Washington: Center for Applied Linguistics.

Labov, W. (1971). The Study of Language in its Social Context. In J.A. Fishman (Ed.), *Advances in the Sociology of Language I*. The Hague: Mouton.

Long, M.H. (1985). A Role for Instruction in Second Language Acquisition: Task-Based Language Training. In K. Hyltenstam & M. Pienemann (Eds.), *Modelling and Assessing Second Language Acquisition*. Clevedon: Multilingual Matters Ltd.

McLaughlin, B. (1978). The Monitor Model: Some Methodological Considerations. *Language Learning 28*, 309-332.

Munby, J. (1978). *Communicative Syllabus Design*. Cambridge: CUP.

Nelson, K. E. (1981). Toward a Rare-Event Cognitive Comparison Theory of Syntax Acquisition. In P.S. Dale & D. Ingram (Eds.), *Child Language–An International Perspective*. Selected Papers from the First Intern. Congress for the Study of Child Language. Baltimore: University Park Press.

Pienemann, M. (1984). *Learnability and Syllabus Construction*. In Hyltenstam & Pienemann (Eds.), *Modelling and Assessing Second Language Acquisition*. Clevedon: Multilingual Matters Ltd.

Skutnabb-Kangas, T. (1976). Bilingualism, Semilingualism and School Achievement. *Linguistische Berichte, 45*, 55-64.

Stubbs, M. (1976). *Language, Schools and Classrooms*. London: Methuen.

Wilkins, D.A. (1976). *National Syllabuses*. Oxford: OUP.

Wong Fillmore, L. (1979). Individual Differences in Second Language Acquisition. In C.J. Fillmore, D. Kempler & W. S-Y. Wang (Eds.), *Individual Differences in Language Ability and Language Behavior*. New York: Academic Press.

This bibliography accompanies "The Anti-Pedagogical Aspects of Krashen's Theory of Second Language Acquisition" by Waldemar Marton, and should appear following page 69.

References

Ausubel, D. P. (1968). *Educational Psychology: a Cognitive View.* New York: Holt, Rinehart and Winston.

Bialystok, E., & Fröhlich, M. (1977). Aspects of second language learning in classroom settings. *Working Papers on Bilingualism, 13,* 2-26.

Canale, M., & Swain, M. (1980). Theoretical bases of communicative approaches to second language teaching and testing. *Applied Linguistics, 1,* 1-47.

Carroll, J. B., 1974. Learning theory for the classroom teacher. In Jarvis (1974), 113-149.

Carroll, J. B. (1975). *The Teaching of French as a Foreign Language in Eight Countries.* Stockholm: Almqvist and Wiksell.

Clark, H.H., and Clark, E.V. (1977). *Psychology and Language: an Introduction to Psycholinguistics.* New York: Harcourt-Brace-Jovanovitch.

Diller, K. C. (1971). *Generative Grammar, Structural Linguistics, and Language Teaching.* Rowley Mass.: Newbury House

Dodson, C.J. (1972). *Language Teaching and the Bilingual Method.* London: Pitman. First published 1967.

Galperin, P. Ia. (1970). An experimental study in the formation of mental actions. In Stones (1970), 142-154.

Hammerly, H. (1985). *An Integrated Theory of Language Teaching and its Practical Consequences.* Blaine WA: Second Language Publications.

Harley, B. (1985). Second language proficiency and classroom treatment in early French immersion. Paper presented at FIPLV, Eurocentres Symposium on Error in Foreign Language Learning, London, September.

Henzel, J. (1978). *Nauczanie Języka Rosyjskiego Metodą Reproduktywno-Kreatywna.* Kraków: Wydawnictwo Naukowe WSP.

Jarvis, G.A. (Ed.). (1974). *The Challenge of Communication.* ACTFL Review of Foreign Language Education, Vol. 6. Skokie IL: National Textbooks.

Krashen, S. D. (1981). *Second Language Acquisition and Second Language Learning.* Oxford: Pergamon Press.

Krashen, S. D. (1982). *Principles and Practice in Second Language Acquisition.* Oxford: Pergamon Press.

Krashen, S. D., Terrell, T. D. (1983). *The Natural Approach: Language Acquisition in the Classroom.* Oxford: Pergamon Press.

Krashen, S. D. (1985). *The Input Hypothesis: Issues and Implications,* London and New York: Longman.

Leontiev, A. A. (1981). *Psychology and the Language Learning Process.* C.V. James (Ed.). Oxford: Pergamon Press.

Lewis, E.G., Massad, C.E. (1975). *The Teaching of English as a Foreign Language in Ten Countries.* Stockholm: Almqvist and Wiksell.

Long, M. H. (1983). Does second language instruction make a difference? A review of research. *TESOL Quarterly, 17, 3:* 359-382.

Marckwardt, A. H. (1975). Changing winds and shifting sands. *English Teaching Forum, Special Issue: The Art of TESOL, Part 1, 13:* 41-43.

Mason, C. (1971). The relevance of intensive training in English as a foreign language for university students. *Language Learning, 21:* 197-204.

Omaggio, A. C. (1983). Methodology in transition: the new focus on proficiency. *Modern Language Journal, 67:* 330-340.

Palmer, H. E. (1964). *The Principles of Language Study.* London: Oxford University Press.

Palmer, H. E., & Redman, H. V. (1969). *This Language-Learning Business.* London: Oxford University Press.

de Sauzé, E. B. (1959). *The Cleveland Plan for the Teaching of Modern Languages with Special Reference to French: Revised Edition.* Philadelphia, Pa.: Winston.

Sharwood Smith, M. (1981). Consciousness-raising and the second language learner. *Applied Linguistics, 11, 2:* 159-168.

Sorace, A. (1985). Metalinguistic knowledge and language use in acquisition-poor environments. *Applied Linguistics 6, 3:* 239-254.

Stevick, E. W. (1980). *Teaching Languages: A Way and Ways.* Rowley, Mass.: Newbury House.

Stones, E. (1970) *Readings in Educational Psychology: Learning and Teaching.* London: Methuen.

Strevens, P. (1980). *Teaching English as an International Language: From Practice to Principle.* Oxford: Pergamon.

Talyzina, N. (1970). The stage theory of the formation of mental operations. In Stones. (1970), 155-162.

Upshur, J. (1968). Four experiments on the relation between foreign language teaching and learning. *Language Learning 18*: 111-124.

Wygotski, L.S. (1971). *Wybrane Prace Psychologiczne.* Transl. into Polish by E. Flesznerowa, J. Fleszner. Warszawa: Panstwowe Wydawnictwo Naukowe.

This bibliography accompanies "Variability and the Natural Order Hypothesis" by Rod Ellis, and should appear on page 158.

References

Adjemian, C. (1976). On the nature of interlanguage systems. *Language learning, 26*: 297-320.

Beebe, L. (1980). Sociolinguistic variation and style shifting in second language acquisition. *Language Learning, 30*: 433-47.

Beebe, L., & Zuengler. (1983). Accommodation theory: an explanation for style shifting in second language dialects. In N. Wolfson and E. Judd (Eds.), *Sociolinguistics and Language Acquisition*. Rowley, Mass.: Newbury House.

Bialystok, E., & Sharwood-Smith, M. (1985). Interlanguage is not a state of mind: An evaluation of the construct for second-language acquisition. *Applied Linguistics, 6*, 101-117.

Dickerson, L. (1975). Interlanguage as a system of variable rules. *TESOL Quarterly , 9*: 401-7.

Dickerson, L., & Dickerson, W. (1977). Interlanguage phonology: current research and future directions. In S. P. Corder and E. Roulet (Eds.), *The Notions of Simplification, Interlanguages and Pidgins*: Actes de 5eme Colloque de Linguistique Applique de Neufchatel, 18-30.

Downes, W. (1984). *Language and Society*. London: Fontana.

Dulay, H., & Burt, M. (1973). Should we teach children syntax? *Language Learning, 23*, 245-58.

Edmundonson, W. (1985). Discourse worlds in the classroom and in foreign language learning. *Studies in Second Language Acquisition, 7*: 159-68.

Ellis, R. (1985a). *Understanding Second Language Acquisition*. Oxford: Oxford University Press.

Ellis, R. (1985b). Sources of variability in interlanguage. *Applied Linguistics, 6*: 118-131.

Ellis, R. (1986). Interlanguage variability in narrative discourse: style shifting in the use of the past tense. *Studies in Second Language Acquisition, 8*.

Ellis, R. (forthcoming). Exploring the effects of linguistic environment in the second language acquisition of grammatical rules.

Fairbanks, K. (1982).*Variability in interlanguage*. Unpublished MS. University of Minnesota, Minneapolis.

Giles, H., & Byrne., J. (1982). An intergroup approach to second language acquisition. *Journal of Multilingual and Multicultural Development*, 3: 17-40.

Gumperz, J. (1982). *Discourse Strategies*. Cambridge: Cambridge University Press.

Hulstijn, J., & Hulstijn, W. (1984). Grammatical errors as a function of processing constraints and explicit knowledge. *Language Learning, 34*, 23-43.

Hyltenstam, K. (1985). L2 learners' variable output and language teaching. In K. Hyltenstam and M. Pienemann (Eds.), *Modelling and Assessing Second Language Acquisition*. Clevedon: Multilingual Matters.

Krashen, S. (1977). Some issues relating to the monitor model. In H. Brown, C. Yorio and R. Crymes (Eds.), *On TESOL '77*. Washington, D.C.: TESOL.

Krashen, S. (1982). *Principles and Practice in Second Language Acquisition*. Oxford: Pergamon.

Krashen, S. (1983). Newmark's "ignorance hypothesis" and current second language acquisition theory. In S. Gass and L. Selinker (Eds.), *Language Transfer in Language Learning*. Rowley, Mass: Newbury House.

Krashen, S. (1985). *The Input Hypothesis: Sources and Implications*. London: Longman.

Labov, W. (1970). The study of language in its social context. *Studium Generale, 23:* 30-87.

Larsen-Freeman, D. (1976). An explanation for the morpheme acquisition of second language learners. *Language Learning, 26*, 125-134.

Long, M., & Sato, C. (1984). Methodological issues in interlanguage studies: an interactionist perspective. In A. Davies and C. Criper. (Eds.), *Interlanguage*. Edinburgh: Edinburgh University Press.

McLaughlin, B. (1978). The Monitor Model: some methodological considerations. *Language Learning, 28*, 309-32.

Meisel, J., Clahsen, H. & Pienemann, M. (1981). On determining developmental stages in second language acquisition. *Studies in Second Language Acquisition, 3*, 109-35.

Pienemann, M. (1980). The second language acquisition of immigrant children. In S. Felix (Ed.), *Second Language Development: Trends and Issues*. Tübigen: gunter Narr.

Rampton, B. (forthcoming). Stylistic variability and not speaking "normal" English: some post-Labovian approaches and their implications for the study of interlanguage. In R. Ellis (Ed.), *Second Language Acquisition in Context*. Oxford: Pergamon.

Rivers, W. (1980). Foreign language acquisition: where the real problems lie. *Applied Linguistics, 1*, 48-59.

Schmidt, R. (1977). Sociolinguistic variation and language transfer in phonology. *Working Papers on Bilingualism, 12*, 79-95.

Selinker, L. & Douglas, D. (1985). Wrestling with context in interlanguage theory. *Applied Linguistics, 6*, 190-204.

Sharwood-Smith, M. (1981). Consciousness-raising and the second language learner. *Applied Linguistics, 2*, 159-69.

Stevick, E. (1980). *Teaching Languages: a Way and Ways*. Rowley, Mass.: Newbury House.

Strong, M. (1983). Social styles and second language acquisition of Spanish-speaking kindergartners. *TESOL Quarterly, 17*, 241-58.

Tarone, E. (1982). Systematicity and attention in interlanguage. *Language Learning, 32:*, 69-82.

Tarone, E. (1983.) On the variability of interlanguage systems. *Applied Linguistics, 4*, 143-63.

Tarone, E. (1985). Variability in interlanguage use: a study of style shifting in morphology and syntax. *Language Learning, 35*.

Zuengler, J. (1985). Phonological aspects of input, in NS-NNS interactions. In S. Gass and C. Madden (Eds.), *Input in Second Language Acquisition*. Rowley, Mass.: Newbury House.

This bibliography accompanies "Rules, Consciousness, and Learning" by Peter af Trampe, and should appear on page 168.

References

Clark, H.H., & Clark, E. C. (1977). *Psychology and Language.* New York: Harcourt, Brace, Jovanovich Inc.

Faerch, C., & Kasper, G. (Eds.). (1983). *Strategies in Interlanguage Communication.* London: Longman.

Gleitman, H., & Gleitman, L. (1979). Language Use and Language Judgment. In Fillmore, C. J. et al. (Eds.), *Individual Differences in Language Ability and Language Behavior.* New York: Academic Press.

Itkonen, E. (1978). *Grammar and Metascience.* Amsterdam: Benjamins.

Itkonen, E. (1976). *Linguistics and Empiricalness: Answers to Criticisms.* Helsinki: Dept. of General Linguistics.

Karlsson, F. (forthcoming). Rules and Strategies. *Linguistische Studien.* Berlin: Akademie-Verlag.

Lakoff, G. (1975). Hedges: a Study in Meaning Criteria and the Logic of fuzzy Concepts. In Hockney, D. et al. (Eds.), *Contemporary Research in Philosophical Logic and Linguistic Semantics.* Dordrecht: D. Reidel.

Lakoff, G., & Johnson, M. (1980). *Metaphors We Live By.* Chicago: The University of Chicago Press.

Lindblom, B. (1982). The Interdisciplinary Challenge of Speech Motor Control. In Grillner, S. et al. (Eds.), *Speech Motor Control.* Oxford: Pergamon Press.

Linell, P. (1982). *The Written Language Bias in Linguistics.* University of Linköping (Sweden): Studies in Communication 2.

McLaughlin, B. (1978). The Monitor Model: Some Methodological Considerations. *Language Learning, 28,* 309-332.

Pica, T. (1985). Linguistic Simplicity and Learnability: Implications for Language Syllabus Design. In Hyltenstam, K. & M. Pienemann (Eds.), *Modelling and Assessing Second Language Acquisition.* Clevedon: Multilingual Matters.

Rose, S. (1976). *The Conscious Brain.* Harmondsworth: Penguin.

Ryle, G. (1949). *The Concept of Mind.* Penguin edition 1980.

Wall, R. (1972). *Introduction to Mathematical Linguistics.* Englewood Cliffs: Prentice Hall.

This bibliography accompanies "Krashen and the Captive Learner" by William T. Littlewood, and should appear on page 205.

References

Bialystock, E., & Sharwood-Smith, M. (1985). Interlanguage is not a state of mind: an evaluation of the construct for second-language acquisition *Applied Linguistics*, 6, 2, 101-17.

Buckby, M. (1980 - 1985). *Action!* (Books 1 - 5). Walton-on-Thames: Nelson.

Ellis, R. (1985a). *Understanding Second Language Acquisition*. Oxford: Oxford University Press.

Ellis, R. (1985b). *Classroom Second Language Development*. Oxford: Pergamon Press.

Felix, S. (1981). The effect of formal instruction on second language acquisition. *Language Learning, 31*, 1, 87-112.

Gardner, R.C. (1985). *Social Psychology and Second Language Learning: The Role of Attitudes and Motivation*. London: Edward Arnold.

Genesee, F. (1976). The role of intelligence in second language learning. *Language Learning, 26*, 2, 267-80.

Gibbons, J. (1985). The silent period: an examination. *Language Learning, 35*, 2, 255-67.

Gregg, K. (1984). Krashen's Monitor and Occam's Razor. *Applied Linguistics, 5*, 2, 79-100.

Hatch, E. (1978). Discourse analysis and second language acquisition. In E. Hatch (Ed.), *Second Language Acquisition*. Rowley, Mass.: Newbury House.

Jones, B. (1986). *French GCSE: A Guide for Teachers*. Milton Keynes: Open University Press.

Krashen, S. (1981). *Second Language Acquisition and Second Language Learning*. Oxford: Pergamon Press.

Krashen, S. (1982). *Principles and Practice in Second Language Acquisition*. Oxford: Pergamon Press.

Krashen, S. (1985). *The Input Hypothesis*. London: Longman.

Krashen, S., & Terrell, T. (1983). *The Natural Approach: Second Language Acquisition in the Classroom*. Oxford: Pergamon Press.

Lightbown, P.M. (1983). Exploring relationships between developmental and instructional sequences in L2 acquisition. In Seliger, H. and M. Long (Eds.), *Classroom Oriented Research in Second Language Acquisition*. Rowley, Mass.: Newbury House.

Lightbown, P.M. (1985). Great expectations: second-language acquisition research and classroom teaching. Ap*plied Linguistics, 6, 2,* 173-89.

Littlewood, W. T. (1984a). *Foreign and Second Language Learning.* Cambridge: Cambridge University Press.

Littlewood, W. T. (1984b). Review of Krashen and Terrell 1983. En*glish Language Teaching Journal, 38, 3,* 217-8.

Long, M. (1983a). Does second language instruction make a difference? A review of the research. T*ESOL Quarterly, 17, 3,* 359-82.

Long, M. (1983b). Native speaker/non-native speaker conversation and the negotiation of comprehensible input. *Applied Linguistics, 4, 2,* 126-41.

McLaughlin, B. (1978). The monitor model: some methodological considerations. *Language Learning, 28, 2,* 309-32.

Page, B. (1983). Graded objectives in modern-language learning. *Language Teaching, 16, 4,* 292-308.

Pienemann, M. (1985). Learnability and syllabus construction. In K. Hyltenstamm and M. Pienemann (Eds.), *Modelling and Assessing Second Language Development.* Clevedon: Multilingual Matters.

Rivers, W.M. (1980). Foreign language acquisition: where the real problems lie. *Applied Linguistics, 1, 1,* 48-59.

Rowlinson, W. (1985). *Personally Speaking.* Oxford: Oxford University Press.

Stevick, E. (1980). *Teaching Languages: A Way and Ways.* Rowley, Mass.: Newbury House.

This bibliography accompanies "The Natural Approach and Language Teaching in Europe" by Reinhold Freudenstein, and should appear on page 214.

References

Bliemel, W., Fitzpatrick, A., & Quetz, J. (1976). *Englisch für Erwachsene, 1.* Berlin: Cornelsen & Oxford University Press.

Dunlop, I. (1985). How do people learn languages? *Zielsprache Englisch, 4*: 1-7. Adapted in this volume as *The True and the New.*

International Certificate Conference. (1984). Certificate in English. Bonn, Frankfurt: Deutscher Volkshochschul-Verband.

Jacoby, D., & Kleine, W. (1978). *Sprachkurs Englisch, 1.* Frankfurt, Wien, *1.* Aarau: Diesterweg, Österreichischer Bundesverlag, Sauerländer.

Krashen, S.D., & Terrell, T.D. (1983). *The Natural Approach.* Oxford, San Francisco: Pergamon, Alemany.

Lado, R. (1964). *Language Teaching.* New York: McGraw-Hill.

Lado, R. (1985). Das Interview. *Praxis des neusprachlichen Unterrichts, 2*: 165-169.

Van Ek, J., & Alexander, L.G. (1975). *Threshold Level English.* Oxford: Pergamon Press.

YES. A New English Course. Große Ausgabe. Band 3. (1979). Dortmund, Hannover: Lensing, Schroedel.

Zimmermann, G. & Wißner-Kurzawa, E. (1985). *Grammatik lehren, lernen, selbstlernen.* München: Hueber.

This bibliography accompanies "The True and the New" by lan Dunlop, and should appear on page 222.

References LINCOLN CHRISTIAN COLLEGE AND SEMINARY

1. Carroll, J. B. (1975). The *Teaching of French as a Foreign Language in Eight Countries*. New York: John Wiley & Sons.

2. Dunlop, I. (1970). Practical Techniques *in the Teaching of Oral English*. Stockholm: Almquist & Wiksell.

3. Dunlop, I. (1975). The *Teaching of English in Swedish Schools*. Stockholm: Almquist & Wiksell.

4. Krashen, S. D. (1981). *Second Language Acquisition and Second Language Learning*. Oxford: Pergamon Press. p. 35.

5. Krashen, S.D. (1982). *Principles and Practice in Second Language Acquisition*. Oxford: Pergamon Press.

6. Krashen, S. D. (1984). *Writing: Research Theory and Applications*. Oxford: Pergamon Press.

7. Krashen, S. D., & Terrell, T. D. (1983). *The Natural Approach*. Oxford: Pergamon Press.

8. Lenneberg, E.H. (1967). *Biological Foundations of Language*. New York: John Wiley & Sons.

9. Lewis, G. F., & Massad, C. E. (1975). The *Teaching of English as a Foreign Language in Ten Countries*. New York: John Wiley & Sons.

10. Scherer, A. C., & Wertheimer M. (1964). A *Psycholinguistic Experiment in Foreign Language Teaching*. New York: McGraw-Hill.